Neural Networks

Neural Networks

Current applications

Edited by P.G.J. Lisboa

Department of Electrical Engineering and Electronics,
University of Liverpool, Liverpool, UK

CHAPMAN & HALL
London · New York · Tokyo · Melbourne · Madras

Published by Chapman & Hall, 2–6 Boundary Row, London SE1 8HN

Chapman & Hall, 2–6 Boundary Row, London SE1 8HN, UK

Blackie Academic & Professional, Wester Cleddens Road, Bishopbriggs, Glasgow G64 2NZ, UK

Van Nostrand Reinhold Inc., 115 5th Avenue, New York NY10003, USA

Chapman & Hall Japan, Thomson Publishing Japan, Hirakawacho Nemoto Building, 6F, 1–7–11 Hirakawa-cho, Chiyoda-ku, Tokyo 102, Japan

Chapman & Hall Australia, Thomas Nelson Australia, 102 Dodds Street, South Melbourne, Victoria 3205, Australia

Chapman & Hall India, R. Seshadri, 32 Second Main Road, CIT East, Madras 600 035, India

First edition 1992

© 1992 Chapman & Hall

Commissioned by Technical Communications (Publishing) Ltd
Printed in Great Britain by St Edmundsbury Press Ltd, Bury St Edmunds, Suffolk

ISBN 0 412 42790 7   0 442 31564 3 (USA)

A catalogue record for this book is available from the British Library

Library of Congress Cataloging-in Publication data available

Contents

Contributors   xiii

Preface   xviii

Chapter One: Introduction
by P. J. G. Lisboa   1
  1.1   Summary   1
  1.2   Motivation   1
  1.3   Historical perspective   2
  1.4   Biological neurones   4
  1.5   Artificial neurones   5
  1.6   Networks of neurones   7
  1.7   Toolkit   9
      1.7.1 *Hopfield network*   11
      1.7.2 *Multi-layered perceptron*   15
      1.7.3 *Kohonen network*   20
      1.7.4 *Temporal differences*   23
  1.8   Choosing the right algorithm   26

Chapter Two: Neural network basics
by G. A. Works   **35**
  2.1   Summary   35
  2.2   Introduction   35
  2.3   What is a 'hard' problem?   36
  2.4   What is an ANS?   37
  2.5   ANS implementations   41
  2.6   Applications   43
  2.7   The future of artificial neural systems   47

Chapter Three: Using adaptive networks for resource allocation in changing environments
by T. M. Bell, W. R. Hutchison and K. R. Stephens   **49**
  3.1   Summary   49
  3.2   Introduction   49
  3.3   BANKET   53
  3.4   Airline revenue management   55
  3.5   Airline marketing tactician™ (AMT)   57
  3.6   Scheduling and task management   60

3.7   Adaptive Network Aircrew Training Scheduler
       (ANATS)   61
3.8   Conclusion   63

Chapter Four: Medical risk assessment for insurance underwriting
by S. B. Ahuja and A. Hsiung   **67**
4.1   Summary   67
4.2   Introduction   67
       4.2.1   *Insurance underwriting*   68
       4.2.2   *Shortcomings of existing methods*   69
       4.2.3   *Neural modelling*   71
4.3   A neural network model for classificatory
       problem solving   73
       4.3.1   *A knowledge representation and processing
                model*   73
       4.3.2   *A spreading activation paradigm*   75
4.4   Architecture of a rating network   77
4.5   A connectionist expert system environment   80
       4.5.1   *Structure of the domain knowledge*   82
       4.5.2   *The knowledge specification language*   83
4.6   Conclusion   86

Chapter Five: Modelling chemical process systems via neural computation
by N. V. Bhat, P. A. Minderman, Jr., T. McAvoy and
N. Sun Wang   **91**
5.1   Summary   91
5.2   Introduction   91
5.3   Back-propagation   93
5.4   Steady-state example   95
       5.4.1   *Model*   95
       5.4.2   *Back-propagation net used*   97
       5.4.3   *Optimizing reactor performance*   98
5.5   Dynamic example   99
       5.5.1   *System considered*   100
       5.5.2   *Back-propagation dynamic modelling (BDM)* 101
       5.5.3   *Results*   103
5.6   Interpreting biosensor data   105
       5.6.1   *Overview*   105
       5.6.2   *Back-propagation results*   106
5.7   Conclusion   108

Chapter Six: The application of neural networks to robotics
by A. Guez, Z. Ahmad and J. Selinsky   **111**
6.1   Summary   111
6.2   Introduction   111
6.3   The inverse kinematic problem in robotics   111
     6.3.1   *Problem statement*   112
     6.3.2   *The proposed method*   112
     6.3.3   *Examples*   114
     6.3.4   *Conclusion*   117
6.4   Learning of robot dynamics using a hierarchical neural network   117
     6.4.1   *Dynamic model*   117
     6.4.2   *Proposed learning method*   118
     6.4.3   *Simulation results*   120
     6.4.4   *Conclusion*   121

Chapter Seven: Neural networks in vision
by P. J. G. Lisboa   **123**
7.1   Summary   123
7.2   Introduction   123
7.3   Biological neural networks for vision   124
7.4   Artificial neural models   129
7.5   Kohonen networks   131
7.6   Back error propagation   137
7.7   Feature extraction   140
7.8   Comparison with statistical classifiers   142
7.9   Overview of applications and conclusion   143

Chapter Eight: Image labelling with a neural network
by W. A. Wright   **149**
8.1   Summary   149
8.2   Introduction   149
8.3   Network   151
8.4   Implementation   152
8.5   Results   157
8.6   Conclusion   160

Chapter Nine: Object recognition with optimum neural networks
by M. Bichsel and P. Seitz   **163**
9.1   Summary   163
9.2   Introduction   164

9.3   Measuring the information flow in neural networks:
       the conditional class entropy   165
9.4   Extension to general sigmoid activation functions   169
9.5   A teaching algorithm for the construction of
       optimum neural networks: minimizing conditional
       class entropy   169
9.6   Shift-invariant classification of symmetry axes in
       binary patterns   173
9.7   Detection of human faces   175
9.8   Conclusion   180

**Chapter Ten: Handwritten digit recognition with a back-
propagation network**
by Y. Le Cun, B. Boser, J. S. Denker, D. Henderson,
R. E. Howard, W. Hubbard and L. D. Jackel   **185**
10.1   Summary   185
10.2   Introduction   185
10.3   Zipcode recognition   186
10.4   Pre-processing   187
10.5   The network   188
10.6   Results   191
10.7   Conclusion   193

**Chapter Eleven: Higher-order neural networks for
invariant pattern recognition**
by S. J. Perantonis   **197**
11.1   Summary   197
11.2   Introduction   197
11.3   Invariant 'dynamical' associative memories   198
11.4   Invariant associative memory properties of the
       Hopfield network and the autoassociating perceptron   200
11.5   Digit recognition using the Hopfield network and the
       autoassociating perceptron   203
11.6   The role of image fuzzing in improving the basins
       of attraction   207
11.7   Invariant pattern recognition using high-order
       networks   212
11.8   Invariant pattern recognition by the method of
       moments   218
11.9   Digit recognition using third-order networks and
       Zernike moment classifiers   219
       11.9.1   *Invariant recognition of typed digits*   222

    11.9.2   *Invariant recognition of handwritten digits*   225
11.10 Conclusion   227

Chapter Twelve: The bionic retina and beyond
by J. G. Taylor   **233**
  12.1   Summary   233
  12.2   Introduction   233
  12.3   The retina   235
  12.4   The primary visual cortex   245
  12.5   Bionic processing   246
  12.6   Conclusion   247

Chapter Thirteen: Conclusion
by P. J. G. Lisboa   **251**
  13.1   Trends   251
  13.2   Meek, myth or mirth?   253
  13.3   Application areas   255
       13.3.1 *Business and finance*   255
       13.3.2 *Automated inspection and monitoring*   256
       13.3.3 *Computer vision*   256
       13.3.4 *Speech processing*   257
       13.3.5 *Robotics and control*   258
       13.3.6 *Optimization problems*   258
       13.3.7 *Medical applications*   259
  13.4   Perspectives   260

Appendix A: Glossary   **269**

Index   **275**

To my favourite living neural networks:

Catherine, Corinne and Ciarán.

To my mother. In remembrance of my father.

Contributors

Z. Ahmad:
  College of Engineering
  Department of Electrical and Computer Engineering
  Drexel University
  Philadelphia
  Pennsylvania 19104
  USA

S. B. Ahuja:
  Nielsen
  Bannockburn Lake Office Plaza
  2201 Waukegan Road
  Suite S-200
  Bannockburn
  Illinois 60015
  USA

T. M. Bell:
  BehavHeuristics
  335 Paint Branch Drive
  College Park
  MD 20742-3011
  USA

N. V. Bhat:
  Department of Chemical Engineering
  University of Maryland
  College Park Campus
  College Park
  Maryland 20742
  USA

M. Bichsel:
Paul Scherrer Institute
c/o Laboratories RCA Ltd.
Badenerstrasse 569
CH 8048
Zurich
Switzerland

B. Boser:
AT & T Bell Laboratories
Crawfords Corner Road
Holmdel
New Jersey O7733-1988
USA

Y. Le Cun:
AT & T Bell Laboratories
Crawfords Corner Road
Holmdel
New Jersey O7733-1988
USA

J. S. Denker:
AT & T Bell Laboratories
Crawfords Corner Road
Holmdel
New Jersey O7733-1988
USA

A. Guez:
College of Engineering
Department of Electrical and Computer Engineering
Drexel University
Philadelphia
Pennsylvania 19104
USA

D. Henderson:
AT & T Bell Laboratories
Crawfords Corner Road
Holmdel
New Jersey O7733-1988
USA

R. E. Howard:
    AT & T Bell Laboratories
    Crawfords Corner Road
    Holmdel
    New Jersey O7733-1988
    USA

A. Hsiung:
    Rentenanstalt
    AI Research and Development Laboratory
    Department of Organization and Informatics
    General Guisan – Quai 40
    CH-8022
    Zurich
    Switzerland

W. Hubbard:
    AT & T Bell Laboratories
    Crawfords Corner Road
    Holmdel
    New Jersey O7733-1988
    USA

W. R. Hutchison:
    BehavHeuristics
    335 Paint Branch Drive
    College Park
    MD 20742-3011
    USA

L. D. Jackel:
    AT & T Bell Laboratories
    Crawfords Corner Road
    Holmdel
    New Jersey O7733-1988
    USA

P. J. G. Lisboa:
    Department of Electrical Engineering and Electronics
    University of Liverpool
    Brownlow Hill
    PO Box 147
    Liverpool

L69 3BX
England

T. McAvoy:
Department of Chemical Engineering
University of Maryland
College Park Campus
College Park
Maryland 20742
USA

P. A. Minderman, Jr.:
Department of Chemical Engineering
University of Maryland
College Park Campus
College Park
Maryland 20742
USA

S. J. Perantonis:
NSPRC Demokritos
Athens
Greece

P. Seitz:
Paul Scherrer Institute
c/o Laboratories RCA
Badenerstrasse 569
Ch 8048
Zurich
Switzerland

J. Selinsky:
College of Engineering
Department of Electrical and Computer Engineering
Drexel University
Philadelphia
Pennsylvania 19104
USA

K. R. Stephens:
   BehavHeuristics
   335 Paint Branch Drive
   College Park
   MD 20742-3011
   USA

J. G. Taylor:
   Department of Mathematics
   King's College
   University of London
   Strand
   London
   WC2R 2LS
   England

N. Sun Wang:
   Department of Chemical Engineering
   University of Maryland
   College Park Campus
   College Park
   Maryland 20742
   USA

G. A. Works:
   Science Applications International Corporation
   10260 Campus Point Drive
   San Diego
   California
   CA 921121
   USA

W. A. Wright:
   Sowerby Research Centre
   Department of Advanced Information Processing
   British Aerospace
   PO Box 5
   Filton
   Bristol
   BS12 7QW
   England

Preface

Neural network technology is a relative newcomer to many application areas. Its widespread use today is fraught with difficulties in achieving optimum performance, monitoring their activity, and integrating them into existing solutions and operating environments. But most of all, there is a learning curve of a purely practical nature that is involved in understanding what neural networks are about, how they operate, and what they can do.

This book reviews some of the important commercially available applications and also provides an accelerated introduction to this fast developing field. It is intended to bring the reader some of the way up that learning curve. It presents a brief overview of basic history and principles of artificial neural networks, and describes some of the most important tools provided by this technology, together with their use in practical applications; this is followed by examples of detailed applications, some of which are already marketed, concluding with a review of current applications, and perspectives for the future.

It is hoped that in the book the reader will be able to find parallels with particular applications of interest to them, opening up new opportunities by providing a window into the current state-of-the-art of neural network applications. For each user of neural network techniques, whether experienced or inexperienced, active or aspiring, committed or sceptical, the purpose of this book will be fulfilled if it gives a new insight, inspires a new application, or provides the catalyst for new solutions to difficult problems.

The emphasis throughout the book is upon the use of artificial neural networks as a new set of tools, which have special computational properties, and how best to exploit their potential in practical applications.

All the articles are thoroughly referenced in order to give the user the opportunity to follow up the details of every aspect of the techniques and principles described.

The introduction reviews some of the motivations and history of this not so new field, indicates what neural networks are and what is new about them, and introduces the basic tools that are used in the applications that follow. In addition to the technical references, a bibliography for start-up is supplied.

Chapter 2 caters for a shorter introduction, leading straight on to specific commercial applications. One of these, explosive detection in aircraft luggage, deals with an automatic inspection problem in a high-risk situation. The other describes adaptive vibration cancellation in a non-linear system.

Chapter 3 describes a solution to the problem of resource allocation in a highly competitive environment, involving aircraft seat allocation, and makes use of algorithms especially suited to forecasting. This is another example of a neural-based solution which has proved its worth in the market-place.

Chapter 4 discusses the design of a particularly important type of structure, a 'hybrid model' which acquires knowledge in the same way as neural networks do, but is more amenable to the provision of explanation facilities. It constitutes, in effect, an 'active expert system', which is derived for yet another difficult task, medical risk assessment for life insurance underwriting.

Chapter 5 describes another example of modelling for control of systems with non-linearities, this time in greater detail and applied to a standard chemical process, pH control of a stirred tank reactor.

Inverse kinematics is central to many robotic applications, and also typical of a wide class of problems known as 'inverse problems'. These are problems where the results of certain actions are known but the correct action to achieve a desired goal is uncertain. Chapter 6 tackles this problem, and also investigates another important and difficult problem in robotics, namely modelling the transient dynamics of coupled systems, by addressing the case of a simple arm manipulator with two degrees of freedom.

The area of image processing is of particular success in the application of neural network techniques, and is also an area where even real biological systems are partly understood, providing guidance in the design of general purpose artificial vision systems.

Chapter 7 gives a short tutorial on real and artificial neural vision, from a purely operational point of view. It centres around a detailed discussion of the behaviour of arguably the two most commonly used neural network learning algorithms, back error propagation and the self-organizing Kohonen network, which are applied to hand-printed numeral recognition, thereby providing results that are easy to visualize. More advanced areas where future developments are likely are highlighted.

This is followed by yet another real-world application, this time image labelling, which represents a first step in the interpretation of natural scenes, in Chapter 8. This is a crucial step in the development of automatic navigation systems, and involves feature detection as well as image classification.

Object recognition and the detection of image symmetries is a particularly difficult task for any vision system. Chapter 9 describes an original and very successful approach to this task, which includes automatic detection of human faces against natural scene backgrounds.

Optical character recognition is singularly well suited for solution by neural network methods, since it contains distributed, redundant information. In practice this means that we are able to perform this task with a minimum amount of conscious intervention. Chapter 10 presents what is certainly one of the most powerful and robust solutions to the recognition of handwritten digits, tested on a large database collected from live mail.

Chapter 11 is concerned with invariant pattern recognition, in contrast with an earlier chapter which looked to recognize image invariants in the form of symmetry axes. This is the problem of identifying patterns independently of the basic geometric transformations of translation, rotation and a limited amount of scaling. Conventional and neural techniques are compared, and their benefits discussed. Although applied to character recognition, the approach that is developed could just as easily be extended to problems in industrial visual inspection.

The last paper deals with the future. A close examination of the early stages of the human visual system is linked, in Chapter 12, to a model that can be implemented in silicon.

Finally, the Conclusion summarizes the current state-of-the-art of neural network applications, listing some of the more important developments and prospects for the future.

I am indebted to Dr. J. McTavish for his invaluable assistance in proof-reading the manuscript.

Permission by the Institution of Electrical and Electronic Engineers (IEEE) and Morgan Kaufman to publish the papers by Thomas J. McAvoy *et al.* and Y. Le Cun *et al.* respectively is gratefully acknowledged.

P. J. G. Lisboa
University of Liverpool

1

Introduction

P. J. G. Lisboa
University of Liverpool, England

1.1 Summary

This opening chapter briefly reviews the fundamental precepts of the neural network approach, from a variety of standpoints – historical, biological, systems and tools. The different sections follow a sequence that can also be read separately, leading to different tours of this new subject area.

1.2 Motivation

Over the last three years, activity in the field of artificial neural networks has increased exponentially. This confluence of effort has led to an enormous volume of research publications, 500 or so during 1989 alone, and even to the creation of at least four new journals as outlets for work specifically related to this new field, the identity of which remains somewhat obscure.

Work in this area is now found routinely at international meetings on subjects as diverse as image processing, robotics, signal processing, optics, medical engineering, manufacturing systems and credit scoring, all in an attempt to set new standards of performance by looking at old problems in a new way. Topical meetings bring together specialists across a wide range of subjects, spanning the complete spectrum from 'purists' dealing with the technological, theoretical, neurophysiological and behavioural aspects of the subject, to domain experts who produce anything from feasibility studies to fully worked-out engineering solutions.

One reason for the new outlook is the realization, bordering upon disappointment, of the limitations of conventional artificial intelligence techniques based primarily upon use of explicit symbolic reasoning. There are, of course, many instances where expert systems have become very well established, even though it is now generally acknowledged that they should not be expected to match the proficiency of human experts, nor should they be regarded as a necessarily accurate model of human reasoning. This can be the case even in tasks on which rule-based systems perform well, an example of which is an experiment where a chess master plays five-a-second chess against a weaker, but still master standard opponent, while adding numbers at the rate of one per second [1]. Despite this attempt to jam his higher-level intellect, the chess player's moves are described as 'fluid and coordinated'. It is not difficult to imagine the moves proceeding via some sort of pattern recognition activity taking place at a level below that of explicit symbolic descriptions of the game.

In addition, developments in electronics technology have provided us with a continuing explosion in computer power, which has made it feasible to experiment extensively with numerical methods, encouraging more pragmatic 'proof in the eating' solutions.

All of this has combined to resolve some long-standing difficulties about distributed information storage systems, as well as the realization that the computation which goes on in these models 'is now of interest to many scientists and engineers with practical problems' [2].

The purpose of this introductory chapter is to provide an overview of neural networks as tools, which are used in later chapters to design solutions to particular problems in engineering and finance. The reader in search of a brief introduction leading shortly to detailed applications, will find it in Chapter 2.

1.3 Historical perspective

This section gives a short cut, rather than a tour, across many years of extensive developments in neural network technology. For that, there are several good reviews already available in the literature, some of which can be found in the bibliography.

The formal realization that the brain in some way performs information processing tasks was first spelt out by McCulloch and Pitts in 1943 [3]. They represented the activity of individual neurones using simple threshold logic elements, and showed how networks made out of many of these units interconnected could perform arbitrary logical operations. Today this is not surprising, as this process is akin to wiring up any logical circuit using binary logic gates. There are, however, important differences. It was correctly inferred that the overall behaviour of the circuit was determined by its connectivity, rather than by the detailed operation of any element; their 'Logical Calculus' had no clock, and the circuits contained closed paths, or 'circles', which means that the outcome of a logical process may depend upon the previous history of much of the system over an indefinite period. Thus, some of the formidable difficulties in the study of complex neural network circuits became apparent immediately their computational ability was formalized.

There followed a period of research into the behaviour of randomly connected systems, when the 'spreading' of collective activation modes through the system was discovered, resulting in stable cycles of sustained activity where the same neuronal firing patterns occurred at regular intervals [4,5]. The connectivity of certain neuronal circuits could also be altered to establish desired correlations between the activity of special nodes in the system, which play the role of input and output nodes [6]. This was an exciting development, since it allowed use of the circuit as a classifier of different input patterns of activity. The network started to acquire a practical role [7].

At the same time as understanding about mechanisms of learning in biological systems grew, the study of neurodynamics intensified [8]. There was, still, no clear understanding of how networks could be set up to solve particular problems, how to set the network connectivities, and the roles of different network architectures. It was in this context that excessive claims were made about the learning capabilities of one scheme in particular, Rosenblatt's perceptron. The original excitement about neural learning machines was curtailed after the publication of yet another computational formalism, this time in a language which, albeit abstract, related closely to practical applications in pattern recognition. Minsky and Papert elegantly showed that there were classes of simple tasks which the perceptron could not perform [9].

While theoretical work in the field continued, developing new and well-founded learning algorithms [10–16], with even a small number of published demonstrator projects [17,18], resurgence of mass interest had to wait for the publication of training algorithms capable of overcoming the limitations of the early perceptron [19,20]. In order to understand what the new developments are, and why the amount of interest in them has grown, it is necessary to consider first some facts about biological neural systems.

1.4 Biological neurones

This section reviews briefly those features of natural systems which are incorporated into artificial neural network models. Chapter 12 pursues one particular system in detail, the retina, through to its implementation using electronic components. More detailed reviews can be found in the bibliography.

A prototype neurone is described in Fig. 1.1. Electrical impulses propagating along the axon (action potentials) activate the synaptic junctions [8]. These, in turn, produce further excitations (post synaptic potentials) which travel along the dendrites towards the next neurone. The electrical behaviour of the neurone is best explained by considering the cell membrane as a dynamic object, with a large number of electrochemical pumps, which continually aspirate sodium ions from inside the neurone, and selectively permeable channels to let in potassium ions. The ion densities either side of the membrane are kept in the ratio of about 10:1, with more potassium inside the cell and sodium outside [8,21]. This creates an electrical potential difference of about −70 mV between the inner and outer surface of the membrane which, because the membrane is so thin, gives rise to an electric field in the membrane of about 10^5 V/cm (enough to cause arcing in air).

The firing rate of each neurone is controlled by the region where the axon joins the cell body, called the hillock zone [22]. The two types of ion mentioned earlier have different sizes, and the cell membrane contains proteins with elongated shapes which act as taps. When the membrane potential at the hillock zone rises above a certain threshold value around −60 mV, the electric field which kept the sodium taps in the adjoining region of the axon closed reduces, and sodium ions flood in. This reduces the electrical potential further along the axon, causing a travelling wave of charge to propagate at a speed of around 3,000 cm/sec, roughly 1/10th of the speed of sound in air. These sodium channels soon close, followed by the opening of channels which let potassium ions out to redress the membrane potential. This is clearly a very simplified picture, and the neurone must restore itself to its proper resting state of balance before sending out the next packet of charge, called the refractory period.

We thus arrive at a model of neuronal activity based upon the transmission of information across synapses. The synapses are termed excitatory, or inhibitory, depending on whether the post-synaptic potentials increase or reduce the hillock potential, enhancing or

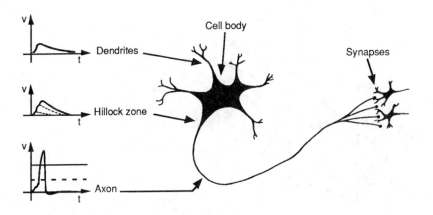

Figure 1.1 A prototype biological neurone.

reducing the likelihood of triggering an impulse there, respectively. The time-scale over which the incoming potentials are integrated depends upon the typical electrical capacitance and resistance of the cell membrane, namely 3×10^{-9} μF and 8×10^6 ohms, which multiplied give 2.4 msec [8], since the potentials discharge through the cell membrane after this time. This explains why the cell body is described as an integrator, yet represented by a linear sum. While a pure integrator would add up every incoming signal and, eventually, always fire, the neurone acts more like a coincidence counter.

1.5 Artificial neurones

A typical simulation of the action of a single biological neurone is shown in Fig. 1.2. The strength of each synaptic junction is represented by a multiplicative factor, or weight, with a positive sign for excitatory connections, and negative otherwise. The hillock zone is modelled by a summation of the signals received from every link [8,22,23]. The firing rate of the neurone in response to this aggregate incoming signal is then described by a mathematical function, whose value represents the frequency of emission of electrical impulses along the axon.

Real neurones have a finite dynamic range from nil response to the full firing rate, so this function is generally non-linear, levelling off at

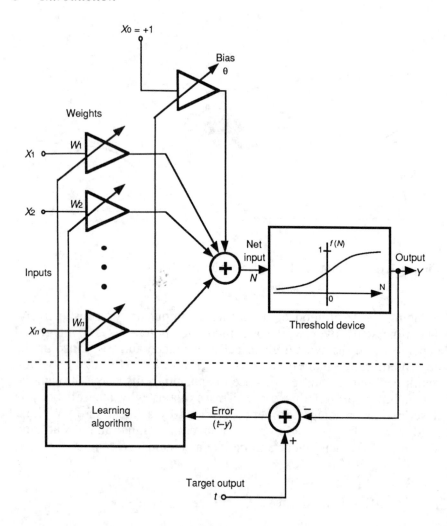

Figure 1.2 A typical model of a neurone.

0 and 1. The additional bias term also shown in Fig. 1.2 determines the spontaneous activity of the neurone, i.e. in the absence of any incoming signal. This can also be viewed as setting the threshold value for the sudden onset of a high firing rate, hence the term non-linear threshold element. These non-linearities play an essential role in the behaviour of neural networks, making an exact mathematical treatment of the subject difficult, yet essential if these networks are to do anything very useful.

There are several variations on the basic theme described here, such as the all-or-nothing response where the smooth non-linear function is replaced by a step [14]. The neurones may also be fully connected, i.e. each one linked to every other one in what is known as a recursive network, or they may be arranged in layers, with information proceeding from one layer to the next, to make a feedforward network. The former case will involve a relaxation period, during which the signals flow around the network until it settles into a stable state. The latter constitutes, in effect, an array of non-linear filters.

1.6 Networks of neurones

In the absence of any accepted definition of what constitutes an artificial neural network, sometimes referred to also as a connectionist model or parallel distributed processor, I shall take the recent view of 'a network of interacting simple units' together with a rule to adjust the strength of the connections between these units in response to externally supplied data.

There are three main ingredients to a neural network, namely:

(a) the disposition of the nodes and links between them;
(b) an algorithm for the first mode of operation of the network, the training phase;
(c) a method of interpreting the network's response during its second mode of operation, the 'recall' phase. The useful properties of the network usually involve non-linearities, which help the stability and robustness properties of the network [24], but also make it difficult to treat analytically.

The question addressed now is whether this type of dilute computational arrangement confers on to the overall structure any properties that are different from, or in any respect an improvement upon, those of conventional computers.

The original motivation for the neural network track is provided by the observation that biological systems, such as the mammalian brain, are able to execute perceptive tasks orders of magnitude faster than the most powerful computers. Examples that come to mind are object recognition, room navigation, reading, hearing, walking, etc. They all involve some form of pattern analysis and take place, to a large extent, automatically, i.e. without the need for conscious intervention.

Therefore it makes sense to attempt to perform these tasks also automatically, learned through practice, without involving explicit high-level symbolic instructions. The situation is all the more surprising because the relaxation time of a neurone is of the order of a few milliseconds, as shown in Section 1.4, and this is around a million times slower than current electronic circuits.

Since these tasks involve a large amount of computation, it follows that something fundamentally different happens in the brain. One immediately obvious difference is the scale of parallelism involved. The human cortex is just 0.2 m^2 in area and 1 mm thick, but it contains an estimated 10^{10} neurones and 10^{14} synapses [25]. It is essentially a two-dimensional structure, layered across its width and divided across its area into specialist functional regions. A substantial amount of information processing is known to occur across the width of the cortex, therefore involving a network that is shallow and broad rather than deep. This has been shown to be the most efficient configuration also for artificial networks.

It is usually referred to as the '100 step rule', namely the observation that low-level recognition tasks are often performed in natural systems in fewer than those many steps. Hence the rapid response, which is necessary to ensure survival, but accomplished using much slower and simpler computational units than modern computers. The volume of computation is achieved instead by resorting to vast numbers of neurones acting in parallel, and it is the combined activity of all of these cells which results in the final pattern recognition ability of the network.

So we come to the recent interest in neural networks. It was triggered by a number of computer experiments (see Rumelhart and McClelland (1986) in the bibliography), which demonstrated that small networks of artificial neurones already display some of the more desirable computational properties of the larger biological counterparts. These are summarized in Table 1.1.

Briefly stated, replacing a small number of well-identified symbolic units with a large number of highly interconnected simple processing units does alter the computational properties of the system. In particular, the ability of the system to cope with corrupted information or implementation defects is expected to increase substantially. Adding more units to the network should improve its performance, and this could provide robustness against component failure without recourse to a direct voting system.

However, the advantages of having information stored in a distributed way among many interconnecting links must be weighted

Table 1.1 A comparison of neural networks and conventional computers.

Neural networks	Conventional computers
Many simple processors	Few complex processors
Few processing steps	Many computational steps
Distributed processing	Symbolic processing
Graceful degradation	Catastrophic failure
Trained by example	Explicit programming

against no longer having clear explanations of what the network is doing at the symbolic level, as indeed is the case in biological systems.

All of the properties described above are intrinsic to networks of many processing units processing information concurrently. The value of 'many', in practice, is much smaller than the half million or so neurones already present in the slug, therefore a distributed approach to the solution to a problem is of little use unless it is carefully applied, a point increasingly appreciated as new applications are developed.

1.7 Toolkit

This section reviews the basic algorithms which are used repeatedly throughout the remainder of the book. They are regarded here as tools, leaving the discussion of particular applications to the following chapters.

In general, algorithms come in a bewildering variety of shapes and sizes, with many different mechanisms for training, and all immersed in professional jargon. Some are said to be supervised, i.e. they require a 'tutor' to train them, while others work entirely by themselves, and are said to be self-organized. Some are fully connected, with all neurones connected to one another, while others are arranged in neat layers, with connections only between adjacent layers. These layers can be connected locally, i.e. linking only with neighbouring nodes in the preceding layer, with static or dynamic receptive fields. Some networks are recursive, involving feedback loops and setting-up cycles which eventually relax into a stable state, while others are one pass only, taking data in at one end and filtering it through to produce the required answers at the other. Some neurones have linear response, others are 'all-or-nothing' (i.e. binary 0 or 1), yet others require a smooth response, ranging continuously between 0 and 1.

Although the different networks all have different properties, with their particular strengths and weaknesses, they may all be viewed under a common umbrella, as distributed associative memories. The process of presenting example data and training a neural network is simply a mechanism to load up the network, effectively storing the samples in the example data. This is what is achieved when the gains of the interconnecting links between nodes in the network are adjusted. The form of the sample data is changed into a new form which depends upon the architecture of the network and the training algorithm used. The information which one wishes to store may consist of sample pattern classifications, regularities in the data, or predictions about the temporal behaviour of a dynamical system, any of which could be done using the same data in conjunction with different networks.

In effect, artificial neural networks are a class of generic filters which store information in a distributed form. The special properties that arise from this result partly from the fact that non-linearities are inherent in neural networks, and are therefore treated naturally by these systems, and partly because of the collective action of many individual elements, which together determine the response of the system as whole. This results in pattern completion capabilities, so that example data presented with missing or corrupted information leads the network towards recalling the completed stored pattern, with the corrupted information filled in or corrected. These networks are said to be content addressable (look ahead to Fig. 1.4). Moreover, new patterns which are related to the examples already stored in the network will trigger the network to recall a response which is intermediate between the responses to the related stored patterns. This is known as an associative memory capacity, and can be regarded as interpolating between the most appropriate responses already taught to the network. There is also the prospect of speed improvements in hardware implementation by replacing serial pipelined conventional algorithms by highly parallel, broad, neural network architectures.

The following are examples of the particular networks described in Table 1.2, how they work, and how they can be applied. They form the core tools of the practical applications described in later chapters. For a more comprehensive review of algorithms, including details of prescriptive formulations aimed at software simulations, there are several specialist in-depth reviews and textbooks listed in the annotated

Table 1.2 Types of network.

Algorithms	Type	Function
Hopfield	recursive	optimization
Multi-layered perceptron	feedforward	classification
Kohonen	self-organizing	data coding
Temporal differences	predictive	forecasting

bibliography at the end of this Chapter.

1.7.1 *Hopfield network*

This has become a historical algorithm because it lends itself to a particularly simple picture of the way it operates.

The Hopfield model [14] is typical of recursive algorithms, in which all of the nodes are connected to one another. A description of a small network with just four nodes, or neurones, is shown in Fig. 1.3. Here, $P1$–$P4$ could represent pixel values in an image with just four pixels. Denoting each link value by Tij, corresponding to the strength of the connection between pixels Pi and Pj, the activity of any one neurone is determined by the overall signal received from all of the other neurones in the network according to whether or not this signal exceeds a given threshold. The mathematical rule for this is the following:

$$
P_{i,\text{new}} \quad \leftarrow \quad
\begin{cases}
1 & \text{if } \sum_{i \neq j} T_{ij}.P_{j,\text{old}} > 1/2 \\
\\
-1 & \text{if } \sum_{i \neq j} T_{ij}.P_{j,\text{old}} < 1/2.
\end{cases}
$$

This rule corresponds to the description of an artificial neurone in Fig. 1.2 replacing the threshold device by an all-or-nothing function, so the node is always fully 'on' or 'off', with corresponding values, this time, of either -1 or 1. By suitably adjusting the connectivity strengths T_{ij} the above transition rule $P_{\text{old}} \rightarrow P_{\text{new}}$ can be made such as to recall only image patterns from a predetermined set. This is done, for one pattern, by setting each link strength either to 1, if the

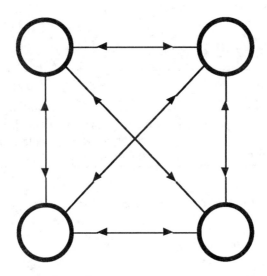

Figure 1.3 Hopfield architecture: a fully recursive network. The states of the network are represented by patterns of activity of the nodes. The links, indicated by arrows, determine the network activity.

pixels at either end of the link in that particular pattern are both 'on' or both 'off', or otherwise to −1. The link strengths for all patterns are added together to give an integer number which is the value of that link.

Hopfield's main contribution was to show that the action of the above transition rule corresponds to sliding image patterns down valleys, called basins of attraction, in a landscape where at the bottom of the valleys lie the patterns in the predetermined set. Given an incomplete or corrupted image, as it slides down the slopes in this contrived landscape, its wrong pixel values will flip over to recover one complete image, which lies at the bottom of a basin of attraction. For this reason, the functions which describe these landscapes are called energy functions, and the whole process is akin to the principle of least action, which drives physical systems in equilibrium with their environment to states of least energy − an example is an object free falling under gravity. The effect of this process on a trial image is illustrated in Fig. 1.4. This simple model has severe limitations, and must be extended to allow for continuously valued neural activity in order to derive full performance from the network [26,27].

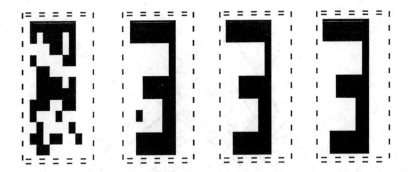

Figure 1.4 Content addressable property (left to right): part of a stored pattern, corrupted by noise, recovers the complete pattern which, then, simply self-reproduces.

The network can either be trained to restore set patterns, in which case a typical landscape, adapted to the data, will repeat application of a training algorithm such as the one mentioned above, or it can be operated in reverse, by defining a cost function which is appropriate to a practical application, and only then mapping the adjustable parameters in the problem into neural network components, usually represented by configurations of nodes into the network. This leads to a powerful optimization algorithm, provided this does not require an excessive number of additional constraints to map the network into the space of allowed solutions. Either way, some energy landscape will result, with dips at the desired basins of attraction. Figure 1.5(a) depicts one such landscape for an elementary bi-stable electronic circuit, the flip-flop. In this simple case there are only two nodes (one for each amplifier) and two stable states where the nodes are inverted, i.e. one is +1 and the other −1. According to the above rule, the nodes are connected by a link with strength $T^{1,2} = -2$, and therefore the energy surface is given by $E = T_{1,2}.P_1.P_2 = -2.P_1.P_2$.

Training networks to perform more difficult tasks results in more complicated landscapes for the energy function, such as the one shown in Fig. 1.5(b) (the subject of this figure is discussed in more detail in Chapter 11). This illustrates one of the main difficulties with this model, namely the existence of spurious valleys far away from the desired one at the centre of the screen. Should the image roll down into one of these local minima it will remain trapped and never fully recover the desired stored state. In the solution of optimization

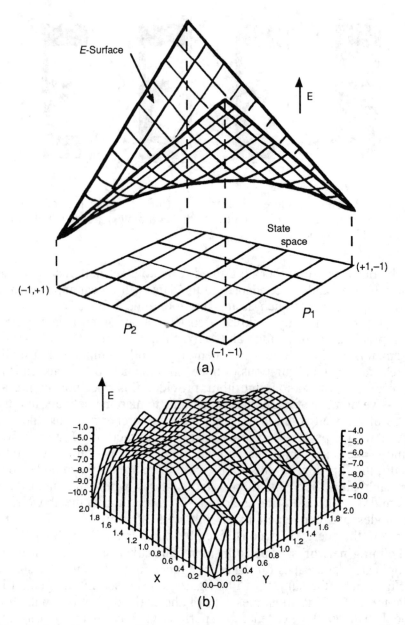

Figure 1.5 Energy surfaces of two trained Hopfield networks: (a) the flip-flop circuit, (b) a larger network trained to centre images of the digits 0–9. The figure shows the landscape obtained by moving the image on a 20 × 20 pixel screen by one pixel in either direction. Periodic boundary conditions mean that the four corners all represent the centre of the screen.

problems, this results in answers which are either far away from the desired near-optimal value or, more likely, invalid configurations of the nodes in the network, outside the set of configurations which maps on to the space of allowed solutions.

Nevertheless, the simple picture of the operation of a content addressable memory remains a useful one, and the Hopfield model has been applied successfully to a number of optimization problems, where the energy landscape is built to represent the function which the network is intended to minimize.

1.7.2   *Multi-layered perceptron*

The multi-layered perceptron is arguably the most popular neural network architecture, and certainly the trigger of the current widespread explosion of activity in this area. It is also known by the name of the algorithm used to train it, back error propagation [19,20, 28].

A typical architecture is shown in Fig. 1.6. The network is arranged in layers, but now only nodes in adjacent layers are connected. Moreover, the layers are differentiated. The first layer has its excitation levels set by an externally imposed input pattern. The function of the network is to reproduce certain target output patterns of excitation at the last layer of nodes, represented here at the top of Fig. 1.6. This filtering action is achieved by adjusting the gain of each interconnecting link according to a mathematical expression which compares the activity patterns at the output nodes with the desired target patterns and propagates the difference, or error, back through the network contributing a small adjustment to the strength of each link. This is in fact the process described, for a single neurone, in Fig. 1.2 under 'Learning algorithm'.

The learning algorithm performs simple gradient descent, altering the value of each weight or bias parameter in the direction for which the change in that particular parameter moves the output activity patterns nearer to their target values. This training method can also trap the network configuration in local minima of this error function, which halts the training process – or 'learning' as it is often referred to. However, this turns out not to be as much of a problem in practice as it might appear. We shall return to this in the concluding chapter.

This algorithm has the considerable virtue of resolving a long-standing difficulty about training in multi-layered structures. This is

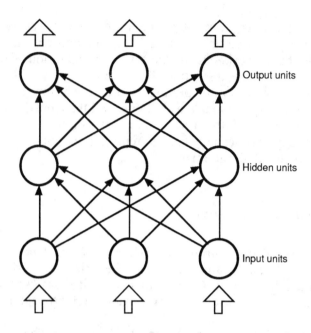

Figure 1.6 A multi-layered perceptron with two layers of weights represented by the arrows between nodes.

called the 'credit assignment problem' which, succinctly put, is the problem of what values should be assigned to the activity levels of the hidden units, since their values are not set directly by the 'teacher', which supplies only the input patterns and corresponding target values. The answer used in this network (and it is not the only solution of this problem) is to let the network decide by setting the connectivities to reduce the discrepancy between the actual outputs of the network, and what they should be. The ability to train multi-layered networks removes the difficulties raised by Minsky and Papert, and opened the floodgates to many practical applications.

This is illustrated in Fig. 1.7, which shows two network architectures which perform the famed 'exclusive-OR' task, i.e. either X or Y but not both, described in Table 1.3. This is something that networks without hidden nodes cannot do, and posed a formidable objection to those networks, which include the previously popular Rosenblatt's perceptron.

The precise values corresponding to 'low' and 'high' signals are not important in this example, and were chosen for convenience, as will

Table 1.3 The XOR task

X	Y	Z
0	0	0.1
0	1	0.9
1	0	0.9
1	1	0.1

be seen later. The two different network architectures, however, have different properties during training, with the second one far less prone to local minima than the first [29].

These networks perform best in classification tasks. A simple picture of the way in which they operate can be arrived at by considering a single node in the hidden layer, as shown in Fig. 1.8(a). For two inputs only, the combinations of input excitations which achieve the activation threshold for that node are given by $X*W + Y*V + BIAS = 0$, which is represented by a straight line. The training process can therefore be regarded as an adjustment of the position of this straight line to correctly separate data that ought to be classified differently (e.g. the As and Bs in Fig. 1.8(b)).

The activity of the hidden nodes, in general, can be shown to result in a partitioning of the input space to allow the next layer of weights, attached to the output nodes, to perform correct classification of the patterns in the sample data [30]. This is illustrated for a single node in Fig. 1.8. A good illustration of the general case is provided by Fig. 2.6 in Chapter 2. The example of the 'exclusive-OR' problem results in one of two different configurations for the weights, one of which is illustrated by the 'decision boundaries' in Fig. 1.9.

The associative memory ability of these networks can be understood by noting that the output surfaces produced after training, when applied to fresh data, in effect interpolate between the correct classifications of neighbouring training samples [31]. This is shown in Fig. 1.10 for the network in Fig. 1.7(a). The effect of training to input values of 0 and 1 would only sharpen the edges of the ridge.

Multi-layered networks can be used as content addressable memories, but they operate in a different way from the Hopfield model. They are sometimes also extended to include terms that are quadratic and higher order in the input activations, which is an old trick to reduce the number of layers needed for accurate pattern classification.

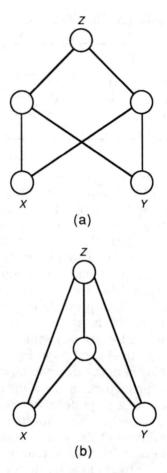

Figure 1.7 Two network architectures that solve the 'exclusive-OR' problem: (a) planar network, (b) simple example of a general architecture consisting of a two-layer network and a single-layer network in parallel.

The most important aspect of the application of these networks however, is to ensure that once trained, the classification ability extends, or generalizes, to fresh data. Examples of this design process can be found in Chapters 2, 5, 7, 8, 10 and 11.

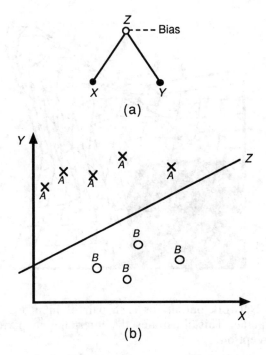

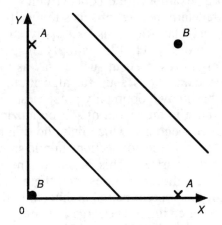

Figure 1.8 The action of one hidden node in a perceptron network. All of the hidden and output nodes in the multi-layered perceptron have 'bias' terms associated with them, although this is usually not drawn for simplicity.

Figure 1.9 Decision boundaries of a solution of the 'exclusive-OR' problem. Each straight line represents the action of one of the two hidden nodes in the network of Fig. 1.7(a).

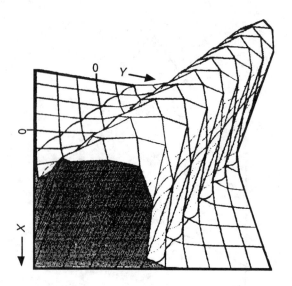

Figure 1.10 Network output for each pair of input (*x.y*) spanning a sector of the plane. This illustrates the interpolation performed by the multi-layer perceptron.

1.7.3 *Kohonen network*

Unlike the previous examples, the connectivities in this network are neither set by a predetermined set of states to recall, nor by attempting to reproduce correct classifications externally supplied by a tutor. The Kohonen network [11], [23] simply inspects the data for regularities, and organizes itself in such a way as to form an ordered description of the data. It is a useful algorithm to use for vector quantization, and has known optimality properties.

The main difference in the layout of self-organizing networks is the presence of lateral connections, which link nodes in the same layer, as indicated in Fig. 1.11. These connections mimic similar connectivities found in the cerebral cortex. This is one of the best theoretically understood of all neural architectures, and there is reason to believe that the function of this type of neural architecture in the cortex is also related to information coding. The large incoming arrow in Fig. 1.11 represents a pyramid of links bringing information from the input data into each node in the network, while the outgoing arrows denote the excitation value of each node in response to data.

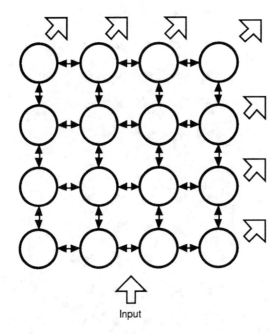

Input

Figure 1.11 A Kohonen self-organizing network. Every node 'sees' the input pattern in the same way. The outgoing arrows denote the output activity of the network, and although only drawn at two of the boundaries, they represent the excitation of each and every node in the network.

The operation of the network can be seen by considering the organization of a small network which is presented with three directions in space, represented in Fig. 1.12 by arrows. This is the input data. Initially, the links between each node and the input data have random values, which represent arbitrary directions.

Now let us carry out the following steps:

(a) Present one input sample, consisting of the first arrow.
(b) Select the node whose direction is closest to this arrow.
(c) Adjust the link weights for this node and its nearest neighbours, by a small amount, towards the direction of the input sample.
(d) Take the next input sample, which is represented by another arrow, and return to (a).

This process is repeated until the links between the nodes and the input window, where the input data are presented one at a time, stop

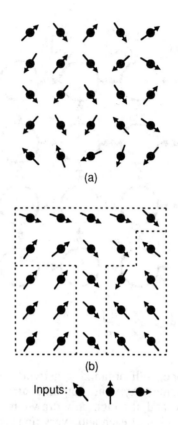

(a)

(b)

Inputs:

Figure 1.12 Operation of a Kohonen network: (a) random initial state, (b) organized weight distribution of a trained network, with boundaries separating the directions nearest to each of the three prototype states.

changing. As training proceeds, the size of the neighbourhood is reduced.

The trained network would have each node set to the directions shown at the bottom of Fig. 1.12. The network displays a topological organization if the changes between the directions of neighbouring nodes as one travels across the network are smooth. A set of link values derived for handwritten character recognition is shown in Chapter 7, Fig. 7.10.

The competition between different nodes in the network, which selects the neighbourhood where the links change for each input sample, can be implemented electronically, and is thought to be realized in biological networks, by inhibitory connections laterally between adjacent nodes in the network, which are shown in Fig. 1.11.

Another graphical example of the process of self-organization is shown in Fig. 1.13. Here, the input data consists of coordinates on the plane sample from a circular density function. The Kohonen network is organized in two dimensions, as the square net shown in Fig. 1.11. If the network were one-dimensional, that is to say with neighbouring nodes connected along a line, with two neighbours each, the final representation of the network would consist of a long string meandering around the circle, instead of a two-dimensional net. This example gives an idea of the power of this network, which can be used to quantize geometrically complex surfaces in any number of spatial dimensions. An example could be spreading a regular net around the fuselage of an aircraft, to help in the selection of grid points for finite element analysis.

1.7.4   *Temporal differences*

This is one of a few neural network algorithms which are especially suited to modelling time-dependent processes [18,32]. The main difference between temporal differences and back error propagation is that the former is able to learn goal-directed functions, where the eventual outcome of each action performed by the network is not known until several steps later. One example of this is optimal aircraft seat allocation, which is the subject of Chapter 3.

An early demonstration of this method is the control of an inverted pendulum, by moving a car left or right. This is represented graphically in Fig. 1.14. The architecture used in this problem is an extreme case of a small-sized neural network. It comprises just two neurones, depicted in the schematic in Fig. 1.15. One is a motor neurone, labelled 'controller', which decides which direction to apply a fixed force to the car. The other 'supervisory' neurone attempts to predict the likelihood that the current sequence of controller actions will eventually lead to failure, by dropping the pole.

This type of training method is also called reward/penalty, and reinforcement learning. The first term describes the fact that the controller uses the penalty or failure signals to gradually learn to avoid those pathways in input space which lead to wrong control actions. The second term reflects the way in which the supervisory element updates its forecasts of the likelihood of failure. Each

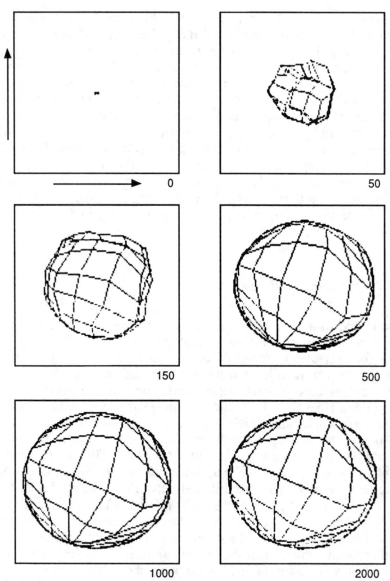

Figure 1.13 Map of two-dimensional weights for a Kohonen network trained to represent a non-uniform circular distribution of points in the plane. The initial weights have small random values, and therefore cluster near the centre of the screen. The two-component weight vector at each node is represented by a single point in the plane. The points corresponding to nearest neighbour nodes in the network are linked by a line to illustrate how the network self-organizes as it trains. This is shown after different numbers of iterations.

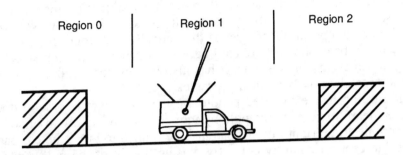

Figure 1.14 The inverted pendulum is balanced by moving the car in either direction, so applying a force of fixed strength to the bottom of the pole.

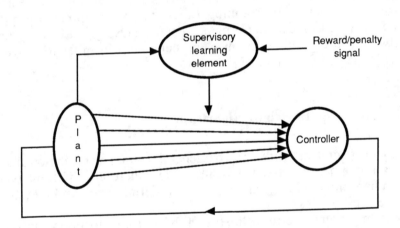

Figure 1.15 Schematic diagram of the network used to balance the pole, and keep it in the centre region. The supervisory learning element forecasts the likelihood of system failure, defined by dropping the pole. The controller is a single node, whose weight parameters are adjusted by the likelihood of signal failure supplied by the supervisory element.

prediction of the eventual outcome of the control process is compared with the previous one, and the difference is used to update the connectivity strengths between the supervisory neurone and the plant states. If a reward signal were used instead, the connectivity strengths would increase if succeeding forecasts agree, and reduce otherwise, hence the term reinforcement. This process of training by correlating one's own guesses with one another is a 'boot-strapping' mechanism, whose convergence is always difficult to ascertain. However, the method of temporal differences is theoretically well founded, and not only has it been shown to extend back error propagation in a sensible way to time varying systems, it has also had its convergence proven for a large class of dynamical processes.

Returning to the inverted pendulum, the two-neurone system does indeed learn to balance the pole by moving the car rapidly in opposite directions at the right rate. It can also be trained to bring the car back into the centre region by correctly biasing the tilt of the pole, but we have found that it is able to perform both of these actions only if it is first trained to balance the pole without reference to where the car is, and only then is a penalty signal for car position introduced. The mode of learning shows some interesting effects, since the system spends a long time training without any significant improvement in performance, before the running times without dropping the pole suddenly increase. The performance deteriorates again as the system partly 'unlearns' how to balance the pendulum in order to move it towards the centre region.

1.8   Choosing the right algorithm

Although neural networks can be generally thought of as non-linear filters implementing associative memories, there are different types depending on which algorithm is used to define them, and they have different properties.

The previous section illustrated how four different network structures may be applied, but there are many other techniques available for classification, optimization, and competitive learning (e.g. [33–38]). There are also techniques which are more closely related to standard statistical methods [39,40] (also Chapter 8), optimal encoders [41] (which is applied in Chapter 9), and expert systems [42]. The approaches described earlier form the backbone of the neural techniques used throughout this book, and their practical properties are increasingly well documented [43–49]. Clearly, these computational paradigms all have their limitations, just like any other numerical methods. The novelty lies in the way in which the novel computing techniques are able to contribute new and effective solutions to problems that have continually challenged the power of more conventional methods.

In conclusion, it is a case of 'horses for courses' – new and old techniques have their own areas of proficiency, and the neural techniques have to be suited to the problem in hand, combining different network architectures where necessary. In both cases there are no magic answers or pandora black box methods of solution: therefore domain knowledge about the practical problem is important and will normally have to be included. The numerical methods, of whichever type, may just enable us to completely solve different problems where our ability leads us only as far as to pose them correctly.

It is the intention of the remainder of the book both to illustrate this design process with practical examples, and to give a brief insight into the status of current applications.

Acknowledgement

It is a pleasure to acknowledge the contributions from colleagues and students, in particular S.J. Perantonis, who through their own application to this work furthered my understanding as much as theirs. In particular, some of the illustrations are reprinted from thesis work by J.K. Leung, K. O'Donovan, L. Russel and S. Kirwin. Thanks are due also to Sandra Collins for her tireless work and meticulous illustrations in several chapters of this book.

References

1. Dreyfus, H. and Dreyfus, S. Why expert systems do not exhibit expertise. *IEEE Expert*, 86-90 (1986).

2. Anderson, J.A. Networks for fun and profit. *Nature*, **323**, 406-407 (1986).

3. McCulloch, W.S. and Pitts, W. A logical calculus of the ideas immanent in nervous activity. *Bull. Math. Biophys.*, **5**, 115-133 (1943). For a review, see Perkel, D.H. Logical neurons: the enigmatic legacy of Warren McCulloch. *Trends in Neurosci.*, **11**, 1, 9-12 (1988).

4. Rapoport, A. "Ignition" phenomena in random nets. *Bull. Math. Biophys.*, **14**, 35-44 (1952).

5. Smith, D.R. and Davidson, C.H. Maintained activity in neural nets. *J. Assoc. for Comp. Machinery*, **9**, 268-279 (1962).

6. Block, H.D. The perceptron: a model for brain functioning. I. *Rev. Mod. Phys.*, **34**, 1, 123-135 (1962). See also Block, H.D., Knight, B.W., Jr. and Rosenblatt, F. Analysis of a four-layer series-coupled perceptron. II. *Rev. Mod. Phys.*, **34**, 1, 135-142 (1962). The original presentation was in the book by Rosenblatt, F. *Principles of Neurodynamics: Perceptrons and the Theory of Brain Mechanisms*, Spartan Books, Washington, DC (1962).

7. Little, W.A. The existence of persistent states in the brain. *Math. Biosc.*, **19**, 101-120 (1974). A more general training process is described in Hebb, D.O. *The Organisation of Behaviour*, Wiley, New York (1949).

8. Griffith, J.S. *Mathematical Neurobiology – An Introduction to the Mathematics of the Nervous System*, Academic Press, London (1971).

9. Minsky, M. and Papert, S. *Perceptrons – An Introduction to Computational Geometry*, MIT Press, Cambridge, MA (1969).

10. Kohonen, T. Correlation matrix memories. *IEEE Trans. on Comp.*, **c-21**, 4, 353-359 (1972).

11. Kohonen, T. *Associative Memory – A System Theoretic Approach*, Springer-Verlag, New York (1977).

12. Willshaw, D.J. and von der Marlsburg, C. How patterned neural connections can be set up by self-organization. *Proc. R. Soc. Lond. B.*, **194**, 431-445 (1976).

13. Grossberg, S. *Studies of Mind and Brain: Neural Principles of Learning, Perception, Development, Cognition and Motor Control*, Reidel Press, Boston (1982). See also Fu (1971) and Hinton and Anderson (1981) in the bibliography.

14. Hopfield, J.J. Neural networks and physical systems with emergent collective computational abilities. *Proc. Natl. Acad. Sci. USA*, **79**, 2554-2558 (1982).

15. Computing with neural networks. Technical comments. *Science*, **325**, 1226-1229 (1987).

16. Fukushima, K., Miyake, S., and Ito, T. Neocognitron: a neural network model for a mechanism of visual pattern recognition. *IEEE Trans. Syst. Man and Cybern.*, **SMC-13**, 5, 826-834 (1983).

17. Barto, A.G., Sutton, R.S. and Anderson C.W. Neuronlike adaptive elements that can solve difficult learning control problems. *Ibid*, 834-846 (1983).

18. Bergen, J.R. and Julesz, B. Rapid discrimination of visual patterns. *Ibid*, 857-863 (1983).

19. Le Cun, Y. Learning process in an asymmetric threshold network. In Bienenstock, E., Fogelman Soulie, F. and Weisbuch, G. *Disordered Systems and Biological Organization*, Springer-Verlag, Berlin and Heidelberg, 233-240 (1986).

20. Rumelhart, D.E., Hinton, G.E. and Williams, R.J. Learning representations by back-propagating errors. *Nature*, **323**, 533-535 (1986). See also Rumelhart and McClelland (1986) in the bibliography.

21. Eccles, J. The synapse. *Sci. Am.*, 56-66, Jan. (1965).

22. Peretto, P. and Niez, J.J. Stochastic dynamics of neural networks. *IEEE Syst. Man and Cybern.*, **SMC-16**, 1, 73-83 (1986).

23. Kohonen, T. The "neural" phonetic typewriter. *IEEE Comp.*, **21**, 3, 11-22 (1988). See also Kohonen (1988) in the bibliography.

24. Lisboa, P.J.G. and Perantonis, S.J. Convergence of recursive associative memories obtained using the multi-layered perceptron. *J. Phys. A: Math. Gen.*, **23**, 4039-4053 (1990).

25. Anderson, J.A. Cognitive and psychological computation with neural networks. *IEEE Syst. Man and Cybern.*, **SMC-13**, 5, 799-815 (1983).

26. Hopfield, J.J. and Tank, D.W. "Neural" computation of decisions in optimization problems. *Biol. Cybern.*, **52**, 141-152 (1985).

27. Hopfield, J.J. Artificial neural networks. *IEEE Circuits and Devices*, 3-10, Sept. (1988).

28. Pineda, F.J. Generalisation of back-propagation to recurrent neural networks. *Phys. Rev. Lett.*, **59**, 19, 2229-2232 (1987).

29. Lisboa, P.J.G. and Perantonis, S.J. Complete solution of the local minima in the XOR problem. *Network: Comp. in Neural Systems*, **2**, 119-124 (1991).

30. Webb, A.R. and Lowe, D. The optimised internal representation of multilayered classifier networks performs nonlinear discriminant analysis. *Neural Networks*, **3**, 4, 367-375 (1990).

31. Broomhead, D.S. and Lowe, D. Multi-variable functional interpolation and adaptive networks. *Complex Systems*, **2**, 3, 269-303 (1988).

32. Sutton, R.S. Learning to predict by the methods of temporal Differences. *Mach. Learn.*, **3**, 9-44 (1988).

33. Kirkpatrick, S., Gelatt, Jr., C.D., and Vecchi, M.P. Optimisation by simulated annealing. *Science*, **220**, 4598, 6671-680 (1983).

34. Bachmann, C.M., Cooper, L.N., Dembo, A. and Zeitouni, 0. A relaxation model for memory with high storage density. *Proc. Natl. Acad. Sci. USA*, **84**, 7529-7531 (1987).

35. Durbin, R. and Wilshaw, D. An analogue approach to the travelling salesman problem using an elastic net method. *Nature*, **326**, 689-691, April (1987).

36. Angeniol, B. and de La Croix Vaubois, G. and Le Texier, Y. Self-organizing feature maps and the travelling salesman problem. *Neural Networks*, **1**, 289-293 (1988).

37. Carpenter, G.A. and Grossberg, S. ART 3: hierarchical search using transmitters in self-organizing pattern recognition architectures. *Neural Networks*, **3**, 2, 129-152 (1990).

38. Yair, E. and Gersho, A. The Boltzmann perceptron network: a soft classifier. *Neural Networks*, **3**, 203-221 (1990).

39. Specht, D.F. Probabilistic neural networks and the polynomial adaline as complementary techniques for classification. *IEEE Trans. Neural Networks*, **1**, 1, 111-121 (1990).

40. Yao, H.C. and Manry, M.T. Iterative improvement of a Gaussian classifier. *Neural Networks*, **3**, 437-443 (1990).

41. Bichsel, M. and Seitz, P. Minimum class entropy: a maximum information approach to layered networks. *Neural Networks*, **2**, 133-141 (1989).

42. Gallant, S.I. Connectionist expert systems. *Comm. of the ACM.*, **31**, 2, 152-169 (1988).

43. Baum, E.B. On the capabilities of multilayer perceptrons. *J. of Complexity*, **4**, 193-215 (1988).

44. Baum, E.B. and Haussler, D. What size net gives valid generalization? In Touretzky, D.S. (ed.). *Advances in Neural Information Processing Systems*, I, Morgan Kaufmann, San Mateo, CA, 81-90 (1989).

45. Mirchandani, G. and Cao, W. On hidden nodes for neural nets. *IEEE Trans. Circuits and Systems*, **35**, 5, 661-664 (1989).

46. Baldi, P. and Hornik, K. Neural networks and principal component analysis: learning from examples without local minima. *Neural Networks*, **2**, 53-58 (1989).

47. Gallant, S.I. A connectionist learning algorithm with provable generalization and scaling bounds. *Neural Networks*, **3**, 191-201 (1990).

48. Gallant, S.I. Perceptron-based learning algorithms. *IEEE Trans. Neural Networks*, **1**, 179-191 (1990).

49. Kangas, J.A., Kohonen, T.K., and Laarksonen, J.T. Variants of self-organizing maps. *IEEE Trans. Neural Networks*, **1**, 1, 93-99 (1990).

Annotated bibliography

This list is not intended to be exhaustive and naturally reflects the familiarity and preferences of the author.

Historical reviews

Fu, K.S. (ed.). *Pattern Recognition and Machine Learning*, Plenum Press, New York (1971). Proceedings of a joint Japan-US seminar held in 1970. It is divided into two parts, one for each of the subjects in the title. It contains a wealth of information on developments at that time, some of which are still relevant today.

Hinton, G.E. and Anderson, J.A. (eds.). *Parallel Models of Associative Memory*, Erlbaum, Hillsdale, NJ (1981). Regarded as a classic, anticipated conceptually some of the developments that took place later on during that decade. The emphasis is on behavioural and psychological aspects of artificial neural models.

Cowan, J.D. and Sharp, D.H. Neural nets. *Quart. Rev. of Biophys.*, **21**, <u>3</u>, 365-427 (1988). A compact review article which reviews the history, main algorithms, theoretical background and application potential of the neural approach to computation, with extensive references.

Biological issues

The brain, *Scientific American*, **241**, <u>3</u> (1979). Highly readable collection of eleven articles, with subjects ranging from the overall organization of the brain, through a detailed description of the neurone, and the mechanisms of vision and movement, to particular chemical processes.

Durbin, R., Miall, C. and Mitchison, G. (eds.). *The Computing Neuron*, Addison-Wesley, London (1989). More theoretical, deals mainly with the correspondence between neural network models and details of the nervous system.

Reviews of general interest

Rumelhart, D.E. and McClelland, J.L. *Parallel Distributed Processing: Explorations in the Microstructure of Cognition*, MIT Press, Cambridge, MA (1986). *Volume I: Foundations*. Extended presentation of the back-propagation training algorithm, among others. Arguably the book that opened the floodgates.

McClelland, J.L. and Rumelhart, D.E. *Parallel Distributed Processing: Explorations in the Microstructure of Cognition*. MIT Press, Cambridge, MA (1986). *Volume II: Psychological and Biological Models*. More concerned with the behavioural and psychological aspects of the new learning paradigms.

Rumelhart, D.E. and McClelland, J.L. *Explorations in Parallel Distributed Processing: A Handbook of Models, Programs and Exercises*, MIT Press, Cambridge, MA (1988). Sequel to the previous book, is accompanied by PC disks with example software.

Kohonen, T. *Self-Organization and Associative Memory*, 2nd edn, Springer-Verlag, Berlin and Heidelberg (1988). Somewhat mathematical, gives a thorough introduction to associative memory, pattern recognition and self-organization, including Kohonen's widely used algorithm. Also discusses the physiological foundations of this approach to associative memory.

Overview articles

Lippmann, R.P. An introduction to computing with neural nets. *IEEE ASSP Mag.*, **4**, 4-22 (1987). Describes the main algorithms, with computational prescriptions for each, and their behaviour in simple example tasks.

Lippmann, R.P. Pattern classification using neural networks. *IEEE Comm. Mag.*, **27**, 11, 47-63 (1989). Extensive review of neural techniques, presented in context with conventional classifiers. The main advantages and disadvantages of each algorithm are discussed briefly, but thoroughly.

Textbooks

Wasserman, P. *Neural Computing: Theory and Practice*, Chapman and Hall, New York (1989). A basic introduction for the non-specialist. Covers the field in some detail and is easy to read.

Mead, C. *Analogue VLSI and Neural Systems*, Addison-Wesley, New York (1989). Aimed at readers with a background in electronics; discusses artificial neural models from the viewpoint of a silicon implementation, leading to detailed descriptions of visual, auditory and motor sensors.

Hecht-Nielsen, R. *Neurocomputing*, Addison-Wesley, New York (1990). A detailed and extensive introduction to the field, written in tutorial style for the technically minded reader.

Source books

Klimasauskas, C.C. (ed.) *A Bibliography of Neurocomputing*, MIT Press, London (1989). Structured bibliography with emphasis on practical techniques and applications.

Wasserman, P. and Oetzel, R. *Neural Source: The Bibliographic Guide to Artificial Neural Networks*, Chapman and Hall, New York (1990). Extensive bibliography covering all aspects of the field, with over 4000 references.

2

Neural network basics

G. A. Works
Science Applications International Corporation, USA

2.1 Summary

Artificial neural network theory, combined with the computing power of today's computer and integrated circuits, has moved from the laboratory on to the factory floor. This paper is an overview of the history, theory, implementations, and applications of artificial neural systems. Two applications, explosive detection in checked baggage and adaptive vibration cancellation, are described.

2.2 Introduction

Although it may seem that neural networks, or artificial neural systems (ANS), is a new technology, what we see today is the culmination of decades of research. From the dawn of history philosophers have attempted to answer the question 'How does man think?'. As calculating machines and cipher engines led to the first computers in the 1930s and 1940s, the questions 'Can we make a machine to think?' and 'What can a computing machine do?' became important. The work of Turing provided the first theoretical answers to these questions [1]. By the 1960s, procedure-based programs like Newell, Simon and Shaw's General Problem Solver were proving theorems, playing chess, and engaging in other activities that seemed to require human intelligence [2–3]. The term artificial intelligence (AI) came into popular use, and prominent researchers in the field, such as Marvin Minsky, suggested that procedure-based computer programs were on the verge of thought [4].

At about the same time, other researchers accepted the brain's massively parallel structure as the model for intelligent systems.

McCulloch and Pitts [5,6], Rosenblatt [7], Lettvin *et al.* [8], Hebb [9] and many others were investigating the properties of biological neurones, and building the theoretical base for ANS [5–9]. What was missing was any practical way to apply these concepts to solve real problems. Integrated circuits were still in the laboratory, and computers of the time had tiny memories and speeds measured in kilo-instructions per second (KIPS). Programming languages, terminals and operating systems bore little resemblance to today's standards. Without more powerful tools productive ANS research, much less practical application, was nearly impossible.

During the past two decades procedure-based AI programs have solved many real-world problems, but they have not solved the hard pattern recognition and adaptive control problems that even the simplest of animals solve constantly. Human intelligence now appears to be composed of countless interacting processes, each dealing with a tiny aspect of the world; Minsky [4] now speaks of a 'community of mind'. At the same time, computer capacity has improved by a factor of approximately one million. Much of the current ANS 'boom' represents the coupling of the ideas of the 1960s with the power of today's computer technology to solve real-world problems. Additionally, many researchers have entered or returned to the field, drawn by the perception that ANS is a technology whose time has come.

2.3 What is a 'hard' problem?

Most of the problems that engineers can solve can be modelled as linear systems, which satisfy the equation:

$$F(aX + bY) = aF(X) + bF(Y), \tag{2.1}$$

where F is the system transfer function and X and Y are scalar variables, vectors, or time functions. The solutions to this equation are complex exponential functions, which are the eigenfunctions of linear systems. We analyse linear systems with a rich body of linear system theory, such as Fourier analysis. When we must deal with a non-linear system, we try to describe it as 'piecewise linear'.

Most real-world problems are not linear, and cannot be understood as piecewise linear. The Mandelbrot set of fractal images, for example, is generated by iterating the equation:

$$Z_k = Z_{k-1}^2 + C \qquad\qquad (2.2)$$

where C is a position in the complex plane, and colouring the pixel located at C according to the value of k at which Z exceeds a threshold. Although the only non-linearity is a quadratic term, the fractal pattern generated has infinite complexity. Mixing of fluids, turbulent flow, failure of mechanical structures, hydraulic systems, economic forecasting, human behaviour, image and speech recognition are a few of many more complex examples. Our mathematical tools for analysing non-linear systems are few and weak, and usually give us only existence proofs rather than hard answers. Chaos theory, strange attractors, basins of attraction, and fractals are concepts applicable to non-linear systems.

We can learn a great deal about complex non-linear systems even though we have no comprehensive mathematical tools. One way to describe this knowledge is to state rules describing the behaviour of a system. This is the approach taken by the author of the textbook, or a knowledge engineer writing an AI program. Another way is to map significant states of the system into some more compact internal representation so that later occurrences of these states can be recognized. This is the approach used in teaching by example, or by an ANS. Both approaches are valid ways of modelling complex systems, although some systems clearly lend themselves to one approach more than to the other, as Fig. 2.1 illustrates.

2.4 What is an ANS?

Artificial 'neurones' are highly simplified representations of some of the functions of real, biological nerve cells or neurones. To distinguish this simplified representation from the biological neurone, many authors use the term processing element (PE). Although there are several simplified models, the semi-linear PE shown in Fig. 2.2 is the most commonly used.

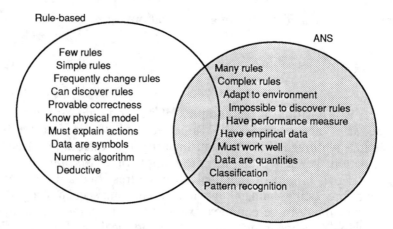

Figure 2.1 Rule-based and ANS-oriented problems.

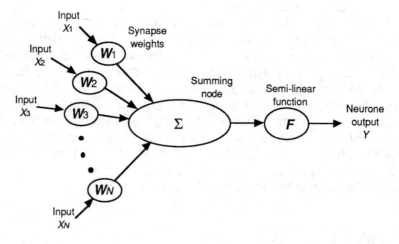

Figure 2.2 Semi-linear processing element.

The semi-linear PE accepts many input signals and produces one output, which is a semi-linear function of the weighted sum of inputs. Various semi-linear functions are in use including the arc tangent function, the sigmoid $F(x) = 1/(1 + e^{-x})$, portions of a sine function, and functions made up of three or more straight line segments. The important requirement of the function is that it must map any input into a finite range of outputs, usually 0 to 1, and must be monotonic. For some purposes, it is also necessary that the function be differentiable. The equation describing the response of a PE to input signals is often called the PE's propagation equation. For the semi-linear PE, this equation is:

$$Y = F(\Sigma X_k W_k). \tag{2.3}$$

PEs can be interconnected in various topologies, shown in Fig. 2.3, including feedforward, partially recurrent, fully recurrent, random, and many other specialized topologies. These different interconnection topologies have specific characteristics that make them useful for particular applications. Feedforward networks are the simplest, because the output from the network at any instant depends only on the current input signals and the connection weights. In all other topologies the network is a feedback system with an internal state, so the output at any instant also depends on the internal state of the network.

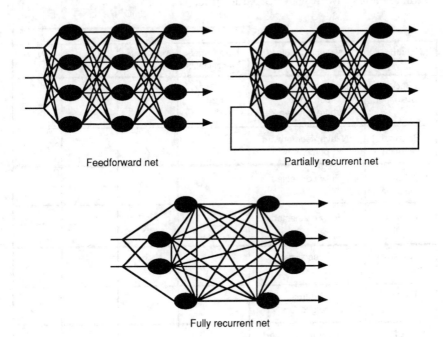

Feedforward net   Partially recurrent net

Fully recurrent net

Figure 2.3 ANS network topologies.

The connection weights in a network can be constant or can change in response to the inputs and states of the network. Constant weights are useful in networks that perform some particular mapping, such as mapping an image of the letter 'A' to the ASCII code for 'A', or which implement specific basins of attraction, so that the network settles into a particular state in response to an input. Changing weights are useful in networks that adapt or learn, such as adaptive control systems and trainable pattern recognizers. Weight changes are described by ordinary differential (or difference) equations, so changing weight networks are non-linear dynamical systems.

An ANS paradigm is a combination of a network topology, the PE propagation equation, and the weight change difference equations. Hundreds of ANS paradigms have been published and presented, although most of them are variations on a few basic schemes. There is no single ANS paradigm that is best suited for all problems. In fact, many successful ANS applications employ specialized networks designed for the problem at hand. Figure 2.4 lists some characteristics of a few ANS paradigms.

Algorithm	Network topology	Function			
		Mapping and classification	Association	Clustering	NP-complete
Back-propagation	N-layer feedforward perceptron, arbitrary networks	X	X		
Boltzman learning	N-layer feedforward perceptron	X	X		
Boltzman machine	Fully connected				X
Hopfield net	Fully connected		X		X
Adaptive resonance	Specialized		X	X	
Feature map	Nearest neighbours			X	
RCE (NESTOR)	3-layer feedforward perceptron	X			

Figure 2.4 ANS paradigms.

2.5 ANS implementations

Most ANS networks today are implemented as software simulations on general purpose or special purpose computers. Networks can also be implemented directly as semiconductor circuits, or using electro-optical or optical technology. Ferroelectric, chemical and superconductive technology has also been proposed. Figure 2.5 compares the capabilities of several current and future implementations in terms of total network interconnections, and connection updates per second. As shown, software simulations can take advantage of dense semiconductor memory technology to implement very large nets, while ANS chips and optical techniques can implement very fast nets. Compared to biological neural nets, today's ANS networks are still very simple.

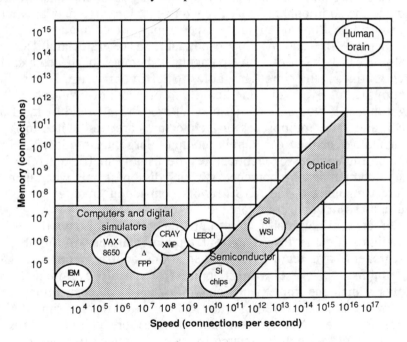

Figure 2.5 ANS implementations.

The principal issue in software implementations is that ANS models are computationally intensive. The semi-linear model requires one multiplication and one addition for each input connection during forward-propagation. During weight update computations the computation load is much greater for most algorithms, although some 'fast-learning' algorithms (such as Nestor Incorporated's RCE algorithm) avoid this computation at the expense of reduced information stored per connection. Some weight update algorithms require at least 32-bit floating point and sometimes 64-bit floating point computation to converge to an optimal weight set for a network. A moderately large 10 000 connection back propagation network trained on 20 000 training vectors can easily require 10^{12} floating point operations to compute a set of connection weights. This computation would consume several CPU weeks on a modern mid-size computer. After training however, this network could be used as a constant weight network with a propagation time of a few milliseconds.

Special purpose computers, or ANS accelerator cards, can speed up ANS training and propagation by factors of 100 or more as well as provide the additional memory needed to develop large networks with desktop PCs. Important issues in special purpose computers for ANS are memory size and memory bandwidth. Accelerator architectures that process data out of a host computer's memory, or use data cache architectures, may not be able to efficiently use their full computational power on heavily dot-product-oriented ANS algorithms. It would seem that parallel processing would be ideal for ANS, and some multiprocessor architectures are well suited to ANS computation, if they can rapidly compute large dot products. Fine-grained multiprocessor architectures are usually inefficient for ANS due to communication bottlenecks, which disappear only when there is a direct mapping of the ANS network connection topology on to the multiprocessor connection topology.

Direct semiconductor chip implementations of specific ANS paradigms are the fastest current implementations. A number of researchers have reported implementations of many common ANS paradigms. Of these, a most impressive recent development was Holler's analogue implementation with over 10 000 connections [10]. A few vendors are offering small quantities of much simpler ANS chips for sale. Several companies have more complex chips in development that will be offered for sale in the next two years. One issue with ANS chips is whether the chip is a building block that can be interconnected with other chips to make large networks, or is itself a complete network of fixed size. A second issue concerns how the chip interfaces to the outside world and possibly other similar chips. ANS chips may require many signal pins, and may use analogue (voltage, current or pulse rate) or digital (parallel or serial) interfaces. A third issue is the speed of the chip, which for an analogue chip may depend on output loading. A fourth issue concerns whether the chip contains some built-in learning mechanism, and if not, how the connection weights are loaded (at manufacture, one-time programming by the user, or rewritable).

Networks implemented with ANS chips (and other direct hardware techniques), whether analogue or digital, can be highly fault tolerant. The failure of a connection or PE in a large network typically causes only a small degradation in network performance, but the failure of a single connection or transistor in a complex microprocessor causes total failure of the microprocessor (and usually the system of which it is a part). This characteristic has profound implications for the way we build semiconductors. As the complexity of a conventional chip increases, the manufacturing yield and reliability decrease exponentially. This is the reason that we do not build circuits the size of semiconductor wafers (180–340 cm^2), but limit chip area to approximately 1 cm^2. The manufacturing yield of a semiconductor ANS network can be independent of network complexity. This fault tolerance is indeed fortunate for biological neural systems; our brains lose about 1000 neurones every day.

2.6 Applications

Pattern recognition and classification is one of the most common ANS applications. Pattern classifiers accept an input feature vector, and produce an output class code. The feature vector corresponds to a point in feature space and the class code is the label assigned to the region in feature space in which the point lies.

Figure 2.6 shows the performance of one, two and three layer feedforward networks on two classification problems, the exclusive-OR and the meshed regions problems. In the exclusive-OR problem two disjoint regions in feature space must be classified as 'A' and two other regions classified as 'B'. Neither conventional template-matching classifiers nor single-layer ANS networks can solve this problem, which requires a minimum of two layers. The more difficult meshed regions problem requires a three-layer network, which Lippmann has shown to be sufficient to solve arbitrarily complex classification problems [11].

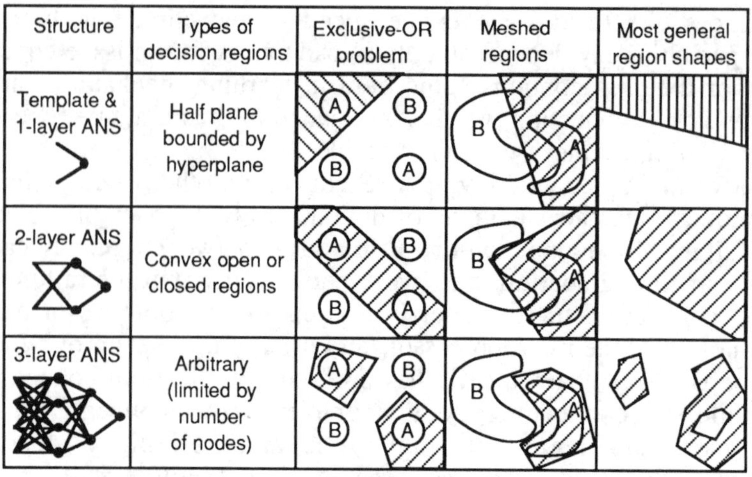

Structure	Types of decision regions	Exclusive-OR problem	Meshed regions	Most general region shapes
Template & 1-layer ANS	Half plane bounded by hyperplane			
2-layer ANS	Convex open or closed regions			
3-layer ANS	Arbitrary (limited by number of nodes)			

Figure 2.6 Pattern classification using feedforward ANS networks.

A good example of ANS pattern classification is Shea and Lin's [12] TNA explosive detection system for checked baggage that SAIC recently began delivering under contract to the Federal Aviation Administration, shown in Fig. 2.7. These systems are now installed at Heathrow, Kennedy, Dulles and several other high-risk airports. The system uses thermal neutrons to irradiate the baggage, causing chemical elements in the baggage to emit characteristic gamma rays. The gamma rays escape from the suitcase and are sensed by detectors around the cavity, providing an image that shows the amount and location of key elements, particularly nitrogen, in the baggage. Features extracted from this image are the input to the ANS pattern classifier that determines whether explosives are present, and whether the explosives are in sheet or bulk form. We compared the performance of several ANS paradigms with respect to probability of detection and false alarm rate, including Adaptive Resonance II (ART II), counter-propagation, and back-propagation. Linear and quadratic discriminant algorithms were also tested. Back-propagation provided the lowest false alarm rate, as shown in Fig. 2.8.

Non-linear adaptive control is a second major area of ANS applications. Non-linear control problems arise in areas such as hydraulics, robotics, vehicle control, deformable structures, traffic control and others. ANS networks can be used in place of linear filters to extend standard linear adaptive control schemes described by Widrow and Stearns [13] and others. Figure 2.9 shows four typical

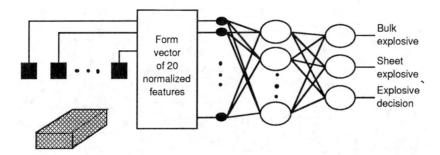

Figure 2.7 Explosive detection system.

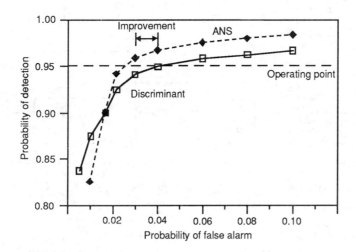

Figure 2.8 ANS and linear discriminant performance.

ANS non-linear control systems based on feedforward networks that can be used to predict or model the inputs and outputs to a system, or to correct its output. Other approaches make use of recurrent ANS networks.

One example of a continuous-training ANS-based non-linear control system is the Equalizer vibration cancellation system that SAIC recently developed. This system employs a hydraulic actuator attached to a structure to move a compensating mass in such a way as to cancel vibration at one point on the structure. In a more complex form, two actuators were used to provide two-axis vibration cancellation. Non-linearities are inherent in the system because the

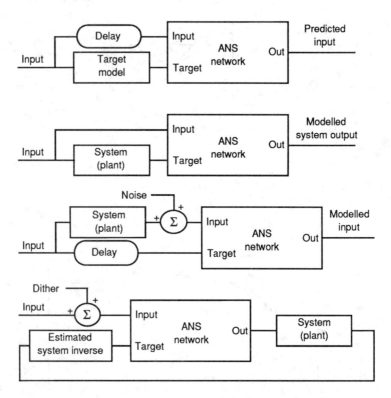

Figure 2.9 ANS non-linear adaptive control systems.

hydraulic actuator is controlled by an electrically operated spool valve, and fluid flow through the spool valve is turbulent in some valve positions. The control system must be adaptive both because the driving vibration is not constant, and because the hydraulic fluid viscosity changes with temperature. Figure 2.10 shows a block diagam of a single-axis Equalizer.

The Equalizer employs a feedforward network that accepts the past 15 msec of time history of acceleration from the vibration source and from the compensator mass, and generates the spool valve control signal. The error term, which the network learns to minimize, is the acceleration of the platform to be stabilized. A position term is also added to the error term so that the network keeps the compensator mass near the centre of its range of travel. Filters are needed to remove amplifier voltage offset from the acceleration error signal, and to prevent the position signal from affecting vibration cancellation. The system continuously trains with a modified back-

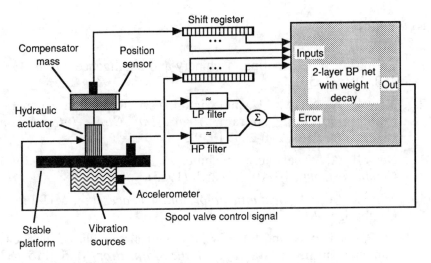

Figure 2.10 Single-axis Equalizer for vibration cancellation.

propagation algorithm, changing its control function in response to the changing dynamics of the structure. The Equalizer was implemented on a high-speed ANS accelerator card (a Delta II Floating Point Processor) running at a 1000 sample per second rate, and provided approximately 30 dB cancellation for fundamental vibration frequencies below 100 Hz.

2.7 The future of artificial neural systems

Current ANS research includes systems of multiple interconnected networks and efficient hardware implementations of connections and PEs. Many researchers are finding that work in ANS is an aid to unravelling the workings of animal nervous systems, and that the study of animal nervous systems inspires ideas for new ANS architectures. An International Neural Network Society (INNS) has been formed, and universities throughout the world have added courses in ANS. ANS is firmly established as a useful adjunct to conventional processing tools. It has the potential to become an information processing paradigm rivalling the Von Neumann digital computer.

References

1. Turing, A.M. Computing machinery and intelligence. *Mind*, 433-460, Oct. (1950).

2. Newell, A., Shaw, J.C. and Simon, H.A. Report on a general problem-solving program. *Proc. Int. Conf. Information Processing*, Paris, 256-264 (1959).

3. Newell, A. The chess machine. *Proc. 1955 Western Joint Computer Conf.*, 101-108, March (1955).

4. Minsky, M. (ed). *Semantic Information Processing*, MIT Press, Cambridge, MA (1968).

5. McCulloch, W.S. and Pitts, W.H. A logical calculus of the ideas immanent in nervous activity. *Bull. Math. Biophy.*, **5**, 115-133 (1943).

6. McCulloch, W.S. *Embodiments of Mind*, MIT Press, Cambridge, MA (1965).

7. Rosenblatt, F. *Principles of Neurodynamics*, New York, Spartan Books (1959).

8. Lettvin, J.Y., Maturana, H., McCulloch, W.S. and Pitts, W. What the frog's eye tells the frog's brain. *Proc. IRE*, **47**, 1940-1951 (1959).

9. Hebb, D.O. *The Organization of Behavior*, Wiley, New York (1949).

10. Holler, M., Tam, S., Castro, H. and Benson, R. An electrically trainable artificial neural network (ETANN) with 10240 floating gate synapses. *Int. Joint Conf. Neural Networks*, II, 191-196 (1989).

11. Lippmann, R.P. An introduction to computing with neural nets. *IEEE ASSP Mag.*, **4**, 2, 4-22, April (1989).

12. Shea, P.M. and Lin, V. Detection of explosives in checked airline baggage using an artificial neural system. *Int. Joint Conf. Neural Networks*, II, 31-34 (1989).

13. Widrow, B. and Stearns, S.D. *Adaptive Signal Processing*, Prentice-Hall, Englewood Cliffs, NJ (1985).

3

Using adaptive networks for resource allocation in changing environments

T. M. Bell, W. R. Hutchison and K. R. Stephens
BehavHeuristics, Inc., USA

3.1 Summary

This chapter discusses a broad class of problems where the objective is to find an optimal solution to the allocation of one or more finite resources within an environment that is unstable – a class of problems that Wasserman has called 'non-linear optimization' problems [1].

3.2 Introduction

In terms used within the artificial intelligence research community, these more complex resource allocation problems are a type of 'planning in uncertainty'. Simpler resource allocation problems, like the 'travelling salesman problem' [2,3], lack some of the essential elements of planning, such as the definition of response elements and their sequential dependencies. Langlotz and Shortliffe [4], Hutchison [5] and Skinner [6] have contrasted two general approaches to planning problems – symbolic logic (which can be first-order or non-monotonic) and decision-theoretic. Research into symbolic logic seems most applicable when the goal is construction of a new plan which complies with a set of constraints. Rule-based expert systems are a favoured approach by proponents of symbolic logic in problem solving. While logical inference can search a solution space for a plan that meets a set of logical constraints, these methods are poor at exerting preference for one course of action over another. Decision theory, on the other hand, offers a method of choosing between different courses of action on the basis of the probability and value of possible outcomes. In fact, Langlotz *et al.* have shown that decision theory concepts are implicit in rule-based systems [7]. For the above reasons, BehavHeuristics prefers a decision theory approach for problem solving in general, and for solving resource allocation problems in particular.

Optimal resource allocation involves the management of resources (e.g. manpower and equipment) in some process over time such that some definable outcome is maximized (i.e. the value of the outcome can be compared to the cost of the resources). The process may be anything that consumes resources in order to produce a desired product. Manufacturing, training, marketing and project management are all examples of this kind of process.

Producing an optimal solution to a complex resource allocation problem is difficult enough when the problem environment is stable. When the resource pool or the resource-consuming process is altered, the previously optimal but static solution must often be discarded and a new optimal solution derived. This can be expensive in terms of time, effort, and computing resources. An efficient, yet adaptive solution is therefore preferable in these situations. In addition to residing within a dynamic application environment, several other characteristics of resource allocation problems suggest their suitability to solutions that make use of adaptive network technology:

- Multiple activities or entities compete for a limited set of resources.
- Many input factors can interact with each other in a complex fashion, and often many different objectives (i.e. values or utilities) must be weighed in making allocation decisions.
- Most of these relationships are probabilistic, which make them not amenable to expression as rules, nor appropriate for most optimization methods.
- As the basis for learning, there is either a large database with examples of inputs and corresponding outputs, or the ability to simulate the application environment (e.g. knowing the failure models of equipment being scheduled).

While these characteristics make an adaptive network approach uniquely suited for such problems, it should be clear that designing a network architecture to solve them is no simple task.

Resource allocation can be a tricky business. It is based on forecasts that are not discrete quantities, but continuous variables having probability distributions. This is well known in portfolio management, but not so clearly recognized in other allocation applications. For example, a forecast may predict that demand for full-fare seats on a flight will be 50. To make optimal decisions one must also know the probability that it might be 60 or some other number. In the case of airline demand and no-show forecasts, it is reasonable to assume normal distributions, which reduces the problem to estimating the standard distribution. This parameter can be estimated from statistical analysis of the forecasts and outcomes. However, we have developed adaptive network methods which can produce better estimates of variability.

Second, unlike some of the more classical problems solved by adaptive networks, resource allocation never permits a network to converge on a correct solution because the best solution changes as the world changes. This means the network must continue to adapt at a rate matching the rate of change in its problem domain, using real-time feedback from the environment as it becomes available. Networks are well suited to this kind of adaptation, but getting the learning parameters right is challenging. This is especially difficult because learning rates that fit rapidly changing relationships can easily wash out more slowly changing relationships, such as season of the year or trend.

The problem of continuous adaptation is enormously compounded in the case of forecasting problems because the feedback for a forecast is by its nature delayed, and delay of feedback hampers adaptation. Imagine a simplistic network model for forecasting airline ticket demand six months ahead, when many critical commitments must in fact already be decided. If the six-month forecasts are only updated six months later – when their results are known – the airline environment may have changed so significantly during that period that the new model was already out of date and causing costly errors. Booking information is a continuous time series, requiring learning algorithms that can utilize this flow of information more efficiently. The solution to this problem is closely related to the solution for the next.

Finally, there is usually more than one outcome variable to consider, which requires that they be combined in some sort of utility function or objective function. For example, if only the immediate revenue effects of denied boardings are considered, to the exclusion of their adverse impact on customer goodwill, flights will too often be overbooked. Sometimes an objective function can be constructed using one of several methods that have been developed for multi-objective optimization [8]. However, the airline problem is like most resource allocation problems in having not only multiple objectives, such as revenue, market share, and goodwill, but also different time frames within which these occur. For example, ignoring customer goodwill earns more revenue today but less in the future. What is needed is a function that can be maximized in the present which will also result in the maximization of long-term values for the airline. Those familiar with the methods of dynamic programming will recognize this problem as fitting those methods. However, dynamic programming becomes computationally intractable with problems of any degree of complexity, such as those of interest here.

Fortunately, methods exist that can be used in conjunction with adaptive networks to offer reasonable solutions to the last two challenges. BehavHeuristics uses architectures that are similar to the 'three-net' architecture described by Werbos [9], which combines 'temporal differences' methods [10], with adaptive networks. In order to handle some of the challenges inherent in the resource allocation applications, however, BehavHeuristics has had to develop several additional technical refinements.

BehavHeuristics has successfully developed solutions to resource allocation problems using a hybrid approach that makes use of adaptive network systems within a decision theory context. These solutions have three elements in common:

(a) a causal model of the process based on a trained adaptive network,
(b) a method for determining the value or utility of a solution, and
(c) a method for optimally managing the allocation of resources to the process.

Each of these solutions was developed using BehavHeuristics' proprietary adaptive network software known as BANKET™ (BehavHeuristics Adaptive Network Knowledge Engineering Toolkit). The remainder of this chapter will discuss the general features of BANKET, and how it has been applied to (1) the problem of selective discounting of an airline seat inventory (i.e. revenue or 'yield' management), and (2) a complex scheduling problem with multiple constraints.

3.3 BANKET

BANKET is the result of several years of independent research and development [5,11]. It is a shell structure for developing and supporting adaptive networks, and is currently hosted within the Smalltalk-80™ Objectworks™ environment from Parc Place Systems. Smalltalk is an object-oriented programming and delivery system, and therefore supports a style of system development known as exploratory programming or rapid prototyping [12]. Smalltalk (and BANKET) will run on a large number of computers, including the IBM PC, AT and 386 systems (and their clones), the Macintosh II, and workstations from Sun, Tektronix, DEC and Apollo. It can be integrated with databases and local area networks. This software environment offers many practical advantages which are beyond the scope of this chapter.

BANKET is the embodiment of a theoretical viewpoint on adaptive behaviour which combines the fields of behavioural science and behavioural systems analysis with the viewpoints of several other scientific disciplines which study adaptive systems [13]. A behavioural view of adaptive networks has been proposed by Hutchison *et al.* [11], [14], and similar viewpoints have recently been reviewed by Donahoe and Palmer [15] and Kehoe [16]. Many issues which are now of interest to adaptive software developers have long been studied in the behavioural literature: learning, control over system behaviour by complex inputs, models of choice between behavioural alternatives, and the integration of symbolic and distributed knowledge within intelligent systems [17].

BANKET is an adaptive network software environment that has been and is being used by BehavHeuristics in the development of a number of practical applications. It includes a number of features that are consistent with a behavioural approach to intelligent systems [18]. According to this approach, there are three major components to the contingencies of reinforcement and punishment which govern operant behaviour: responses, consequent stimuli, and antecedent stimuli.

Responses are the outputs of any system that has been designed to solve a problem effectively. Consequent stimuli are sources of feedback from the system's environment that can be used to differentially strengthen (reinforce) or weaken (punish) the system's responses. To indicate how satisfactorily a particular response solves some problem, a utility function is typically employed (see below). Antecedent stimuli are environmental events that identify for the system different problem types that could be solved by an appropriate response. BANKET provides methods for representing antecedent stimuli, including preprocessing and automatic/adaptive scaling to capture non-linear stimulus effects. It has the ability to maintain a 'sparse matrix' of connections to hidden units, and to insert or remove these units automatically as needed during training to optimally fit the domain. It provides, where appropriate, various learning acceleration processes including noise injection such as simulated annealing and forced random responding. It also contains methods for representing inter-response dependencies and control by temporal processes, both of which are essential for scheduling and other time-dynamic resource allocation solutions. The method of temporal differences [19] is implemented to provide feedback for learning during an extended process, rather than having to wait until a process is completed for learning to occur.

Much of the power of BANKET in producing real-world applications comes from the integration of the adaptive network approach with another important methodology – an implementation of behavioural economics [20–22]. Networks require feedback in order to learn, but in most real-world problems the outcome of interest is not uni-dimensional. For example, in a training programme the objectives are to maximize learning, minimize cost, minimize idle time, maximize student satisfaction, etc. Since these cannot always be achieved simultaneously, a function must be developed which combines them [8]. BANKET contains a set of procedures for developing such functions, which correspond to the 'primary utility functions' of dynamic programming. This function can be used in network learning through 'temporal differences' methods described by Barto *et al.* [10], implementing an approximation to dynamic programming [9]. Since conventional dynamic programming is computationally intractable for most complex problems, the availability of a primary utility function provides an exciting building block for resource allocation.

The method of temporal differences is implemented in BANKET to provide feedback for learning during the course of an extended process, rather than waiting until process completion for learning to occur. The temporal differences method was identified by Sutton [19] who acknowledged its basis in Rescoria and Wagner's [23] behavioural theory of conditioning. In fact, the concept of temporal differences is related to an entire body of research on higher-order conditioning [24]: the primary utility function corresponds to primary reinforcement, while the secondary utility function corresponds to secondary, or 'conditioned' reinforcement.

In some applications, algorithms can be mathematically derived to serve as utility functions; this is a major function of knowledge engineering in these cases. In other application areas where the utility function cannot be described directly, BANKET generates scenarios for a human expert to judge on the basis of 'situational value' [25]. The database of scenarios thus elicited can be used to train a separate network to match the human judgments of overall utility. Utility functions can be based on the best judgments of a single expert, or can be an aggregate of the judgments of several experts. BANKET can also discount future values and derive net present values of outcomes, and can integrate probabilistic events for various probability models and derivative expected values.

All of these features make BANKET amenable to optimal resource allocation by behavioural decision theory. Since it can effectively forecast event probabilities (when trained with sufficient and appropriate data), and since it can use a utility function that has either been provided algorithmically or derived through human judgements, it is ideally suited to compute expected values of outcomes. In resource allocation problems, different outcome actions compete with each other; the action with the highest expected value will be chosen.

3.4 Airline revenue management

Airlines, like all industries, are ultimately controlled by the economic laws of supply and demand. These are managed by setting the capacity and pricing variables that are under an airline's direct control. Since capacity can be changed only very slowly, pricing is the primary mechanism. Until a few years ago, airlines fought major battles using broad pricing offensives. For example, prices overall were lowered by 15% to meet demand overall on all flights in certain markets. Such price drops were unnecessary on some flights, and inadequate to overcome competition on others.

Today there is a strong trend towards more flexible pricing, so that competition will be optimized on every departure. This capability has become recognized by industry analysts as being perhaps the most crucial asset an airline can have to remain profitable, given that profitability often hinges on a difference of one or two seats sold per flight departure. However, since a major airline can have an inventory of half a million future departures being sold at any given time, the prospect of flexible pricing is a daunting task!

Airlines sell a very perishable commodity – namely, seats on an aircraft – of which some portion (often as much as one third) does in fact 'spoil' every time an aircraft departs with empty seats. This problem corresponds closely to those faced by other industries [26], such as empty rooms for hotels and idle cars at a car rental company; somewhat less obviously, it also corresponds with poorly managed shelf space in retail stores, and idle workers and/or inventory in a manufacturing setting. If the seats (rooms, cars, etc.) would otherwise be empty, selling it for any price above its low marginal cost would be preferable to leaving it empty.

Airline marketing specialists respond to demand on a flight-by-flight basis by allocating limits for bookings in each fare class, such as making many discount-fare seats available on a flight with little demand from full-fare business customers. However, airlines want to avoid yield dilution: selling seats at low cost to customers who would have been willing to pay a higher fare. They also want to avoid high-yield spill: selling so many discounted seats that later-booking full-fare customers end up being turned away.

The second, interrelated part of the marketing specialist's problem is that many customers who have booked seats end up as no-shows, leading airlines to overbook more passengers than they have physical capacity to carry. However, the number of no-shows is quite variable, so that despite overbooking there will often be empty seats that could have been sold. At other times so many ticket holders will show up that some will be denied boarding. A few people on each flight may show up without prior reservations (go-shows), and are usually willing to pay higher fares if a seat is available.

The marketing expert's skill lies in accurately predicting passenger demand for each class of ticket, as well as the percentage of no-shows and go-shows under various conditions. Then the challenge is to make optimal trade-offs between the factors mentioned above, taking into account the expected degrees of variability in each case. A further complication is that the costs of errors are not symmetrical: for example, the cost of a denied boarding can be much higher than the cost of an empty seat.

The above description should make clear that every departure requires and merits significant effort, especially since each departure constitutes a nearly unique marketing environment. There are many variables to consider for each flight, such as time of day, day of week, seasonally or holidays, the origin and destination city-pair, ticket prices, strength of competition, and a host of other factors. This effort must be multiplied by the vast number of flights to monitor. A small airline with 100 departures per day and monitoring bookings 360 days in advance would have to be actively monitoring 36 000 departures simultaneously. This number would rapidly inflate to 720 000 for a major airline of 2000 departures per day. Hundreds or thousands of dollars in marginal revenue on each one of these flights depend on accurate judgment. Performing this task well is worth hundreds of millions of dollars annually to a major airline. Even small improvements in accuracy are extremely valuable.

The complex pattern of interacting factors makes it difficult for marketing experts to articulate the factors that influence a subjective forecast of demand. This, combined with the large number of potential interactions and non-linear contributions of the decision factors, makes the problem an unnatural fit to the production-rule approach of a typical expert system solution. Even if the experienced analyst could identify all the determinants of accurate judgment, the large and unwieldy rule base needed to represent this knowledge would be difficult to update if conditions should change. The same difficulties also pose severe problems to conventional operations research and statistical methodologies. Linear programming models, for instance, are the traditional method of choice for solving optimization problems. But when many variables – all of which may not be linear – interact with each other, linear programming methods become computer intensive and thus impractical.

3.5 Airline marketing tactician™ (AMT)

The BehavHeuristics product family known as AMT was initially described by Hutchison and Stephens [27]. Since then, the product has been enhanced considerably and has received excellent reviews in its day-to-day performance at Nationair Canada. It is currently being evaluated by several major US and international carriers.

AMT provides daily monitoring and recommendations for each departure. The system accesses current data on advance bookings and limits from the airline's computerized reservation system and maintains an internal database of fares, routes, equipment, schedules, etc. associated with each flight. In normal operation, the system formulates recommendations for actions for each departure being reviewed prior to consultation sessions with the airline's marketing specialists. Users can then examine the recommendations for a particular flight across departure dates, for a date across flights, or any selected group of flights defined by characteristics such as percentage of changes being recommended.

AMT uses a two-step process, step one being the production of forecasts by the network and step two being the allocation of seats to fare classes using standard optimization methods. Two main networks are used for forecasting: one to predict demand for seats in each fare class, and the other to predict no-show and go-show rates in each fare class. The inputs for each network are the variables that influence demand and no-shows respectively, which may be binary or categorical, such as day of the week, or continuous, such as price. Time is also a critical input variable, since the network needs to know at what point in the booking period the input data reflect. Additionally, there are interdependencies among the different classes of the system, such as the fact that offering a large number of discount seats may undermine demand for higher-fare seats. These dependencies, which can be seen as demand elasticities, must be represented in the network by way of cross-connections. On the output side of the networks, there is a continuous-valued output in each network for each fare class, indicating the magnitude of the forecast (i.e. bookings and no-shows).

Network training makes use of historical data from the airline's reservation system. This is supplemented with input from revenue analysts regarding competitive position and special events. Forecasts can thus be compared with actual results to determine the training feedback. BehavHeuristics uses a proprietary variation of the back-propagation algorithm for this training. By also incorporating temporal differences methods, accuracy is improved, especially for long-term forecasts. BANKET's self-configuring abilities construct a network structure which maintains only those 'hidden layer' nodes that represent significant interactions. Input scaling is automatically adjusted during training to form a 'piecewise linear' approximation of non-linear variables. Since the network is trained with all readily available data that may play a role in determining demand, it represents a causal model of consumer behaviour and the booking process. Each airline's competitive environment is unique, so an individualized forecasting network is developed for each installation of the product. The utility function for AMT can be adjusted to include subjective input from key decision makers in the organization. In this way, it captures and retains corporate values and policies.

An adaptive system which self-configures requires very few a priori assumptions. And since it can be incrementally retrained with most recent data, it is a dynamic model that can track evolving trends in the market-place as they occur. Because BANKET incorporates temporal differences methods, updating the model can occur from one review horizon to the next, instead of waiting until the actual outcome of the flight departure is provided by a post-flight audit.

The first generation of this product controlled the entire allocation process by an adaptive network (but the two-step process is preferred because the system converges on solutions faster, and because users find this two-step process easier to monitor, since the forecasts can be checked against later outcomes, and the optimization methods can be more easily understood), and it is certainly possible to train a network to make a fare class allocation decision given a certain business scenario. The traditional method of choice for solving optimization problems is often linear programming, but when there are many variables which may not be linear and which interact with each other, linear programming methods become computationally intensive and impractical. For these reasons, the adaptive network solution is preferable to linear programming. However, BehavHeuristics has since found that a hybrid system more closely approaches optimality in an efficient way, and enables users to have the intermediate results (the demand forecasts). An algorithm based on marginal economics known as Expected Marginal Seat Revenue (EMSR) conducts a seat-by-seat bidding process to give each seat to the fare class with the greatest expected value (the product of fare and probability of booking the seat in the particular class). It is interesting to note that the network, in the first generation of AMT, automatically implemented EMSR. BehavHeuristics then derived and split the processes – independently arriving at the EMSR algorithm before it was described in detail by Belobaba [28].

BehavHeuristics has recently completed the preliminary phase of tests that will compare AMT's forecasting accuracy to that of several alternative methods, using actual airline data. AMT's forecasts have thus far proved to be extremely accurate. It achieved far better results than any of the other methods, to a degree that would be worth in the order of a hundred million dollars to the airline. BehavHeuristics is proceeding with comparisons using additional information about each flight, which should allow AMT to excel by an even greater degree.

3.6   Scheduling and task management

BehavHeuristics views scheduling as a variation on the concepts represented in AMT, which could be said to schedule seats into different fare classes. Both are examples of resource allocation in changing environments. Yet true scheduling is difficult for several reasons:

- Schedules must usually satisfy many constraints at once.
- There will typically be many alternative legal schedules, and it is not feasible to examine all of them.
- The final quality of a schedule cannot usually be evaluated until the entire schedule – which may be very long – has been constructed; this makes 'credit attribution' among the scheduling events very difficult.
- If multiple events can occur in parallel and may compete for resources, the desirability of scheduling each event will depend on which other events are scheduled at the same time, which presents an extremely challenging interdependency.
- Events may occur during the life of the schedule that will disrupt the original plan.

BehavHeuristics conceptualizes scheduling problems within a project management framework in which there is a set of activities to be completed. Each activity has a given duration; some activities have prerequisites; each activity requires resources; each resource is available according to a given calendar; each resource has certain fixed and variable costs. Numerous other constraints are often in effect. The 'resource levelling' capabilities now available in many project management packages merely enforce constraint checking, often leading to sub-optimal resource allocation in schedules. The scheduling optimization technology developed by BehavHeuristics can be used in conjunction with existing project management software packages, thus addressing the market provided by the large installed base of such systems. In addition, BehavHeuristics believes that using a standard conceptual framework should speed market acceptance by matching existing users' concepts and skills.

3.7 Adaptive Network Aircrew Training Scheduler (ANATS)

Using BANKET, BehavHeuristics developed prototype scheduling software for Link Flight Simulation, a division of CAE-Link Corporation, which demonstrates the feasibility of applying adaptive network software to solve resource allocation problems of this type. Called ANATS, the prototype demonstrated that the characteristics of adaptive networking techniques fit these applications extremely well and are able to produce correct and near-optimal schedules [29].

ANATS focused on a particular type of scheduling problem, that of scheduling various student cohorts for miliary aircrew training (a cohort is any group of students with the same training requirements; e.g. pilots, co-pilots, navigators, flight engineers, and loadmasters). In one example, several months were scheduled for up to 200 students at a time, with up to 100 training activities each, requiring numerous resources to be applied in different combinations, and with training plans having varying start dates and degrees of complexity.

Instructional systems present a complex scheduling problem, and thus provided a good test of the adaptive network approach. Resources, such as classrooms, instructors, and computer-based facilities need to be allocated efficiently to avoid unnecessary costs. The same resource pool may be needed to teach different student cohorts each of whom are completing separate academic objectives. Course design may require students to participate within their own cohort, as a member of a mixed group of cohorts, or according to a self-paced format. Many additional constraints must be satisfied: length of the training day depending on type of activity, when 'breaks' can or must be scheduled, how much time should be devoted to different activity types, how many students can participate in an activity at one time, etc.

ANATS uses a one-step process for scheduling; the network makes resource allocations directly. This method is preferred because it has the advantage of avoiding the need for developing optimization algorithms to take every decision factor into account, which in many cases are very complex and not fully understood. The system operates on data files that define the training scenario to be scheduled. This includes the characteristics of each cohort, the activities each cohort will complete and the sequential dependencies among these activities, and the pool of available resources to be used for completing these activities. A schedule is created by considering each hour in sequence, beginning with a given start date and time, and assigning activities to all students who are available for training at that hour. Activities are assigned according to the availability of needed resources and the relative value of possible activities for each cohort (defining these values is the first task of the network). When different cohorts compete for the same resources, assignment is made to cohorts such that the overall schedule will be optimized (this is the second task of the network). The schedule is complete when all students have been assigned resources for their required activities.

A major challenge lies in identifying and integrating all the kinds of values that should be considered in the objective or utility function. In the case of training, a schedule should minimize resource costs, maximize student throughput, minimize student idle time, maximize student satisfaction, etc. As in the airline seat allocation example, networks provided the ability to generate optimal schedules by first defining a primary utility function, then by integrating temporal differences methods which allowed them to optimize the function over time.

Another challenge to optimal scheduling is that disruptions will be inevitable; for example, a resource may fail at any time. Specific failures cannot be predicted, but general failure characteristics of resources are known. ANATS takes into consideration a 'failure model' for each resource which describes statistically its probability of failure at any given time. For example, many physical devices fit a MTBF (Mean Time Between Failure) model, with a given mean, standard deviation, most recent failure or maintenance, etc. Even resources such as human instructors have been known to be unavailable at times for which they were otherwise scheduled! The adaptive network is trained in a simulated scheduling environment where resources become unavailable according to their respective models, so the resulting schedule is optimal not for a hypothetical ideal world, but for the real world. Thus, ANATS schedules in such a way that failures are least likely to produce a state in which no other activity can be performed – it avoids painting itself into such corners.

After a schedule has been created it can be examined according to resources or students, either for single days or for a week at a time. Changes to the schedule can be effected by swapping resources, by adding special events (e.g. unscheduled maintenance), and by rescheduling from some point in the schedule to its conclusion.

One of the most valuable functions of the system lies in its resource estimation capabilities. Schedules that approximate optimal resource utilization can be generated by comparing different-sized resource pools against different training requirements (e.g. student load and/or flexibility in training plans). By studying various what-if scenarios, a schedule can be produced that accomplishes all training objectives with a minimum number of resources.

There are many other scheduling challenges within the airline industry, such as flight, aircrew, aircraft maintenance, and gate or slot scheduling. Each has unique difficulties that could benefit from the solutions prototyped in ANATS. BehavHeuristics has already designed some of the systems to address these problems. Beyond the airlines, virtually every industry must ultimately cope with the scheduling of its personnel and other resources to accomplish its defined tasks. The degree to which this can be optimized will have a direct bearing on the company's bottom-line.

3.8   Conclusion

Two applications have been described that demonstrate the value of an approach that combines the strengths of adaptive networks with those derived from decision theory, behaviour science, and behavioural economics. This hybrid approach is effective for solving dynamic resource allocation problems because it incorporates the well-accepted concept of expected value as a basis for making decisions, and it integrates methods for making use of changes in value in time-dynamic processes. Adaptive networks provide a method of solving the problems of choice between situational values through time, without having to make static assumptions that could prove erroneous. BehavHeuristics has found the world to be rich in problems whose structure matches this solution paradigm, and looks forward to meeting the challenges that many of them will ultimately bring to bear.

References

1.   Wasserman, P.D. *Neural Computing: Theory and Practice*, Van Nostrand Reinhold, New York (1989).

2.   Hopfield, J.J. and Tank, D. "Neural" computation of decisions in optimization problems. *Biol. Cyb.*, **52**, 141-152 (1985).

3.   Kirkpatrick, S., Gellatt, Jr., C.D., and Vecchi, M.P. Optimization by simulated annealing, *Science*, **220**, 671-680 (1983).

4.   Langlotz, C.P. and Shortliffe, E.H. Logical and decision-theoretic methods for planning under uncertainty. *Artificial Intelligence Mag.*, **10**, 39-47 (1989).

5.   Hutchison, W.R. Cognitive vs. behavioral approaches to artificial intelligence. *Newsletter for the Behavioral AI Network*, 5, Dec. (1984).

6.   Skinner, B.F. Cognitive science and behaviorism, in *Upon Further Reflection*, Prentice-Hall, Englewood Cliffs, NJ, 93-111 (1987). Reprinted from *Brit. J. of Psych.*, **76**, 291-301 (1985), and from *Newsletter for the Behavior Artificial Intelligence Network* (1987).

7.   Langlotz, C.P., Shortliffe, E.H. and Fagan, L.M. Using decision theory to justify heuristics. *Proc. of the 6th National Conf. on Artificial Intelligence*, American Ass. for Artificial Intelligence, Menlo Park, CA, 215-219 (1986).

8.   Rosenthal, R.E. Principles of multi-objective optimization. *Decision Sciences*, **16**, 133-152 (1985).

9.   Werbos, P.J. Generalization of back-propagation with application to a recurrent gas market model. *Neural Networks*, **1**, <u>4</u>, 339-356 (1988).

10.   Barto, A., Sutton, R. and Anderson, C. Neuron-like adaptive elements that can solve difficult learning control problems. *IEEE Trans. Syst., Man and Cybern.*, **SMC-13**, <u>5</u>, 834-846 (1983).

11.   Hutchison, W.R. Behavior analytic models for artificial intelligence. *Assoc. for Behavior Analysts*, Columbus, Ohio, May 24-27 (1985).

12.   Sheil, B.A. Power tools for programmers. *Datamation* (1983).

13.   Hutchison, W.R. Behavior analysis and other adaptive systems theories within the "functional camp" of artificial intelligence. *Newsletter for the Behavior Artificial Intelligence Network*, **2**, 3-18, March (1985).

14.   Hutchison, W.R. and Stephens, K.R. Artificial intelligence: demonstration of an operant approach. *Assoc. for Behavior Analysis*, Milwaukee, WI, May 23 (1986).

15. Donahoe, J.W. and Palmer, D.C. The interpretation of complex human behavior: some reactions to *Parallel Distributed Processing*, edited by J.L. McClelland, D.E. Rumelhart, and the PDP Research Group. *J. of the Experimental Analysis of Behavior*, **51**, 399-416.

16. Kehoe, E.J. Connectionist models of conditioning: a tutorial. *J. of the Experimental Analysis of Behavior*, **52**, 427-440 (1989).

17. Hutchison, W.R. and Stephens, K.R. Integration of distributed and symbolic knowledge representations. *Proc. of the 1st Int. Conf. on Neural Networks*, **2**, 395-398. IEEE Press, Piscataway, NJ (1987).

18. Stephens, K.R. and Hutchison, W R. Behavior analysis and intelligent machines. *Cybernetic* (in press).

19. Sutton, R.S. *Temporal Credit Assignment in Reinforcement Learning*. Doctoral dissertation, University of Massachusetts (1984).

20. Hursh, S.R. Economic concepts for the analysis of behavior. *J. of the Experimental Analysis of Behavior*, **34**, 219-238 (1980).

21. Rachlin, H., Green, L., Kagel, J.H. and Battalio, R.C. Economic demand theory and psychological studies of choice, in Bower, G.H. (ed.). *The Psychology of Learning and Motivation, Volume 10*, Academic Press, New York (1976).

22. Staddon, J.E.R. (ed.). *Limits to Action: The Allocation of Individual Behavior*, Academic Press, New York (1980).

23. Rescoria, R.A. and Wagner, A.R. A theory of Pavlovian conditioning: variations in the effectiveness of reinforcement and nonreinforcement. In Black, A.H. and Prokasy, W.F. (eds.). *Classical Conditioning, Volume 2: Current Research and Theory*, Prentice-Hall, Englewood Cliffs, NJ (1972).

24. Fantino, E. Conditioned reinforcement: choice and information. In Honig, W.K. and Staddon, J.E.R. (eds.). *Handbook of Operant Behavior*, Prentice-Hall, Englewood Cliffs, NJ (1977).

25. Baum, W.M. Chained concurrent schedules: reinforcement as situation transition. *J. of the Experimental Analysis of Behavior*, 22, 91-102 (1974).

26. Makens, J.C. Yield management: a major pricing breakthrough. *Piedmond Airlines*, 30-33, April (1988).

27. Hutchison, W.R. and Stephens, K.R. The airline marketing tactician (AMT): a commercial application of adaptive networking. *Proc. of the 1st Int. Conf. on Neural Networks*, **4**, 753-756. IEEE Press, Piscataway, NJ (1987).

28. Belobaba, P.P. *Air Travel Demand and Airline Seat Inventory Management*. Doctoral dissertation, Massachusetts Institute of Technology (1987).

29. Bell, T.M., Stephens, K.R. and Hutchison, W.R. *ANATS: Adaptive Network Aircrew Training Scheduler, Final Report*. IR&D Contract #5-04915, Link Flight Simulation Division, CAE-Link Corporation, Binghamton, NY (1989).

4

Medical risk assessment for insurance underwriting

S. B. Ahuja and A. Hsiung
Rentenanstalt, Switzerland

4.1 Summary

We develop the theory that experience is an unconscious aspect of learning derived from the recognition of salient features of input case scenarios encountered over a period of time. This information, or case knowledge, is subsequently used by an expert to augment his knowledge to enable him to make decisions in the future which are 'safer' and more representative of his prior experiences.

In this chapter, a novel yet pragmatic approach to building life insurance underwriting systems is presented. In the context of a recently proposed 'neurally inspired' model for knowledge-based decision making, a hybrid learning mechanism is devised that incorporates both the supervised and unsupervised experience-based, learning processes that are believed to contribute to the development of an expert. This approach allows the gradual evolution of an expert's quantitative and qualitative decision-making skills to be emulated under a unified framework for decision making.

4.2 Introduction

Financial risk assessment forms the kernel of most business decision making. In order to evaluate a financial risk, be it for the loss of life, equipment, or trade, one must recognize the characteristics of the associated risk to be able to estimate the probability and extent of future claims in the event of a loss. Whether it is underwriters in an insurance company, or loan officers in a lending institution, the people who are responsible for making such estimations are expected to be able to assess as precisely as possible the magnitude of risk that the institution will be required to cover. Such people are usually experts in their respective problem domains, with a comprehensive knowledge about the relevant characteristics that are likely to influence the factor of risk. Besides a 'diagnostic' skill that is gained through repeated practice and tutoring in order to classify typical case-scenarios correctly, with experience these individuals develop a certain 'feel' for the domain which enables them to improve their assessment of the size of risk for a given case.

One can usually find within each domain a set of rating manuals, which attempt to provide objective criteria or rules for assessing a case, but the final decision must be made by the underwriter. While doing so, the expert is largely relying on his own subjective criteria, ranging from observations made over similar cases in the past to other preconceived personal beliefs about which characteristics are important for risk assessment. Recognizing the significance of this disparity between a 'novice' (with a rating manual) and an 'expert', the role of rating manuals has been transformed from that of stating a dictum, to simply presenting suggestive guidelines [1]. This limitation on the use of rating manuals to being just a 'working tool', however, defeats the original purpose for which they were intended – to bring more objectivity into the subjective task of underwriting.

4.2.1   *Insurance underwriting*

Life insurance underwriting is a judgement task that requires an assessment of the medical risk in a given case. It is assumed that if one has knowledge of the effects of existing physical and/or functional impairments on the life expectancy of the particular case being processed, together with information about the subject's state of health and habits, then it is possible to assess reasonably well the risk that is to be insured. With relatively few exceptions, the main characteristics of the life underwriting process are:

(a) Diagnosis/classification
- identify any impairments, from information available within medical documents;

- confirm the identified impairments, based on specified criteria to determine insurability.

(b) Assessment
- compute a rough estimate of the death risk, as an average extra mortality rate for the subject class with those impairments;
- refine the estimate of death risk, based on certain prognostic factors that project a better or worse outcome for members of that subject class.

4.2.2 *Shortcomings of existing methods*

Using a rating manual and the above sequence of steps, one can assess the death risk reasonably well, but only in the ideal case-scenarios for which this method is specifically designed. Life underwriters, however, usually ignore the manual guidelines since they rarely apply in real-life scenarios. The rating manuals acknowledge that in cases which do not exactly match the given classification criteria, an underwriter needs to estimate the death risk by making a 'symptomatic' assessment of the case.

To make an assessment of the death risk based on the specified diagnostic, classificatory and prognostic factors, the underwriter needs either to be a trained medical professional, or be able to glean this information from the documents presented by the subject – an expectation that is quite difficult to fulfil in practice! Furthermore, all the missing pieces of information must be compiled before attempting to classify an impairment to determine the insurability of the case. Even when a complete medical profile is easily obtained, it is a time-consuming and expensive process, and one is unlikely to match the specified criteria exactly in every case. The ambiguity in rendering a classification (and the subsequent assessment based on this ambiguity) is worse in cases where multiple, related impairments are present.

In other words, there is a lack of adequate diagnostic and classificatory procedures in existing life insurance underwriting approaches, which makes the process of risk assessment rather difficult and extremely inconsistent. The tight diagnostic and classificatory constraints specified in rating manuals make current approaches extremely brittle to be of any use for a general population – uncertainty and incomplete information is the norm rather than an exception in medical diagnosis. And even on the rare occasion when the desired constraints are satisfied, the factors used for refining and combining extra mortality rates for risk assessment are largely *ad hoc* and require subjective extrapolations over relatively broad ranges of rates. Moreover, since the significance attributed to a prognostic factor after classification is not based on any comparative statistical analyses, the relative importance assigned to each factor is somewhat arbitrary.

An inconsistency in the original diagnostic process, followed by an arbitrary rate assignment, renders the task of risk assessment rather vague. For example, one underwriting manual suggests that in the case of chronic organic tuberculosis, a recent normal ESR (erythrocyte sedimentation rate) is a healthy sign and good enough to 'balance out' a history of relapsing infection: clearly an *ad hoc* decision, which may at times contradict medical reality!

In the field of artificial intelligence (AI), the past two decades have seen the evolution of several methods and tools for constructing diagnostic systems. A question that is commonly asked and which several people have attempted to answer is which of these methods is the 'best'. Previous studies have demonstrated that no single method has a clear performance advantage over another. Where minor differences were found, it could be argued that these were differences in the problem-specific information rather than fundamental differences in the methods [2–7]. In all of these studies, the performance of a method was judged relative to another on the basic premise that the desired functionality could principally be achieved through any of the methods. The main issue at stake has been the accuracy of each system to predict the outcomes in a selected set of test cases, where the correct outcomes were known in each case.

The development of an intuitive 'feel' for the domain, a judgement skill that is routinely displayed by life insurance underwriters, is however, a functionality which it is impossible to replicate using classical AI representations like scripts [8], frames [9], schemata [10–11], and production rules [12]. Classical AI techniques do not allow a system to assimilate new information about prior case-scenarios, which is an intrinsic part of the decision-making process. The comparison of any new approach to perform this task, therefore, will necessarily have to be made with respect to humans rather than against any of the existing systems.

4.2.3   *Neural modelling*

In the context of LIBRA/Dx, a neural network model for diagnostic reasoning [13], we propose a practical method of capturing, quantifying, and emulating both the diagnostic (objective) and the assessment (subjective) logic followed by life insurance underwriters. In this chapter we briefly describe its unique decision-making paradigm that enables the gradual augmentation of domain knowledge through an experience-based, unsupervised learning process called episodic learning.

The term 'neural model' is used here to refer to models of processing mechanisms which assume that all information processing takes place through the interactions of a large number of simple processing elements that are connected to each other in the form of a network. The primary distinguishing feature of such models is the absence of a central controller or executive to coordinate the processing within a system, as is commonly the case in conventional serial models of computation [14]. The relative autonomy with which each processing element can carry out its computations makes parallel activation models extremely attractive for solving problems that have traditionally required inordinate amounts of processing time using serial models. Our approach here is more from an engineering perspective rather than the cognitive or neurophysiological.

Diagnostic reasoning is a high-level cognitive task that involves trying to explain a set of symptoms by postulating a set of 'disorders' or impairments. Existing symbol processing models of diagnostic reasoning do not provide adequate mechanisms to support the interactions among knowledge structures, which are necessary to capture the generative capacities of human diagnosticians in novel situations. Achieving such interactions has been one of the greatest difficulties with implementing models of diagnostic reasoning which can reason in the presence of imprecise or incomplete information.

LIBRA/Dx has its knowledge representational basis in the symbol processing approaches of AI, and an underlying neurone-like processing microstructure that allows knowledge structures to reconfigure themselves in the context of each case being processed, thereby capturing the ability to respond in unforeseen situations. A diagnostician typically starts off with overlapping descriptions of disorders which specify sets of manifestations that are likely to be observed, in the event that any of the corresponding disorders were to occur. In general, however, the manifestations in a specific case may indicate the presence of multiple disorders, since no single disorder can account for all the observed manifestations in spite of the absence of certain expected ones. LIBRA/Dx enables the knowledge to be arranged such that relevant pieces configure themselves dynamically in each context to form tailor-made explanations. This process thus enables the identification of appropriate knowledge pieces which then assemble to form a coherent, context-sensitive explanation which supports inference. The combination of such a representational scheme with the locally constrained parallel activation processing mechanism constitutes its diagnostic engine.

The diagnostic model of LIBRA/Dx operates on the theory that simultaneous satisfaction of multiple local constraints among domain concepts is sufficient to construct a plausible global explanation for a set of observed signs and symptoms. We further hypothesize that the experience necessary for risk assessment is an unconscious aspect of learning, which results from the gradual development of a sensitivity to certain local relationships between select attributes of a number of input case scenarios. Over a period of time the sensitization process slowly evolves into a global interpretation of the facts that are observed in a case, which determines how we react in both novel and familiar situations. It is this case knowledge which forms the basis of the expert's intuition, or subjective beliefs; it augments his domain knowledge to help him make 'safer' decisions that are more reflective of his prior experiences.

The remainder of this chapter is divided into four sections. The second section gives an overview of LIBRA/Dx, the parallel activation model for diagnostic reasoning. This model forms the basis for our approach towards augmenting domain knowledge through the temporal (time varying) evolution of a rating network (RN). The third section describes the architecture and function of significance maps for the construction of such a network. In the next section we briefly describe ACE (A Connectionist Expert System Environment) which is being used to build the proposed life insurance underwriting system.

4.3 A neural network model for classificatory problem solving

LIBRA/Dx is based on the theory that diagnostic reasoning takes place through the interactions of several relevant domain concepts, connected to each other in the form of a causal network. Several prototype models of this reasoning approach have shown that satisfying local constraints on spreading activation through a causal network can demonstrate meaningful global behaviour in the network, including circumscribed activation, competitive inhibition and stability [13].

4.3.1 *A knowledge representation and processing model*

The model is based on an underlying associative network of nodes that represent domain concepts or 'knowledge atoms' [15]. These nodes are connected to each other through links that represent associations (both causal and non-causal) among the knowledge atoms. The network consists of a set of hierarchically layered nodes, in which the nodes in one layer connect only with the nodes in an immediately adjacent layer, as shown in Fig. 4.1.

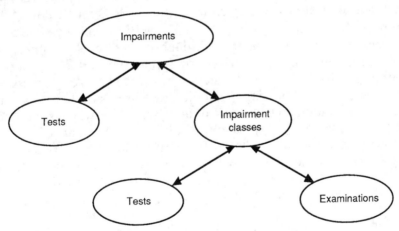

Figure 4.1 Architecture of a causal network.

There are two kinds of nodes within such a network. Nodes whose activation does not change during the course of problem solving are called router or stuck-at nodes. Nodes whose activation changes during the course of problem solving are called memory or accumulator nodes. A node in the network is said to be active if it has a non-zero level of activation. Nodes with a zero activation level are said to be inactive. An active node can have a positive or a negative activation level which lies in the interval $(-1.0, +1.0)$. The activation values can be thought of as having the following interpretations: positive activation signifies the presence of the concept which is represented by that node; negative activation signifies the absence of the concept which is represented by that node; and zero activation signifies no knowledge about the presence or absence of the concept represented by that node.

A node on one layer is connected to other nodes in an adjacent layer via bi-directional links. In any given network one can define a connectivity matrix for the nodes of two adjacent layers. Each entry in the matrix specifies the association between a pair of nodes in mutually adjacent layers if it exists, and the strength (weight) of this association. These weights lie in the interval $(-1.0, +1.0)$, with a negative weight implying a preventive association or an inhibitory link and a positive weight implying a supportive association or an excitatory link. The sets D and M represent any two adjacent layers in the parallel activation model framework. Each node d_i in layer D is connected to a set of nodes, man (d_i), in layer M through downward causal links. Similarly, each node m_j in layer M is connected to a set of nodes evokes(m_j), in layer D through upward evoking links. In each direction the associative strengths may either represent conditional probabilities or subjective causal and evoking strengths, respectively. If conditional probabilities are used as weights, for any given manifestation node the sum of all upward link-weights must add up to $+1.0$, while for any given disorder the sum of all downward link-weights must add up to $+1.0$. These constraints need not be necessary or relevant when subjective causal and evoking strengths are used as weights. In the context of the parallel activation model the following characteristics are to be noted:

(a) For any given manifestation node that is said to be present, all plausible disorders that can account for its presence get activated initially.

(b) Among alternative disorders with the same manifestation, only one disorder stays active by competitively inhibiting all the others. (Of course, some of the inhibited disorders may get reactivated subsequently, to account for other observed manifestations.)

(c) Each observed manifestation is accounted for by at least one disorder that stays active.

(d) Disorders that are found to be active at the end of the problem-solving session are those that present a globally most plausible explanation for the observed manifestations.

4.3.2   *A spreading activation paradigm*

It is useful to think of the associational links between the nodes of adjacent layers as constraints, which could be a numeric value denoting how activated one node can become when its corresponding associated neighbour is fully activated. Since these constraints are only local to the specific nodes that are involved, they are to be satisfied only locally. In existing activation models, both neural networks and other cognitively oriented networks, the activity of a node that spreads to its neighbours is not determined by the level of activity possessed by the recipient node. In such models the incoming activation for a node is a weighted sum (or some other, possibly non-linear function) of the activities of its neighbours to which it is directly connected [15–19].

More recently, a competition-based parallel activation model has been proposed [20] where, when a node assumes an activity level above its normal (threshold) resting level, its neighbours actively compete for the activity possessed by that node. The ability of the neighbouring nodes to compete for a shared node's activity is proportional to their own respective activation levels. The activation that each neighbouring node acquires is at the expense of that which becomes available to the others and vice versa.

In contrast to this approach, however, we identify two separate aspects of contention that exist between neighbouring nodes that become competitors and form an inhibitory cluster. The idea of competition is introduced by permitting the evoked disorders of manifestation m_j in an adjacent disorder layer, to actively compete for the total output activity of m_j. The ability of disorder node d_i to complete for m_j's output activity $a_j(t)$ is proportional to its own activation level $a_i(t)$ and to the weight of its association with m_j. This computation enables highly activated nodes to extract a proportionately larger part of m_j's finite activation, leaving a successively smaller portion for competitors with lower activations.

In diagnostic reasoning, whenever supporting evidence is found for one disorder among several plausible alternatives, then not only does it encourage the belief that a disorder is present, it also discourages the belief that one of its alternatives is present instead. In other words, each node in an inhibitory cluster actively seeks to drain its competitors of their respective activations. Since competing disorders influence each other via the manifestation that they all share, this drain of activation among competitors can be interpreted as a correction of the original support that is received by each competing disorder d_i from the common manifestation node m_j. The measure of belief (MB) in the presence of a disorder node d_i due to each of the manifestation nodes m_j that are present from its man(d_i) set, is computed as the sum of the contributions that are made by each of the individual manifestations.

Similarly, the measure of disbelief (MD) in its presence is computed as the sum of the activation that is drained from it by all of its competitors that share its active manifestations. One other phenomenon that is believed to occur during diagnostic reasoning is that the belief in the presence of a manifestation is diminished if other manifestations which share a common cause with it are not observed. This effect can be expressed as a proportionately lower belief in the presence of their common cause. We compute the active fan-out $ACTFO_i$ as a weighted measure of the portion of the manifestations of d_i that are in fact found to be present. Using these definitions, one can compute the net flow of activity into a disorder node d_i at time t as:

$$F_i(t) = \tanh[MB_i(t) \cdot ACTFO_i - MD_i(t)]. \qquad (4.1)$$

Given this competition-based parallel activation approach to satisfying local constraints in a causal network, a global interpretation of the effects is possible by allowing the network to stabilize. The activation of node d_i at time $(t+1)$ is equal to the activation at time t, plus the net flow of activation $F_i(t)$ into the node, minus its decay over each discrete time step:

$$a_i(t+1) = a_i(t) + \beta \cdot [F_i(t) \cdot \{1 - a_i(t)\} - \delta_i \cdot a_i(t) - \theta_i] \qquad (4.2)$$

where β is a constant that is used to control the size of time slice during numerical simulation; δ_i is the rate at which the activation of node d_i decays in the absence of stimulus; and θ_i is the threshold or the natural resting level of activation for node d_i. This paradigm has been tested in different diagnostic contexts and the results were found to compare favourably with those from an existing symbol processing model of diagnostic reasoning. A more detailed description of the LIBRA/Dx paradigm can be found in [13].

4.4   Architecture of a rating network

Having generated the most plausible classification for the case under consideration, the next step is to assess its associated death risk. Given the existence of a specific impairment, one can easily compute or read off from an existing rating manual the average extra mortality for that subject class [1]. Recall from above, it is not the average extra mortality rates specified in the rating manuals that are of questionable validity, but the decision to classify the given case into a particular subject class so that its corresponding average extra mortality rate can be applied. The parallel activation paradigm ensures that the diagnosis (classification) rendered is the one that is most plausible, in the context of all the examination and test results which are presented for a case.

The average extra mortality rates for a subject class can place one only in the 'neighbourhood' of a reasonable rate, since certain other characteristics of subjects may make them more, or less at risk for a worse outcome in the future. These characteristics could include unquantifiable information about the subject's predisposition to a worse outcome, such as his current health profile, his past family history, history of operative/surgical procedures, and perhaps other contra-indications such as the presence of compounding impairments. Since these characteristics provide a prognosis on the eventual better or worse outcome for a case, they are commonly referred to as prognostic factors. An expert normally has a personal belief about which of these factors are likely to contribute to a worse (or better) outcome for the given case. It is not normal for an expert to be able to quantify the contribution made by each factor, however, except to have some symbolic belief (e.g. extremely low, moderate, very high, etc.) in its likelihood to have a worse effect on the eventual outcome. But it is interesting to note that the expert is able to 'modulate' these beliefs in the context of other factors which are also found to be present in a particular case, although these adjustments tend to be more or less arbitrary, depending largely upon his past experience.

What we need then is a mechanism which can take into account the relative (local) importance of each prognostic factor in the presence of an impairment, and which can gradually develop a sensitivity to particular combinations of these factors over a population of input case-scenarios. We would also like to see a global order emerge from this sensitization process, which enables the system to effectively decide how it must interpret the influence of multiple prognostic factors on the future outcome, especially in the presence of more than one impairment. In this section, we attempt to reconstruct an expert's assessment logic, but without the arbitrariness that is intrinsic to this function. Our approach is derived from the basic principles underlying the formation of one-dimensional topological maps as proposed by Kohonen [18]. The assumption we make here is that the entire space of input patterns $\{C_k\}$ (constellations of prognostic factors) over all impairments can be ordered in some topological way such that $C_1, Pt, C_2, Pt, C_3...$, where Pt represents this transitive ordering relation on the constellations of prognostic factors.

We propose the construction of a rating network: an organization of significance maps, which transforms the significance of the prognostic factors to predict a worse outcome in the presence of an impairment into a placement within an array of nodes. Each prognostic factor for an impairment is given a symbolic significance level which denotes its 'promise' in predicting a worse than average outcome in the future. These significance levels form the parameter of interest for adaptation, with the following interpretations:

R: reject
VL: very low
L: low
M: medium
H: high
VH: very high
A: accept.

A symbolic level of R implies that the given case should not be insured, while level A implies that the case can be accepted without assigning an extra mortality rate for the impairment. The symbolic scale spans a numeric range of [0–1], with the symbols distributed over the following sub-ranges: (0–0.05), (0.05–0.15), (0.15–0.4), (0.4–0.6), (0.6–0.85), (0.85–0.95), and (0.95–1.0) respectively. As in any topologically organized system, the goal is to make sure that in the presence of any given input (set of prognostic factors) elements that are nearby respond similarly. But the system must achieve this global organization only through a local self-adaptation process that is restricted to a small physical 'neighbourhood'.

For each impairment we construct a one-dimensional output array of processing nodes, with a connectivity vector W_k consisting of weight elements $W_{kn} \in [0,1]$, defined for each output node k that is connected to a random set of n input nodes, one each for the different prognostic factors that are relevant to that impairment. For a given case with a known impairment, the vector $X - (x_1, x_2, \ldots, x_n)$ denotes the significance levels of its n prognostic factors, where $x_i \in [0,1]$. On the application of a pattern of observed prognostic factors, the maximally activated output node p and two (or more) of its immediate neighbours, adapt the weights connecting them to the active prognostic factors.

The aim is to strengthen the weights along the same direction as the active prognostic factors, so that over time the statistical properties of the input population get implicitly encoded within the weight matrix. The output array for each impairment is in turn connected above, to the nodes of another one-dimensional array, which forms the output of the life underwriting system. Each node at the higher level is connected to a random set of nodes in the lower level, with the same constraints imposed on the weights as were described for the connections betwen prognostic factors and the output nodes at the first level. The rating network schema is shown in Fig. 4.2. At the second level also, we use the same set of equations to determine the spread of activity and adaptation of weights between the nodes, as described for level one.

After a number of iteration steps, the output nodes at the two levels start to get sensitized to different patterns of prognostic factors. Note, however, that the developing of maximal sensitivity in response to certain patterns of prognostic factors is not what is of primary interest to us, since we are not necessarily interested in assigning a specific numeric significance to an observed pattern. What is of interest here is the creation of a global topological organization, such that the active nodes after the presentation of a pattern of prognostic factors reflect its composite significance simply by their physical placement in the significance map.

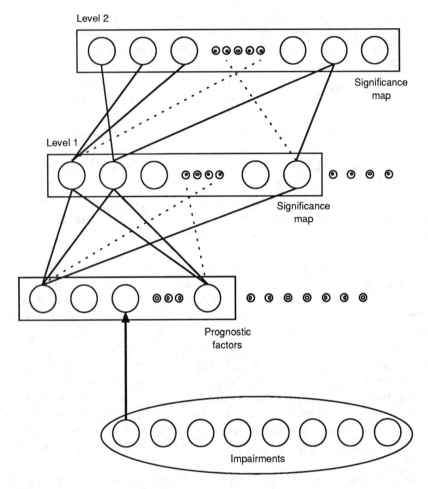

Figure 4.2   A rating network.

4.5   A connectionist expert system environment

The life insurance underwriting system described in the earlier sections is being built using ACE (A Connectionist Expert System Environment). Connectionist (or neural) models offer a promising alternative to classical, logic-based expert systems [21], with a radically new perspective on the basic computational architecture that is deemed necessary for capturing the characteristics which are normally expected of an 'expert'. The main reason behind this realignment within the AI community is the powerful emergent property of globally meaningful behaviour based on purely local interactions between domain concepts that arises from the underlying processing and representational mechanisms which are employed by neural models [22]. Suggestive of the kind of processing and architecture that is thought by some to exist in the human brain, the major advantages of this new approach (as compared to the classical AI models on which expert systems of today are based) include: tolerance to malformed and incomplete input, a capability to generalize, graceful degradation of performance in the presence of physical faults and, above all, a consistent mechanism to learn from examples and experience.

The fundamental problem of how to represent domain and case knowledge so as to be able to reason with it, however, still remains. Although research literature in this field aptly points out the fundamental issues underlying the use of local versus distributed representations [23], these distinctions are made largely on the grounds of cognitive validity and computational viability. In building application expert systems, the engineering issue of selecting a representation format is also the issue of selecting the appropriate reasoning (spreading activation) and learning paradigms. The representation, activation and learning strategies must be suited to capture the functional and statistical properties of the application domain, if indeed one desires to model them. To select an optimal combination of all these relevant parameters requires that any application development effort be preceded by a prototypical experimental phase, where different activation and learning paradigms can be studied for their modelling abilities in the context of various representational formats. This task is impossible without the help of some neural network generators, which are built on much of the same philosophy as the ubiquitous expert system shell tools. The primary motivation behind building ACE, therefore, was to enable the rapid prototyping of expert systems which use neural processing paradigms as opposed to the traditional AI techniques such as statistical pattern classification, rule-based deduction, or hypothetico-deductive inferencing.

4.5.1   *Structure of the domain knowledge*

For the purposes of life insurance underwriting, we partition the domain knowledge into two functionally distinct sets of concepts.

1. **Examination and test results.** Knowledge in this category represents the input for the system. This information can usually be found in medical reports or solicited from medical experts on request when needed. It consists of multiple classification hierarchies, which group the results from different examinations and diagnostic procedures under logically related concepts. For example, input information about a specific case is separated into: the subject's profile (e.g. age, profession, medical history), anatomy (e.g. height, weight, obvious deformities), habits (e.g. smoking, alcohol, drugs) etc. and into results from the following examinations: neurological (e.g. mental status, sensory, motor, reflexes), cardiovascular (e.g. blood pressure, pulse, electrocardiogram), respiratory, gynaecological, etc. Results from laboratory tests and other diagnostic procedures (e.g. blood tests, X-rays, urine analysis) comprise the test hierarchy. Figure 4.3(a) shows a portion of such a hierarchy for the results from a neurological examination. Each node in this conceptual hierarchy can be thought of as an attribute, with each of the nodes connected to it from below as its possible values. At any given time during problem solving only some of these values are known for the case being processed, and the remaining are acquired through an active goal-oriented information-seeking process that is inherent to ACE.

2. **Physical and functional disorders.** Medical disorders that are of any relevance to life insurance underwriting are included here and separated into: pathologies of physical organs (or organ systems) and the diseases that can affect them, and impairments of functional systems (e.g. endocrine, urinogenital, cardiovascular). These concepts represent information that can be inferred based on the values that are known for the input attributes in a specific case. Figure 4.3(b) shows a portion of the disorder hierarchy for tuberculosis, which is itself contained within the hierarchy of infectious and parasitic diseases. A 'node' within a disorder's hierarchy is associated with another node within an examination and test result's hierarchy through a causal link, provided the presence of that disorder is likely to cause the associated symptoms to be observed.

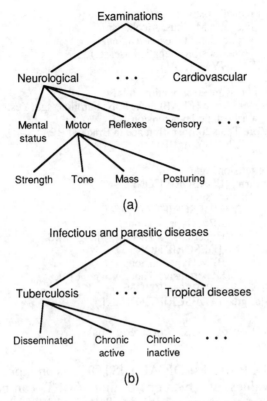

Figure 4.3 (a) An examination hierarchy; (b) a disorder hierarchy.

4.5.2   *The knowledge specification language*

Recognizing the fact that knowledge for most high-level applications exists in the form of semantic networks for domain concepts, ACE provides a high-level knowledge specification language (KSL), that can be used by a domain expert to build a knowledge base for the chosen domain in exactly the same way as if it were for a traditional expert system.   For instance, KSL allows its users to describe the domain concepts and the mutual dependencies that may exist between them in the form of an associative network.   Two types of domain concept can be specified: input attributes and inferred attributes.   The former denote information that must be solicited from the user at run time, while the latter denote information that can be inferred from the facts that are known at a given time.   Figure 4.4 shows a portion of the medical underwriting knowledge base as specified using KSL.

```
Past Medical History: mlt (
    Diabetes Mellitus, Alcoholism,
    Peptic Ulcer Disease, Angina,
    Hypertension, Hepatic Disease.)
    {SYNONYM: PMH}.

Blood Pressure Examination: mlt (
    Hypertension [ELABORATION: Familial: sgl (Yes, No)],
    Orthostatic Hypotension,
    More Than 20mm difference in Brachial BP.)
    {SYNONYM: BP}.

Hypertension: sgl (
    Primary [ELABORATION:
    Treated: sgl (
        Yes [DESCRIPTION:
        BP = Hypertension;
        Hypertensive Therapy = long term],
        No [DESCRIPTION:
        BP = Hypertension;
        Hypertensive Therapy = none].)],
    Secondary [DESCRIPTION: . . . . ],
    Malignant {DESCRIPTION: ....].)
```

Figure 4.4 Portion of a KSL knowledge base.

In the example, PAST MEDICAL HISTORY is an input attribute with six possible values, of which one or more (MLT) can be present at a time. PMH is a synonym for this attribute and it can be used instead of the full name to refer to this attribute. Similarly, BLOOD PRESSURE EXAMINATION is another input attribute with three possible values. Note that the first possible value HYPERTENSION can be further elaborated on the basis of whether it is FAMILIAL or not. Such elaborations allow possible value hierarchies of arbitrary depth to be created with minimal specification effort. The next attribute HYPERTENSION (different from the possible value of the same name) is inferred and it can have only one of three possible values: PRIMARY HYPERTENSION, SECONDARY HYPERTENSION and MALIGNANT HYPERTENSION. The possible value PRIMARY HYPERTENSION can be further elaborated, based on whether it is MEDICALLY TREATED or not, and is causally linked to the input attributes BLOOD PRESSURE EXAMINATION and HYPERTENSIVE TREATMENT listed in its description attachment.

The KSL parser interprets the knowledge constructs contained in the knowledge base and converts them into the data structures for an intermediate network specification language (NSL). This intermediate language allows someone who is sophisticated in the field of neural modelling to develop spreading activation and learning paradigms that are appropriate for decision making in the chosen application domain. Functions can be freely defined and referred to in building more complex ones. It is this powerful and flexible capability which allows different neural network paradigms to be constructed and tested in the context of a given application. The activation paradigm for LIBRA/Dx was specified using the syntax of NSL. ACE takes the network specification generated by KSL and the functions created using NSL to generate a connectionist expert system that is tailored to the specifics of the application domain. Figure 4.5 shows the functional schema for the ACE system.

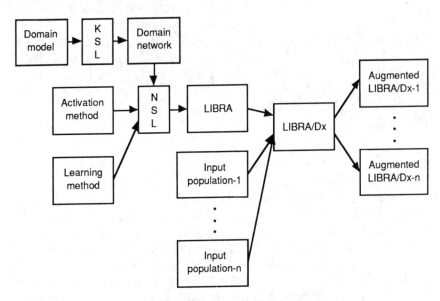

Figure 4.5 ACE – a connectionist expert system environment.

Based on the results that are reported for certain select examinations in a subject's medical reports, as a first diagnosis LIBRA/Dx generates the set of most specific disorder classes (physical or functional) which can explain the observed signs and symptoms. Note that this restricts the amount of subsequent information which is sought for a final, more precise diagnosis. Once a disorder class has been identified, the activation paradigm is applied with some additional examination and test results, to clearly isolate the specific disorders which comprise an explanation: the most plausible set of impairments that can account for all of the observed signs and symptoms.

Inferencing is initiated through an <u>OBTAIN <inferred-attribute></u> command, which takes the information that is known so far and arrives at a diagnosis by spreading activation through the causal network. The OBTAIN command can be issued for an inferred attribute at any level of the attribute hierarchy. If during problem solving additional information is required by the system, it makes an implicit call to the command, <u>ASKFOR <input-attribute></u>, which generates a question for the user to answer. If additional information needs to be volunteered to the system, ACE provides an <u>ASSERT <attribute = value></u> command which can be issued either before issuing an OBTAIN command, or after its execution to assign specific values to an attribute. ACE provides several other commands that create a powerful user front-end which allows an interactive dialogue to be carried out with the expert system, without the user having to know which specific inferencing technique is being used to arrive at the results. A further detailed description of ACE, including the syntax for KSL and NSL, the list of ACE and LIBRA commands, and other system level information can be found in [24].

4.6   Conclusion

Life underwriters in an insurance company are routinely required to estimate the likelihood of a future claim against the institution in the event of a loss of life. Their know-how of the medical domain is limited to a 'diagnostic' classificatory skill that is inculcated through repeated practice and tutoring with typical case-scenarios, on the basis of which they must correctly classify every case. With experience, however, they are expected to develop an astute insight about the size of risk which is being undertaken for a given case. Relying primarily on their own subjective criteria and using unspecified formulations, ranging from observations made over similar cases in the past to other preconceived personal beliefs about the characteristics which are important for risk assessment, underwriters finally assign a level of risk to the case being considered.

In the context of LIBRA/Dx, a neural model for diagnostic reasoning, we have proposed a practical method of quantifying and emulating both the diagnostic (objective) and the assessment (subjective) capability of life insurance underwriters. We believe that a neural network processing mechanism lends itself more readily to the kinds of knowledge interaction that are necessary, in order to reproduce the generative capacities of human diagnosticians to respond to novel situations. Based on the creation of topologically organized significance maps, we have presented a means of capturing experience through the gradual development of a sensitivity to local co-occurrence relationships between selected attributes (prognostic factors) of a population of input case-scenarios. This sensitization process slowly imposes a global order on the significance that is assigned to a pattern of prognostic factors, which allows a consistent assessment of the risk in every case. It is this case knowledge which encodes the expert's intuition, or subjective beliefs, and which augments the internal representations of his domain knowledge to help him make 'safer' decisions in the future which are more reflective of his prior experiences.

We are currently involved in compiling a representative sample of 'training patterns' from actual case scenarios in life insurance underwriting, which will be used to generate the topologically organized significance maps. First, the results from LIBRA/Dx will be tested against a test-bed of previously assessed cases, to determine the validity of its classifications. This will be followed by a comparison of the subsequent assessment made by the system, against those cases from this set for which claims had to be settled over the past. This will provide conclusive evidence if indeed our approach can lead to a better premium/claim ratio in life insurance underwriting, on the average.

References

1. Hefti, M. L. (ed.). *Swiss Re (SR) Life Underwriting Rating Guidelines*, Swiss Reinsurance Company, Zurich, Switzerland (undated).

2. Aikins, J. *Prototypes and Production Rules – A Knowledge Representation for Computer Consultations*, Memo HPP-80-17, Stanford Heuristic Programming Project, CA (1980).

3. Croft, D. and Machol, R. Mathematical models in medical diagnosis. *Ann. Biomed. Eng.*, **2**, 69-89 (1974).

4. Fliess, J., Spitzer, R., Cohen, J. and Endicott, J. Three computer diagnosis methods compared. *Arch. Gen. Psych.*, **27**, 643-649 (1972).

5. Fox, J., Barber, D. and Bardhan, K. Alternative to Bayes? A quantitative comparison with rule-based diagnostic inference. *Meth. Inform. Med.*, **19**, 210-215 (1980).

6. Nordyke, R. and Kulikowski, C. A comparison of methods for the automated diagnosis of thyroid dysfunction. *Comp. Biomed. Res.*, **4**, 374389 (1971).

7. Ramsey, C., Reggia, J. *et al. A Comparitive Analysis of Methods for Expert Systems*, TR-1491, Department of Computer Science, University of Maryland, College Park (1985).

8. Minsky, M. A framework for representing knowledge, in Winston, P.H. (ed.). *The Psychology of Computer Vision*, McGraw-Hill, New York, 211-277 (1975).

9. Newell, A. and Simon, H.A. *Human Problem Solving*, Prentice-Hall, Englewood Cliffs, NJ (1972).

10. Norman, D. and Bobrow, D.G. On the role of active memory processes in perception and cognition. In Cofer, C.N. (ed.). *The Structure of Human Memory*, San Francisco, Freeman, 14-132 (1976).

11. Rumelhart, D.E. Notes on a schema for stories. In Bobrow, D.G. and Collins, A. (eds.). *Representation and Understanding*, Academic Press, New York, 211-236, (1975).

12. Schank, R.C. The role of memory in language processing. In Cofer, C.N. (ed.). *The Structure of Human Memory*, Freeman, San Francisco, 162-189 (1976).

13. Ahuja, S.B., Soh, W.Y. and Schwartz, A. A connectionist processing metaphor for diagnostic reasoning. *Int. J. of Intel. Sys.*, **4**, 155-180 (1989).

14. Rumelhart, D.E. and Norman, D. Parallel Models of Associative Networks. In Hinton, G.E. and Anderson, (eds.). Earlbaum, Hillsdale, NJ, 1-7 (1981).

15. Smolensky, P. Information processing in dynamical systems: foundations of harmony theory. In Rumelhart, D. E. and McClelland, J. L. (eds.). *Parallel Distributed Processing – Explorations in the Microstructure of Cognition, Volume 1:* Foundations, MIT Press, Cambridge, MA, 194-281 (1986).

16. Anderson, J.A., Silverstein, J., Ritz, S. and Jones, R. Distinctive features, categorical perception, and probability learning: some applications of a neural model. *Psych. Rev.*, **84**, 413-451 (1977).

17. Feldman, J.A. and Ballard, D.H. Connectionist models and their properties. *Cog. Sci.*, **6**, 205-254 (1982).

18. Kohonen, T. Clustering, taxonomy, and topological maps of patterns. In Lang, M. (ed.). *Proc. of the 6th Int. Conf. on Patt. Rec.*, 114-125 (1982).

19. McClelland, J.L. and Rumelhart, D.E. An interactive activation model of context effects in letter perception: part I. An account of basic findings. *Psych. Rev.*, **88**, 375-407 (1981).

20. Reggia, J.A. Virtual lateral inhibition in parallel activation models of associative memory. *Proc. of the 9th Int. Joint Conf. on Artificial Intelligence*, 244-248 (1986).

21. Gallant, S.L. Connectionist expert systems. *Comm. of the ACM.*, **31**, 2, 152-169 (1988).

22. Hopfield, J.J. Neural networks and physical systems with emergent collective computational abilities. *Proc. of the Nat. Acad. Sci. USA*, **79**, 2554-2558 (1982).

23. Rumelhart, D.E. and McClelland, J.L. *Parallel Distributed Processing – Explorations in the Microstructure of Cognition, Volume 1: Foundations*, MIT Press, Cambridge, MA (1986).

24. Ahuja, S.B., and Soh, W.Y. *The ACE Manual*, Technical Report, Department of Computer Science, University of Maryland, Baltimore County (1988).

5

Modelling chemical process systems via neural computation

N. V. Bhat, P. A. Minderman, Jr., T. McAvoy and N. Sun Wang
University of Maryland, USA

5.1 Summary

This paper discusses the use of neural nets for modelling non-linear chemical systems. Three cases are considered: a steady-state reactor, a dynamic pH stirred tank system, and interpretation of biosensor data. In all cases, a back-propagation net is used successfully to model the system. One advantage of neural nets is that they are inherently parallel and, as a result, can solve problems much faster than a serial digital computer. Furthermore, neural nets have the ability to 'learn'. Rather than programming neural computers, one presents them with a series of examples, and from these examples the nets learn the governing relationships involved in the training database.

5.2 Introduction

One reason for the recent interest in neural computation is that neural nets hold the promise of solving problems that have so far proved extremely difficult for traditional digital computers. Not only are neural nets parallel computing devices and therefore fast, but they are capable of learning by example. The most widely used learning neural net is back-propagation [1].

Back-propagation is an example of a mapping network that learns an approximation to a function, y equal to $f(x)$, from sample x,y pairs. The fact that the function to be learned is non-linear presents no problem to a back-propagation net (BPN). We have used back-propagation successfully on a number of problems typical of those found in the chemical/petroleum industry, including sensor interpretation [2], dynamic modelling [3,4], and in learning how to design distillation control systems. This paper draws together the authors' results in these areas and presents some new results on steady-state modelling of a non-linear chemical reactor.

Figure 5.1 schematically shows an example of a back-propagation neural net used herein. The boxes and circles are neurones, and the lines between the neurones are called interconnects. As can be seen, a back-propagation net has three layers: input, hidden and output. Cybenko [5] showed that a continuous neural network with two hidden layers and any fixed continuous sigmoidal non-linearity, i.e. a back-propagation net, can approximate any continuous function arbitrarily well on a compact set. Although Cybenko's results do not give any insight into just how large a back-propagation net is required, they do show that the fundamental structure of back-propagation is such that it can model any continuous non-linear function.

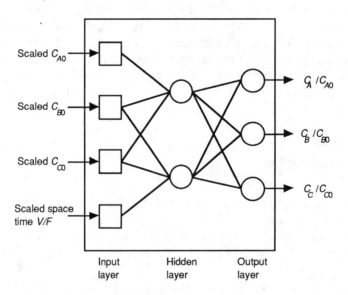

Figure 5.1 BPN for steady-state modelling application.

One of the chief barriers to the more widespread use of advanced modelling and control techniques in the chemical/petroleum industry is the cost of model development and validation. Often modelling costs account for over 75% of the expenditures in an advanced control project. Since neural nets can learn by example, they may offer a cost-effective method of developing useful process models.

This paper discusses the use of neural nets for modelling non-linear chemical process systems. Both a steady-state reactor and a dynamic pH continuously stirred tank reactor (CSTR) are treated, as well as the use of back-propagation for interpreting biosensor data. It is shown that a back-propagation net is capable of learning the underlying relationships. Once a back-propagation model is available, then it can be used directly on-line, even now. When parallel chips are widely available, back-propagation will be even more attractive. Indeed, the back-propagation algorithm can be simulated in a standard digital computer so that no special hardware is required for its implementations. After discussing the back-propagation algorithm, the various examples are treated.

5.3 Back-propagation

The governing equations for a back-propagation net, such as shown in Fig. 5.1, have been derived by Rumelhart and McClelland [6] and are briefly reviewed here. The neurones in the input layer simply store the input values. The hidden layer and output layer neurones each carry out two calculations. First, they multiply all inputs and a bias (equal to a constant value of 1) by a weight and then they sum the result as

$$S_j = \sum_{i=1}^{N} W_{ij} X_i. \tag{5.1}$$

Second, the output of the neurone, O_j, is calculated as the sigma function of S_j as

$$O_j = \sigma(S_j) \tag{5.2}$$

where

$$\sigma(z) = [1 + \exp(-z)]^{-1}. \tag{5.3}$$

Note that not all of the nets use the sigmoidal function as given in equation (5.3), but the ones presented here do. A back-propagation net learns by making changes in its weights in a direction to minimize the sum of squared errors between its predictions and a training data set. The minimization is done using the steepest descent algorithm, which is known to have two main drawbacks. First, the rates of convergence of this algorithm are extremely slow and the improvement per iteration falls sharply. Other minimization techniques, such as the conjugate gradient or Newton's method, have better convergence properties and can be tried in the future. A second drawback is that this algorithm often leads to a local minimum, but this fact has not posed a problem in the actual functioning of the net. Assume that there are R input/output pairs, $x^{(r)}y^{(r)}$, available for training the net. After presentation of pair r, the weights are changed as follows:

$$w_{uv}^{(r)} = w_{uv}^{(r-1)} + \Delta w_{uv}^{(r)} \tag{5.4}$$

with $\Delta w_{uv}^{(r)}$ given by:

Hidden to output weights:

$$\Delta w_{jk}^{(r)} = \sigma(S_k)[y_k^{(r)} - O_k^{(r)}]O_j \tag{5.5}$$

Input to hidden weights:

$$\Delta w_{jk}^{(r)} = \sigma(S_j)\left[\sum_{k=1}^{P}[\sigma'(S_k)] \cdot [y_k^{(r)} - O_k^{(r)}]w_{jk}^{(r-1)}\right]x_i^{(r)} \tag{5.6}$$

and

$$\sigma'(S_k) = \sigma(S_k)[1 - \sigma(S_k)].\tag{5.7}$$

After presentation of the first input/output pair, one proceeds with the second pair, and so on. The weights are changed with each presentation. One might assume that setting all the weights to zero may be an acceptable starting point. If all the weights start with equal values and the solution requires unequal weights to be developed, then the system can never learn. The reason is because the error is propagated back through the neurones in proportion to the value of the weights, as shown in equation (5.6). All the error signals to the hidden nodes remain identical, and the system starts out at a local minimum and remains there. This problem is counteracted by starting the system with a set of randomized weights distributed uniformly between −0.5 and +0.5.

The chosen activation function has a special feature. The function cannot reach its final values of 0 and 1 without infinitely large inputs. The useful region of the activation function is approximately between 0.1 and 0.9, and the variable's input to the net is scaled within this range.

5.4   Steady-state example

5.4.1   *Model*

To illustrate the use of back-propagation, the following isothermal CSTR reaction sequence is considered, where constituent A goes to constituent B with reaction constant k_1 while constituent B goes to constituent C with reaction constant k_2.

$$A \xrightarrow{k_1} B \xrightarrow{k_2} C.$$

The volume of the reactor is V, the feed flow rate is F, and CA and CB are the concentrations of A and B, respectively. At steady state, the mole fractions of A, B, and C in the reactor are given by the following expressions:

$$C_A/C_{A0} = b_1 \tag{5.8}$$

$$C_B/C_{B0} = b_2(C_{B0}/C_{A0}) + (k_1 V/F)b_1 b_2 \tag{5.9}$$

$$C_C/C_{A0} = C_{C0}/C_{A0} + (k_2 V/F)b_2 C_{B0}/C_{A0}$$
$$+ k_1 k_2 (V/F)^2/(b_1 b_2) \tag{5.10}$$

where $b_i = [1 + k_i V/F]^{-1}$ for $i = 1,2$.

It is assumed that historical data on product concentrations are available at the different operating conditions shown in Table 5.1. These data are used to train the net so that it can be used to optimize reactor yield. To generate a data set, k_1 is taken as 0.16 min^{-1} and k_2 as 0.06 min^{-1}. Equations (5.8)–(5.10) show that the product concentrations are a function of both the reactor feed composition and the space time, V/F. Furthermore, although the reaction mechanisms are linear, the kinetic parameters appear in the yield relationships in a non-linear manner. In using neural nets, the underlying reactor kinetics are assumed to be unknown. In generating historical data, six different values of V/F and two different values of feed composition were assumed. Noise (10% Gaussian) was added to these data.

Table 5.1 Process data.

	Feed Composition (A/B/C)	Space Time (–)					
		0.02	0.04	0.08	0.16	0.32	0.64
Learning set	(99%, 0%, 1%) (80%, 5%, 15%)	(A/B/C) data generated from eqs. (5.8)–(5.10) and corrupted with 10% Gaussian noise					
Test set	(90%, 2%, 8%)						

Note: nominal feed composition and space times were also corrupted with 10% noise in the learning set.

5.4.2 *Back-propagation net used*

The back-propagation net used is schematically shown in Fig. 5.1. This net was simulated on a MicroVAX computer. The net inputs are the scaled feed composition and reactor space time. The outputs are the dimensionless product concentrations. One of the issues that has to be decided in configuring a back-propagation net is the number of hidden elements to be used. This number was arbitrarily set at nine for this illustration. The assumed historical data were fed to the net until convergence was achieved. The rate of convergence of the net is slow in this case. Fig. 5.2 shows a plot of the root mean square (rms) error between actual and predicted concentrations as a function of the number of times that a data set was presented to the net. The rms error is the sum of the errors of the A, B, and C concentrations. As can be seen, it takes 10 000 presentations before convergence is achieved. The final net predictions of the concentrations for the low-purity feedstock A versus space time are shown in Fig. 5.3 together with the actual model values. Other concentrations of B and C exhibit similar behaviour. As can be seen, the back-propagation net does an excellent job in learning the underlying governing CSTR model.

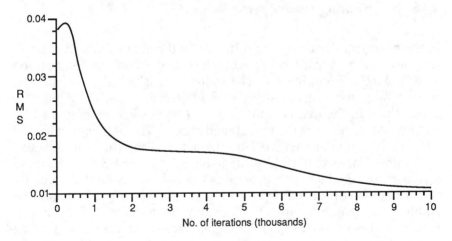

Figure 5.2 Rate of convergence.

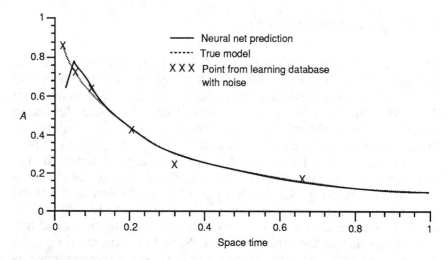

Figure 5.3 Comparison of neural net and model predictions (low-purity feedstock).

5.4.3   *Optimizing reactor performance*

In the historical database, two different feed compositions were used. Here it is assumed that a new feedstock is used, where the composition is 90% A, 2% B and 8% C. The trained net is asked to predict the space time to use to maximize the yield of component B. Figure 5.4 gives a plot of the exit composition of B versus V/F as predicted by the net. Also shown is the model prediction. The optimum values of V/F are 10.0 min as predicted by the net, and the true value is also 10.0 min. The actual yield at this space time is 61.3%. As these results show, the back-propagation net is able to generate essentially optimum operating conditions in this simple example. It should be emphasized that only historical data were used to train the net. However, these data did span the region over which the net was asked to make a prediction. Back-propagation nets do well when asked to interpolate, but their performance is poorer when asked to extrapolate. This point is illustrated in Fig. 5.4 at low space times. As V/F approaches zero, the highest errors between the net results and the actual model results exist.

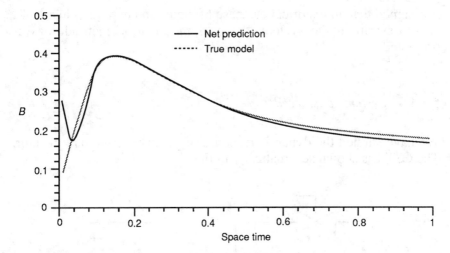

Figure 5.4 Comparison of neural net and model predictions (medium-purity feedstock, test case).

Although this example is simple, it illustrates the potential power of neural computation. By using only readily available historical information, a back-propagation net is able to model the reactor without any knowledge of the detailed kinetic mechanisms involved. Such an approach, if successful on a commercial reactor, would be extremely cost-effective. It is felt that there are many chemical process systems where the approach outlined here could be used successfully. Bioprocesses would appear to be particularly attractive candidates because they are so difficult to model from first principles. The next section discusses the use of back-propagation nets to learn dynamic models from input/output data.

5.5 Dynamic example

Our results on using back-propagation to develop non-linear dynamic models have been discussed in detail in [3,4]. A summary of these results is given here. To illustrate the neural net methodology, the same pH CSTR as discussed in [3,4] is treated. Recently, we have applied the same modelling approach to data taken from an industrial distillation tower [7] that had seven inputs and four outputs. Our results on the industrial data were comparable to those that follow. It is assumed that an historical database of inputs and outputs is available. After describing the system, the back-propagation methodology is presented.

5.5.1   *System considered*

We have studied the dynamic response of pH in a stirred tank reactor. The CSTR is shown schematically in Fig. 5.5.

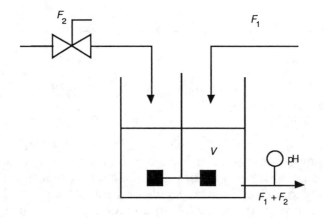

Figure 5.5 pH in a CSTR.

The CSTR has two input streams, one containing sodium hydroxide and the other acetic acid. A dynamic model for the pH in the tank can be obtained using the approach presented by McAvoy *et al.* [8]. By writing material balances on Na^+ and total acetate ($HAC_- + AC^{-1}$), one gets:

Total acetate balance:

$$F_1C_1 - (F_1 + F_2) = Vd\xi/dt \qquad (5.11)$$

Sodium ion balance:

$$F_2C_2 - (F_1 + F_2) = Vd\zeta/dt \qquad (5.12)$$

where

$$\zeta = [Na^+]$$
$$\xi = [HAC] + [AC^-].$$

Combining the HAC and H_2O equilibrium relationships with the requirement for electoneutrality gives

$$\zeta + [H+] = K_w/[H^+] + K_a[HAC]/[H^+]. \tag{5.13}$$

Parameters for the CSTR considered are given in Table 5.2. A training database was developed by forcing the F_2 stream with a 2% pseudorandom binary signal (PRBS) superimposed on its steady-state value. The F_2 and pH responses used for training are shown in Fig. 5.6. In the pH model, equations (5.11) and (5.12) are essentially linear differential equations. Equation (5.13) is a highly non-linear algebraic equation. Thus, the model has highly non-linear steady-state characteristics and essentially linear dynamic characteristics.

Table 5.2

CSTR parameters used	Value
Volume of tank	1000 litres
Flow rate of HAC	81 litres/min
Steady-state flow rate of NaOH	515 litres/min
Steady-state pH	9
Concentration of HAC in F_1	0.3178 mol./litre
Concentration of NaOH in F_2	0.05 mol./litre

5.5.2 *Back-propagation dynamic modelling (BDM)*

To model the pH response shown in Figure 5.6, a back-propagation net was used. The input to the net consisted of a moving window of pH and F_2 values, as illustrated in Figure 5.7. The centre of the window is taken as the current time, t_0. Past and present values of pH and F_2, as well as future values of F_2, are fed to the net. The output from the net is the pH in the future. Thus, the back-propagation modelling approach is similar to traditional autoregressive moving

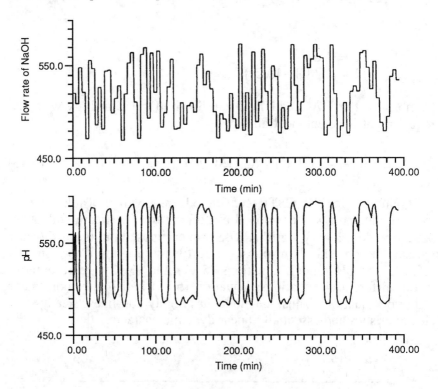

Figure 5.6 Data used for the dynamic CSTR example.

average (ARMA) modelling. Various sizes for the input layer were tried. For the results that follow, the input layer had 15 neurones and the hidden and output layers five neurones. The pH output was predicted one to five time steps into the future. A time step, Δ_t, of 0.2 min is used.

At the beginning of the training process, the window is placed at the beginning of the database. The first 5 pH and 10 F_2 values are input to the net. The desired net outputs are the pH values at $t_0 = 0.5$ plus one through five Δ_t in the future. After the first data presentation, the window moves Δ_t down the database. Again the current and past four pH and F_2 values and the future five F_2 values are input to the net. This process is continued until the end of the database is reached, and then the process is repeated by starting at the beginning of the database until convergence is achieved.

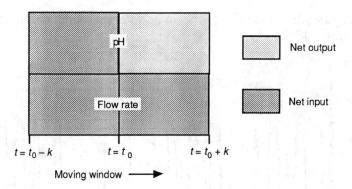

Figure 5.7 Window of data.

5.5.3   *Results*

After convergence, the net gives excellent pH predictions, as the results in Fig. 5.8 show. Although the net predicts pH at one to five times steps into the future, only predictions for the first time step are shown for simplicity. The agreement between predicted and actual pH at the other four time steps is as good as that one time step. Figure 5.9 illustrates the ability of the BDM model to learn the non-linear process characteristics. The net weights were fixed at the values obtained from the training illustrated in Fig. 5.8. For this training, the pH would settle out at 9 if the PRBS signal were stopped. To generate a test set, the steady-state hydroxide flow, F_2 was lowered slightly so that the steady-state pH in the CSTR was 7. Then a 1% PRBS signal was introduced into F_2. As can be seen, the net's response is close to that of the system. In [3] a comparison between a traditional ARMA model and back-propagation is given for this same forcing around pH equal to 7. It is shown that the net does better than an ARMA model in learning the non-linear process characteristics.

Once a trained back-propagation model is available, then it can be used in a straightforward manner for process control. Figure 5.10 presents a schematic diagram showing how the neural model is used. The approach is essentially the same as that used in dynamic matrix control [9], except that the non-linear neural net model is used in place of the linear convolution model. Basically, the optimizer calculates future control moves to minimize a performance index, e.g. a sum of squared errors between desired and predicted future pH values. Alternatively, one can train a net to model the inverse process dynamics and then use this inverse in an internal model control (IMC) configuration [3,4].

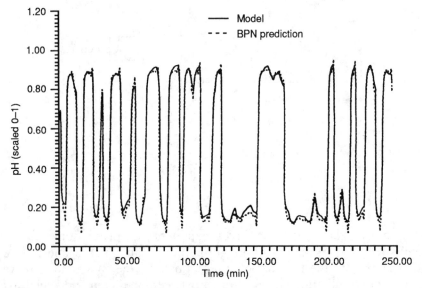

Figure 5.8 Prediction of training data (steady-state pH = 9).

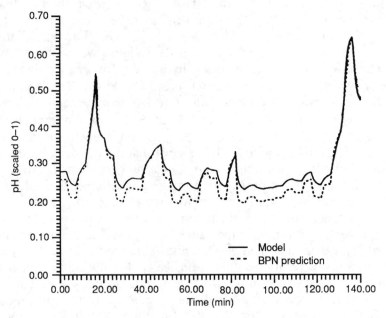

Figure 5.9 Prediction of test data (steady-state pH = 7).

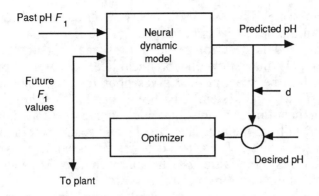

Figure 5.10 Neural net-based predictive control.

5.6 Interpreting biosensor data

5.6.1 Overview

Currently, process industries face the constant challenge of holding down the prices of products vis-a-vis the inflationary trend of raw materials. To meet this challenge effectively, plants must be made more efficient and productivity must increase. Although computer-based methods have been developed to meet these goals, often the required measurements are lacking. One area that holds great promise to achieve these goals is new sensor technology [10]. Traditionally, the process industries have relied on standard measurements such as flow, pressure and temperature. Today, it is becoming increasingly important to measure composition, since this is the key variable in terms of economic importance. Presently, there is a great deal of activity in developing new methods for sensing composition. Most of these new methods, however, have not been applied on-line. It is critically important that promising laboratory techniques be tried on real problems so that measurement science can be transferred to engineering practice. For this transition to occur, reliable and accurate methods for interpreting sensor signals must be available.

We have studied [2] how to interpret signals from light-induced fluorescence spectra for estimating bioconcentrations. Specifically, mixtures of tryptophan and tryosine are considered. The input to the net is the measured fluorescence intensity at various wavelengths. The output from the net is the concentration of the fluoreophores present. Non-linear models describing the fluorescence spectra have been developed [11] that show that a linear least-squares approach to deconvoluting the spectral data gives poor results. The non-linear characteristics of the system must be included. Back-propagation is capable of handling the non-linearities in the spectral data. Both simulated data from the non-linear model and actual experimental data have been studied [2]. The actual data are discussed here. Although a specific sensor system is treated, the approach taken is general, and it can be applied to other sensor systems as well.

For our experimental work, 33 samples containing binary mixtures of tryptophan and tyrosine were considered. The composition and mole fraction of these samples are such that the total composition ranges over three decades from 10^{-4} to 10^{-6} molar. To handle this variation, we took the logarithm of total concentration and then scaled it to the range 0 to 1 before presentation to the back-propagation net. Thus the net outputs were mole fraction and the scaled logarithm of total concentration. Finally, the data were split into a training set and test set by random choice. The test set had 11 elements and the training set 22.

5.6.2 *Back-propagation results*

The inputs to the back-propagation net were the fluorescence spectra at 30 wavelengths. A number of approaches to scaling this intensity data were tried. Taking the logarithm of the intensity produced the best results. Thus a scaling logarithm of intensity was used as the net input. The number of hidden elements in the net was varied from 2 to 10. After convergence, the average sum of squared error in predicting the test set data (PRESS) was used as a means of choosing the optimum number of hidden elements. Figure 5.11 gives a plot of the PRESS versus the number of hidden elements. It was determined that eight hidden elements were optimum. A comparison between the actual test set data and the back-propagation results for eight hidden elements shows excellent agreement is achieved. The average absolute percentage errors compared with the actual values are 5.18% for mole fraction and 9.07% for total concentration. The maximum absolute percentage errors are 25.6 and 25.3% for each variable, respectively.

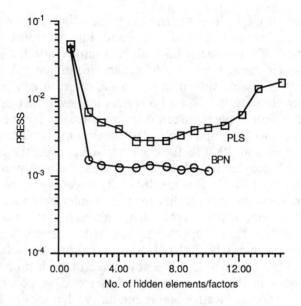

Figure 5.11 Comparison of PLS and BPN.

To determine just how well back-propagation does in deconvoluting the spectral data, a benchmark is needed. Recently, Carey *et al.* [12] have compared several chemometric methods of analysing data such as fluorescence spectra. The methods evaluated include: standard least squares, principal component regression, and partial least squares (PLS). They concluded that the latter two methods are significantly superior to standard least squares. The best technique appears to be PLS [13–15], and this is the method used for comparison here. With PLS, a matrix calibration model of the following form is assumed:

$$Y = XC + E \qquad (5.14)$$

where Y is the measured spectra, C is a calibration matrix, X is the matrix of variables to be predicted, and E is assumed to be a matrix of random noise. The PLS method is used to determine an approximation to the inverse of CC^T from a set of calibration samples. Once the inverse of CC^T is known, it is straightforward to calculate X from spectral measurements on an unknown sample. A key aspect of PLS is that it is essentially a linear technique. As a result, even though it is widely used, it may prove to be inferior to back-propagation. In PLS, one has to decide how many factors to keep in the approximation of the inverse of CC^T. This decision is made using cross-validation in which the calibration data are divided into a training set and calibration set. To compare PLS with back-propagation, the same 11-member test-set sample was used for each technique. A plot of the PRESS for PLS is also shown in Fig. 5.11, where it can be seen that seven factors are optimal. The PLS results for seven factors show that the average absolute percentage errors are 11.68% for mole fraction and 13.73% for total composition. The maximum absolute percentage errors are 50.99 and 20.70% for each variable, respectively. As can be seen, back-propagation does a much better job in predicting the test data than does PLS. This result is very encouraging because PLS appears to have wide applicability for sensor interpretation.

It should be emphasized again that, although a specific sensor is considered, the neural net approach discussed is generally applicable. The only requirement is that one have a calibration set with both inputs and outputs available. The advantage of back-propagation for sensor analysis is that one no longer has to be as concerned with linearity of response. Rather, reproducibility of response becomes a key issue. The characteristics of back-propagation allow one to consider sensor methods that were previously rejected because of their non-linear nature.

5.7 Conclusion

This paper has discussed the use of back-propagation neural nets for learning non-linear models from plant input/output data and for interpreting biosensor data. Because of its ability to identify non-linear relationships and because it is fundamentally a parallel technique, back-propagation is a particularly promising neural algorithm for application in the chemical/petroleum industries. The back-propagation modelling approach was illustrated on two reactor interpretations. The neural net is able to learn the underlying government relationships in all cases. It is concluded that neural nets hold great promise for cost-effective modelling of chemical process systems.

Acknowledgements

This research has been supported by the National Science Foundation under Grant EET 87-20046 and through its support of the Systems Research Center at the University of Maryland. Experimental data were taken at the laboratories of the Chemical Process Metrology Division of the National Institute of Standards and Technology. Collaboration with the Hecht Nielsen Company and the use of its neural coprocessor board are gratefully acknowledged.

References

1. Werbos, P. *Beyond Regression: New Tools for Prediction and Analysis in Behavioral Sciences*. Ph.D. thesis, Harvard University (1974).

2. McAvoy, T., Wang, N., Naidu, S. and Bhat, N. Use of neural nets for interpreting biosensor data. *Proc. Joint Conf. Neural Networks*, Washington, DC, 1227-1233 (1989).

3. Bhat, N. and McAvoy, T. Use of neural nets for dynamic modeling and control of chemical process systems. *Comp. and Chem. Eng.* (in press).

4. Bhat, N. and McAvoy, T. Use of neural nets for dynamic modeling and control of chemical process systems. *Proc. 1989 Amer. Automat. Contr. Conf.*, Pittsburgh, PA, 1342-1348 (1989).

5. Cybenko, G. Continuous value neural networks with two hidden layers are sufficient. *Math. Contr. Signal & Sys.*, **2**, 303-314 (1989).

6. Rumelhart, D. and McClelland, J. *Parallel Distributed Processing: Explorations in the Microstructure of Cognition, Volume 1*, Chapter 8, MIT Press, Cambridge, MA (1987).

7. Bhat, N. and McAvoy, T. Dynamic modelling via neural computing. *Annual AIChE. Meeting*, San Francisco (1989).

8. McAvoy, T., Hsu, E. and Lowenthal, S. Dynamics of pH in CSTR's. *Ind. Eng. Chem. Process Des. Develop.*, **11**, 68-70 (1972).

9. Cutler, C. and Ramaker, B. Dynamic matrix control – a computer control algorithm. *AIChE. 86th National Meeting*, Houston, TX, (1979); also *Joint Automat. Contr. Conf. Proc.*, San Francisco (1980).

10. Amundsen, N. *Frontiers of Chemical Engineering: Needs and Opportunities.* Report to National Research Council (1987).

11. Rinaudo, P. *Analysis of Laser Induced Fluorescence Spectra.* MS thesis, University of Maryland, College Park, Chapter 5 (1987).

12. Carey, W., Beebe, K., Sanchez, E., Geladi, P. and Kowalski, B. Chemomeric analysis of multisensor arrays. *Sensors and Actuators*, **9**, 223-234 (1986).

13. Wold, H. *Festschrift Jerzy Neyman*, Wiley, New York, 411-444 (1966).

14. Joreskog, K. and Wold, H. (eds.). *Systems Under Indirect Observation, Parts I and II*, North Holland, Amsterdam (1982).

15. Geladi, P.and Kowalski, B. Partial least squares regression: a tutorial. *Anal. Chim. Acta*, **185**, 1-17, (1986).

6

The application of neural networks to robotics

A. Guez, Z. Ahmad and J. Selinsky
Drexel University, USA

6.1 Summary

We report on the application of neural networks (NN) architecture to two important problems in robotics. A hybrid architecture is used to solve the inverse kinematics problem with performance superior to that of the classical approach. We also use a hierarchical NN architecture for learning rigid robot dynamics for the purpose of real-time control.

6.2 Introduction

In this chapter we summarize the results of Guez [1,2] in applying NN architecture to problems in robot control. Section 6.3 describes a hybrid architecture used to solve the inverse kinematics problem with performance superior to that of the classical approach. In section 6.3 we use a hierarchical NN architecture for learning rigid robot dynamics for the purpose of real-time control.

6.3 The inverse kinematic problem in robotics

The purpose of a robot is to manipulate objects with its end-effector. The end-effector is at one end of a chain of links, connected with joints; the other end is fixed. The motion of the robot is linked with the transformations between the joints and the end-effector. The activation of the joints result in a motion of the end-effector. In order for the end-effector, carrying an object, to follow a desired path in the world space it is required to activate the joints in a manner that will make the end-effector track the desired trajectory.

Solutions to the inverse kinematics exist in closed form for some robots or may be obtained by iterative methods. However, the procedure to obtain a closed form solution, if it exists, is tedious and the iterative methods have a tendency to diverge when the initial guess to the methods is far from the actual solution.

6.3.1 *Problem statement*

The inverse kinematic problem (IKP) deals with finding the n joint angle values q of the robot that will position the end-effector in a desired position and orientation X in the m-dimensional world space. This may be expressed as:

$$q = f^{-1}(X). \tag{6.1}$$

However, in general this solution is not unique. In many cases (e.g. redundant manipulators) there may result an infinite number of solutions. In these cases additional constraints [3] in terms of the allowed configurations or performance function minimization are used to reduce the number of legitimate joint configurations or to single out a unique preferable one.

6.3.2 *The proposed method*

The formation of the proposed method starts with the robotic manipulator for which the IKP is to be solved and a 'blank' (untrained) multi-layered feedforward neural network of suitable size. Then, training data in the form of pairs of the end-effector position and orientation $X = [\phi \; \theta \; \psi \; x \; y \; z]^T$, and the corresponding joint values $q = [q_1 \; q_2 \; ... \; q_n]^T$, are generated. These data are used for training the NN via the back error propagation algorithm [4]. The position and orientation vector is the input and the corresponding joint values are the desired outputs of the network. After the training is completed the trained NN is coupled with the iterative method, as shown in Fig. 6.1, for the purpose of operation. During the operation phase the desired position and orientation X of the end-effector is provided to the NN. The NN gives the approximate solution q_0 based on the learned connection weights. The approximate solution is taken as the initial guess by the iterative method to give the final solution within the specified tolerance. We consider that the type of solution out of the finitely many solutions is pre-specified to us and therefore training of the NN is restricted to the set of examples that pertain to this specific solution only.

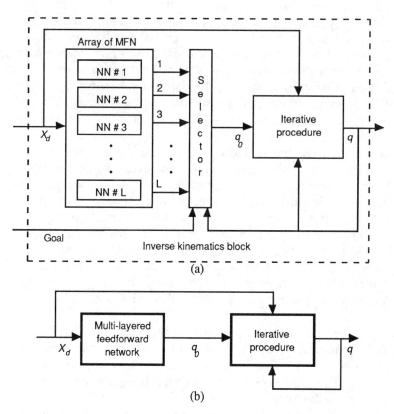

Figure 6.1 Schematics of the proposed method employing the NN to provide the initial guess q_0 to the iterative procedure.

6.3.3   *Examples*

The back error propagation (BEP) algorithm simulating a three-layer perceptron was employed to tackle the problems described below. Continuous inputs and outputs were assumed. The nodes assumed the symmetric sigmoidal non-linearity [5]. Parameters of the NN are as given in reference [2]. Training was terminated when it was seen that the errors were not improving.

1. The human arm. Here we show an attempt to capture the criteria that a human being allegedly optimizes in manipulating different objects by training the NN by a data set corresponding to some specified task. Planar motion parallel to the ground was the considered task. The subject was asked to move an object in free space, in a plane parallel to the ground. Knowing the actual distances between the joints the data set was filtered to achieve a 10.0% tolerance about the respective actual values. The data set thus obtained contained only 43 words out of a total of 78 words. The network for this case consisted of two inputs and three output nodes and two hidden layers, each containing ten nodes.

    Figure 6.2(a) shows the plot of the error in the positioning of the hand resulting for the trained data set, while Fig. 6.2(b) shows the same for a different data set obtained separately from the data set on which the network was trained. The two figures have similar errors indicating that the neural network has generalized on the trained data set. Large errors near $X = 0.5$ m are perhaps due to singularity reasons or insufficient data near that region. Further, it was observed that the values for the elbow joints were learned much better than those for the wrist joint and the shoulder joint.

    As seen earlier, the filtered data set was only 55% of the total data gathered with 10% tolerance which indicates that the precision of the training data may not be adequate. However, it is observed that the NN is able to generalize upon the training data, giving similar results for the untrained data to that of the trained data. This implies that implicit performance indices can be captured via NNs and perhaps identified via weight pruning and analysis.

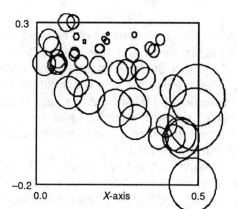

(a) Hand positioning error for the training data.

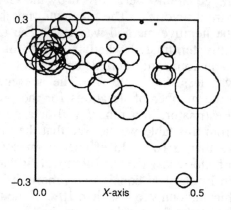

(b) Hand positioning error for other than the training data.

Figure 6.2 Results of single MFN trained on human arm data in a plane perpendicular to the gravity. Shoulder is located at (0,0).

2. PUMA 560. The PUMA 560 parameters were taken from Fu *et al.* [6], page 37. This manipulator, which is a 6-DOF robot, was chosen for ease of generation of data and verification of results since it has a closed form solution. PUMA 560 has eight solutions for a given position and orientation signified by Right/Left – Shoulder, Above/Below – Elbow, and Up/Down – Wrist. In our simulations the training data corresponds to: LEFT Arm, BELOW Elbow and UP Wrist configuration. In the simulations the joint limits used for the sixth joint were –180° to 180° instead

of $-266°$ to $266°$.

The network in this case consisted of six input nodes, one output node each for the six joints and two hidden layers for each joint consisting of 32 nodes in the first layer and eight nodes in the second layer. The average error in the solution given by the NN for each joint taken over 100 samples ranged from $0.16°$ to $6.02°$ while the standard deviation of the error ranged from $11.5°$ to $36.8°$. This solution was seen to be more scattered for joints 4 to 6 as compared with the joints 1 to 3.

Next, the proposed method was compared by giving a fixed estimate to the iterative procedure. This fixed estimate was taken as: $\theta_1 = 0$, $\theta_2 = 0$, $\theta_3 = \pi/4$, $\theta_4 = 0$, $\theta_5 = \pi/4$, and $\theta_6 = 0$, which is a configuration corresponding to that in which the NN was trained, as indicated in the beginning of this section. In the simulations the equations were solved by the Gauss elimination method and partial pivoting. The maximum number of iterations allowed for the iterative method was 100. The iterative method was successfully terminated when the norm of the difference between the desired and actual end-effector position and orientation was less than 1.0E–4. The average and standard deviation for the number of iterations for the proposed method and the fixed estimator, in a run of 100 data points, is given in Table 6.1. From this table we can see that the proposed method achieves more than a two-fold efficiency in computing on the average, with better consistency. Moreover, it was observed that the time taken by the NN equals two time units of the iterative procedure, which amounts to less than 10% of the time required to get the solution by the fixed estimator method.

Table 6.1 Comparison of the proposed solution with the fixed initial guess Newton–Raphson method, for the PUMA 560 manipulator. The data corresponds to 100 samples.

Initial guess for Newton-Raphson method	Number of iterations	
	Average	Standard deviation
Neural solution	9.96	12.95
Fixed	21.09	18.90

6.3.4   *Conclusion*

The proposed hybrid method which takes the solution given by the trained NN as an initial guess to an iterative procedure (Newton–Raphson in our case) combines the advantages of the NN and iterative methods, these being (1) independent of the type of the manipulator and (2) simple to implement. Only forward kinematics is required for this method and, as shown by our simulations, this combination results in an increase in computational efficiency by two-fold for the PUMA 560 (6-DOF) robot. This results in minimal processing within each control cycle and improves real-time control performance.

6.4   Learning of robot dynamics using a hierarchical neural network

Adaptation, in control, is the process of adjusting the controller to comply with the regulation and tracking requirements of the closed loop system. During operation, the controller is given a trajectory by a path planner in order to accomplish some useful task. The controller then adapts the parameters on-line, so as to satisfy the tracking requirements. If the parameters are not known exactly, there will be a transient period of tracking error while adaptation occurs. Thus identification of the true parameters is desirable for increased tracking precision.

Inverse dynamics-based control algorithms are computationally intensive, and may result in prohibitively slow control rates if implemented on serial computers. A parallel implementation of the above adaptive controller is proposed. The proposed implementation utilizes a hierarchical neural network architecture, which would ideally provide very fast control.

6.4.1   *Dynamic model*

A rigid robot is defined as an open kinematic chain of rigid links, which are joined by linear or revolute joints. The dynamic model of a rigid robot manipulator can be written as

$$T(t) = I(q,t)\,\ddot{q}(t) + H(q,\dot{q},t)\dot{q} + B\dot{q}(t) + G(q,t) \qquad (6.2)$$

where
> $q(t)$ is the $n \times 1$ vector of joint linear or angular positions,
>
> $I(q,t)$ is the $n \times n$ matrix of terms related to inertial forces,
>
> $H(q,\dot{q},t)$ is the $n \times 1$ vector of terms related to centripetal and coriolis forces,
>
> B is the $n \times n$ diagonal matrix of viscous friction terms,
>
> $G(q,t)$ is the $n \times 1$ vector of terms related to gravitational forces,
>
> $T(t)$ is the $n \times 1$ vector of driving forces or torques, and
>
> n is the number of degrees of freedom (DOF) of the manipulator (for further details see [6,7]).

The representation – equation (6.2) – is not unique. Different choices of ϕ result in different structures of the known function matrix $Y[q, \dot{q}, \ddot{q}, \ddot{q}']$. In this work, it will be assumed that the parameter vector ϕ will represent the p parameters to be identified.

6.4.2   Proposed learning method

The manipulator's dynamics can be represented by a weighted linear combination of suitable basis functions. The basis functions for a general class of manipulators are known a priori and may be trained into a series of three-layer feedforward network modules prior to use and then combined on-line in a fourth layer using a suitable weight adjustment rule such as LMS [8].

We use a linear control law with added non-linear compensation to control the manipulator. During an initial purely learning phase and whenever the manipulator is not needed for production, exploratory schedules (ESs) are used to isolate and identify the non-linear compensation terms. ESs are trajectories specifically designed for efficient learning of the system dynamics. A block diagram of the closed loop system is shown in Fig. 6.3.

Learning of the non-linear compensation terms is as follows. Let $G_0(q)$, $W_0(q,\dot{q})$ and $I_0(q)$ be the outputs of the $G(q)$, $W(q,\dot{q})$ and $I(q)$ compensation networks respectively, where $W(q,\dot{q}) = H(q,\dot{q},t)\dot{q} + B\dot{q}$. After receiving the desired trajectory, the control that is to be applied to the robot is calculated using the feedback control (FB) from the linear controller and the feedforward control (FF) from the learned non-linear compensation terms.

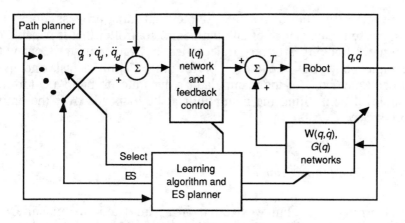

Figure 6.3 Block diagram of the closed loop system.

Learning of the $G(q)$ terms is accomplished during positioning control phases of the trajectory. At the steady state of positioning control, $\ddot{q} = \dot{q} = 0$. Then from equation (6.2) it can be seen that $T = G(q)$. The applied torque at steady state can be used to learn the $G(q)$ compensation network.

Learning of the $W(q,\dot{q})$ compensation terms is performed during constant velocity portions of the trajectory. To isolate the $W(q,\dot{q})$ terms, notice that at $\dot{q} = $ constant, $\ddot{q} = 0$ and $T = W(q,\dot{q}) + G(q)$. But $G(q)$ has already been identified and is available as $G_0(q)$, so that we may isolate $W(q,\dot{q})$ to be used in learning.

The inertia-related terms $I(q)$ may be continuously evaluated using the a priori known relationship $dI(q,t)/dt = H(q,\dot{q}) + H(q,\dot{q})^T$ (see [9]).

After the dynamic equations of the manipulator are known, a feedback linearization or inverse dynamics-based controller [6,10] of the form:

$$T = I_0(k_p e + k_v \dot{e} + \ddot{q}_d) + W_0(q,\dot{q}) + G_0(q) \qquad (6.3)$$

where $e = q_d(t) - q(t)$, and $q_d(t)$ is the position reference signal, is then employed. The closed loop system is then equivalent to:

$$\ddot{q}(t) = k_p e + k_v \dot{e} + \ddot{q}_d(t) \qquad (6.4)$$

which, when k_p and k_v are appropriately chosen, results in an asymptotically stable system. Note that this process does not presuppose the existence of an omnipotent controller that is capable of accurately tracking arbitrary trajectories, but rather it starts out with a simple controller capable of performing a limited task and uses learned knowledge of the manipulator's dynamics to build a controller capable of controlling the manipultor at high speeds over the entire work space.

6.4.3 Simulation results

The learning algorithm was tested on a simulated two-planar DOF manipulator (Fig. 6.4). Note that in these results, exactly computed basis functions were used.

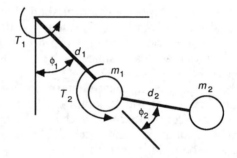

Figure 6.4 Two degree of freedom planar manipulator.

The dynamic equations for this manipulator can be represented as linearly separable non-linear subsystems

$$T_1 = (a_{11} + a_{12}C_2)\ddot{\phi}_1 + (a_{13} + a_{14}C_2)\ddot{\phi}_2 + a_{15}S_2)\dot{\phi}_1\dot{\phi}_2$$
$$+ a_{16}S_2\dot{\phi}_2^2 + a_{17}\dot{\phi}_1 + a_{18}S_2 + a_{19}S_{12} \quad (6.5)$$

$$T_2 = (a_{21} + a_{22}C_2)\ddot{\phi}_1 + a_{23}\ddot{\phi}_2 + a_{24}S_2\dot{\phi}_1^2 + a_{25}\dot{\phi}_2 + a_{26}S_{12} \quad (6.6)$$

where $C_i = \cos(\phi_i)$, $S_i = \sin(\phi_i)$, $C_{ij} = \cos(\phi_i + \phi_i)$, $S_{ij} = \sin(\phi_i + \phi_i)$, and the a_{ij} terms are weighting constants to be identified.

Utilization of the ES for a 2-DOF manipulator result in small tracking errors which may lead to small errors in the parameter identification. As can be seen in Table 6.2 the learning algorithm was able to identify the a_{ij} terms to a very close approximation of their true values. The comparison of the 2-DOF manipulator controller before and after learning via ES showed that the controller performance is significantly improved. Further details of the method and results can be found in [1].

Table 6.2 Performance results of the learning algorithm.

Weight number	True value	Estimated value
a_{11}	30.0	29.51
a_{21}	10.0	10.06
a_{12}	20.0	19.28
a_{22}	10.0	10.20
a_{13}	10.0	9.79
a_{23}	10.0	10.12
a_{14}	10.0	9.47
a_{24}	10.0	10.22
a_{15}	−20.0	−19.28
a_{25}	5.0	5.01
a_{16}	−10.0	−9.97
a_{26}	98.1	98.10
a_{17}	5.0	4.61
a_{18}	196.2	196.19
a_{19}	98.1	98.10

6.4.4 Conclusion

The exploratory schedules have been specified as a desired trajectory that is to be followed to do learning while the manipulator is not doing other useful tasks. The simulation results of the ES for a 2-DOF manipulator showed how small tracking errors may lead to small errors in the parameter identification. The comparison of the 2-DOF manipulator controller before and after learning via ES showed that the controller performance is significantly improved.

References

1. Guez, A. and Selinsky, J. Neurocontroller design via supervised and unsupervised learning. *J. of Intel. and Robotic Systems*, **2**, 307-335 (1989).

2. Guez, A. and Ahmad, Z. Improving the solution of the inverse kinematic problem in robotics by neural networks. *J. of Neural Network Computing*, **1**, 21-32, Spring (1990).

   In addition to references [1], [2] and [10] by the authors of this paper, see also:

   Guez, A. and Ahmad, Z. Solution to the inverse kinematics problem in robotics by neural networks. *IEEE Int. Conf. on Neural Networks, Volume II*, 617-624, (1988).

   Guez, A. and Ahmad, Z. Accelerated convergence in the inverse kinematics via multilayer feedforward networks. *IEEE IJCNN, Volume II*, 341-344, June 18-22 (1989).

3. Yoshikawa, T. Manipulability of robotic mechanisms. *Int. J. of Robotics Research*, **4**, 2, 3-9, Summer (1985).

4. Rumelhart, D.E., McClelland, J.L. and the PDP Research Group. *Parallel Distributed Processing: Explorations in the Microstructure of Cognition, Volumes 1 and 2*, MIT Press, Cambridge, MA (1986).

5. Scott, W. and Huberman, B.A. An improved three-layer, back propagation algorithm. *IEEE 1st Int. Conf. on Neural Networks, Volume II*, 637-643 (1987).

6. Fu, K.S., Gonzalez, R.C. and Lee, C.S.G. *Robotics Control, Sensing, Vision and Intelligence*, McGraw-Hill, New York (1987).

7. Paul, R.P. *Robot Manipulators: Mathematics, Programming and Control*, MIT Press, Cambridge, MA (1981).

8. Widrow, B. and Stearns, S.D. *Adaptive Signal Processing*, Prentice-Hall, Englewood Cliffs, NJ (1985).

9. Slotine, J.J. and Li, W. Adaptive manipulator control: a case study. *Proc. IEEE Robotics and Automation Conf.*, 1392-1400, Rayleigh, NC (1987).

10. Guez, A. *Optimal Control of Robotic Manipulators*, Ph.D. thesis, University of.Florida, Gainesville, Florida (1982).

7
Neural networks in vision

P. J. G. Lisboa
University of Liverpool, England

7.1 Summary

The application of neural networks to computer vision is introduced by reference to the structure of the primary visual cortex. Artificial neural network models are described and their operation as self-organized feature extractors, and in the classification of simple binary images, is discussed. Further applications to computer vision are reviewed.

7.2 Introduction

Artificial neural networks are currently the subject of much theoretical research, and of considerable practical interest in a wide range of applications. This paper provides an introduction to the use of neural models in computer vision, and it reviews the motivation for this approach, some of the best-known algorithms, and current applications.

One of the main motivations for the revival of biologically inspired computation is the apparent ease with which biological systems perform pattern recognition and other tasks with standards of speed and robustness which conventional artificial intelligence techniques find impossible to match. Thus a child can recognize faces, navigate a room, locate objects and read handwriting, easily out-performing the most advanced computer systems of today.

Clearly, there are processes of perception that are naturally adapted, and efficient, for identifying visual patterns, their shape, texture, form, colour, motion, stereopsis, and circuits which perceive depth, size, direction and so on. These processes are supported by suitable information processing channels, which in the main are hardwired in such a way that much of this considerable amount of processing takes place automatically, without any need for conscious intervention or control. In fact, this processing happens even before the image is perceived at the higher levels of the visual cortex, even altering the retinal image, which results in the familiar visual illusions.

An artificial system possessing the attributes of pre-processing which are present in the early visual system would be substantially advanced along the path of achieving low-level natural vision, and the performance benefits that this entails. It turns out that the neural circuits involved are very complex and at present, in the main, poorly understood. One partial exception to this are the feedforward processes along the optic path, reaching from the retina to the primary visual cortex. This system serves as an illustration of the nature of perceptual neural processes in the brain, why they are the way they are, and how computer models attempt to emulate them.

7.3 Biological neural networks for vision

The transmission of the retinal image through to the visual cortex is outlined in Fig. 7.1. There are three main stages along that path, namely the retina itself, an organ called the lateral geniculate bulb (LGB) and the primary visual cortex. None of these stages is simple, either in its function or its architecture. However, to a first approximation, their effect on the retinal image can be approximated using simple linear filters with the profiles shown in Fig. 7.1.

The retina is modelled by a difference of Gaussians (doG) filter, where the two Gaussians have the same centre point in two dimensions and are circularly symmetric, but they have different widths, and different areas [1]. They behave as contrast enhancement filters, which are convolved with the image transmitting only a small fraction of its uniform brightness (the 'd.c.' image components). Next, the LGB can be modelled using another difference of Gaussians filter, still with Gaussians of different widths, but this time equally weighted. They form circularly symmetric edge detectors, along the lines discussed by Marr and Hildreth [2]. Finally, the primary visual cortex contains other types of filter, which are not circularly symmetric. Their characteristics are best understood with reference to a

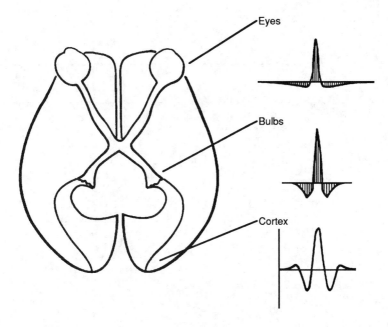

Figure 7.1 Transmission of the retinal image through the visual nervous system to the primary visual cortex. The filter profiles represent the signal processing operations taking place at the retinal ganglion cells, lateral geniculate bulb, and the simple cells in layer IV of the visual cortex.

fundamental uncertainty principle in image processing.

Following on from a relationship between the Fourier transformation and spatial derivatives of the signal, it can be shown that the product of the bandwidth of the signal expressed in the spatial domain and in the frequency domain has an absolute lower bound, which in suitable units is 1/2 per dimension. This is expressed in 2-D by:

$$< Dx >.< Dy >.< Du >.< Dv > \geq 1/4.$$

The phase space cell is illustrated, for 1-D, in Fig. 7.2. The two-dimensional Gabor filters achieve precisely this lower bound for the bandwidth product, and hence represent the elementary shapes with the maximum combined resolution in both domains [3,4].

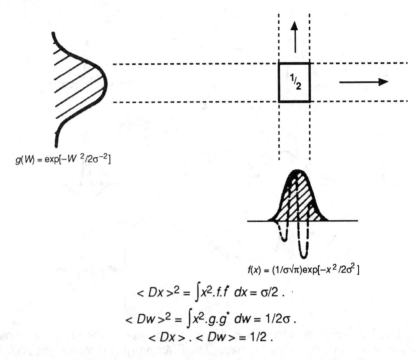

$$g(W) = \exp[-W^2/2\sigma^{-2}]$$

$$f(x) = (1/\sigma\sqrt{\pi})\exp[-x^2/2\sigma^2]$$

$$<Dx>^2 = \int x^2.f.f\ dx = \sigma/2.$$

$$<Dw>^2 = \int x^2.g.g^*\ dw = 1/2\sigma.$$

$$<Dx>.<Dw> = 1/2.$$

Figure 7.2 Phase space cells in 1-D. The unit of frequency appropriate to a minimum area of 1/2 in rads/sec.

These optimal filters also have a clearly defined function in computer vision, consisting of optimal 'bar' and 'edge' detectors generated by the real and imaginary components of each Gabor function, respectively. Their shapes and the corresponding Fourier signatures, obtained by making iso-amplitude cuts, are depicted in Fig. 7.3. What distinguishes them from the 'Mexican hat operators' of Marr is that the new filters are selective of orientation and scaling, as well as resolving position and orientation. This is illustrated in Fig. 7.4. There are a number of free parameters available with which to tune these filters to a specific application, although they are normally used with a 2:1 aspect ratio, a frequency bandwidth of around two, and orientation bandwidth of 30–60 degrees.

A remarkable consequence of modelling these naturally evolved biological mathematical functions is a resolution of the classical dichotomy about what is the preferred domain of image analysis – whether images are best characterized using frequency signatures or

$$G(x,y) = \exp\{-\pi.[x^2\alpha^2 + y^2\beta^2] - 2\pi i.u_0x\}$$
$$F(u,v) = \exp\{-\pi.[(u-u_0)^2/a^2 + v^2/b^2]\}$$

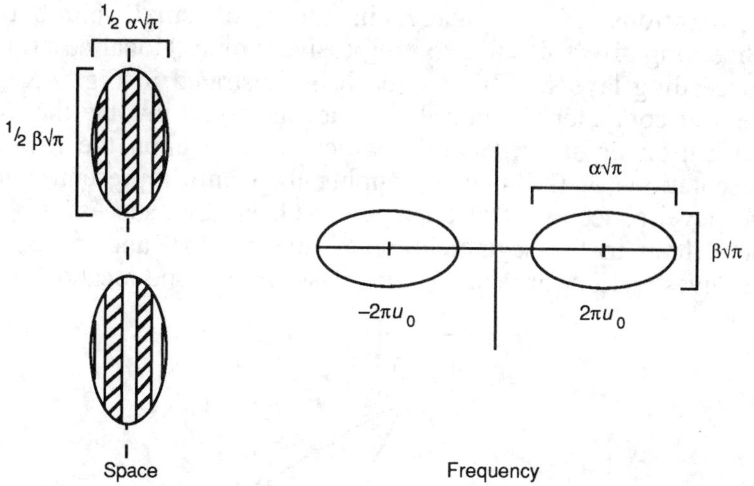

½ α√π

½ β√π

α√π

β√π

$-2\pi u_0$ $2\pi u_0$

Space   Frequency

Figure 7.3 Iso-amplitude contours of a single 2-D Gabor basis function in the space and frequency domains. A mathematical expression for these filters is included.

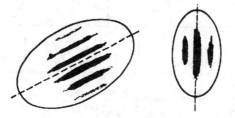

Figure 7.4 Profiles of orientation and frequency selective filters in 2-D. These are optimal 'bar' and 'edge' detectors sensitive to edges of different scales and orientations.

spatial templates. Both of these techniques are subsumed in the Gabor representation, since the two separate domains are simply extreme cases as the coefficients α and β in Fig. 7.3 approach zero and infinity, respectively. Moreover, the area of the fundamental regions of uncertainty in phase space remains at the minimum possible value as the shape of these cells changes from a spike normal to the frequency axis to one normal to the position axis. This ensures optimal resolution throughout the continuum joining the two domains.

The layered structure of the visual nervous system suggests a staged approach to image analysis. This involves starting with localized representations of the image, in terms of small numbers of neighbouring pixels, leading to progressively more global descriptions in succeeding layers. This approach is illustrated in Fig. 7.5. The process of computer vision at higher levels would involve the use of classification or other networks which operate upon the low-level representations of the image, mapping them into representations of higher-level concepts. This approach has been used successfully with Gabor filters in the segmentation of textures [5], and is currently under investigation for facial feature classification and location [3].

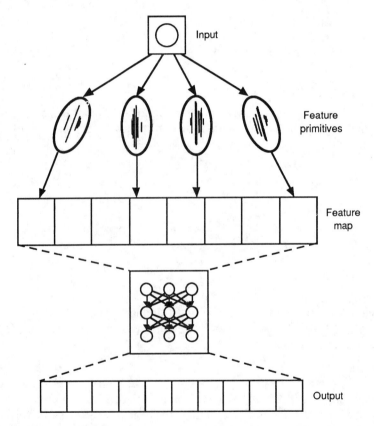

Figure 7.5 Generic functional model for computer vision based on the layered structure of the visual nervous system.

Related models of low-level vision using visual primitives which are localized in the spatio-frequency domain have been studied [6,7], and they show promise not only in achieving results of practical benefit in computer vision, but also in providing common ground for the three 'vision schools' of neuroscience, perceptual psychology, and applied computer vision [4,8,9].

7.4 Artificial neural models

There are currently many different neurally inspired models of computation applied to image processing and computer vision. They range from attempts to emulate known circuitry in the cortex, such as the models described above, to more general techniques derived directly from all-purpose classification and other artificial neural tools described in Chapter 1.

One approach of the former type consists of implementing an array of Gabor filters with a log-polar Fourier structure, as shown in Fig. 7.6. The original image is expressed in terms of these 'pseudo-orthogonal' elementary functions either by a regular convolution, or by a more careful expansion procedure involving an iterative procedure to minimize the Euclidean distance between the original image and its reconstruction from the expansion in terms of this non-orthogonal and overcomplete basis set [9]. The coefficients of this expansion form the new representation of the image.

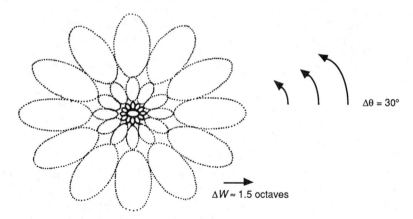

Figure 7.6 Log-polar Fourier structure of a complete set of elementary Gabor basis functions.

A more 'standard' approach to artificial neural computation attempts to achieve 'human-like' performance using large numbers of densely interconnected simple computational elements. In this approach the network constructs its own representations of the incoming signals, and acts as a convenient parametrization of non-linear functions which are used either to enforce the desired relationships between input and output patterns, in the case of the multi-layered perceptron, or to find natural sets of primitive features to represent the data, in the case of the Kohonen algorithm. Both of these networks are described in more detail in Chapter 1.

Recall that this approach is founded upon the understanding that the storage of information in the brain lies in the strength of the connections between the constituent neurones [10]. Neural arrays are, then, networks of non-linear filters which perform mappings between the activity patterns at their input and output layers, forming a highly distributed method of information storage, whose special properties provide a simple explanation, not only for the rapid evaluation of large amounts of computation in the brain, but also for its natural content and associative memory properties.

A taxonomy of some of the widely known models currently used in computer vision is given in Table 7.1.

Table 7.1 Artificial neural networks for vision.

Self-organized	e.g. Kohonen network
Pattern classification	e.g. Multi-layer perceptron
Feedback networks	e.g. ART of Grossberg *et al.*
Information theoretic	e.g. Min.entropy, Sim.anneal
Invariant networks	e.g. Moments, Fourier, etc.
Hebbian learning	e.g. Higher order

This table shows that different algorithms perform distinct functions, including spontaneous generation of elementary features by self-organized networks [11], pattern classification by suitable partitioning of the configuration space using hyperplanes [12,13], networks with feedback which possess feature enhancement properties suitable, for example, for filtering noise near edges [14], networks minimizing entropy [15] which can be used, for instance, for counting faces in video images, and a number of models dealing with the problem of invariance under translations, scaling and rotations [16–18]. These questions are the subject of later chapters in this book.

Returning for a moment to the parallel with neuro-physiology, it is interesting to speculate about the nature of feedback networks in relation to the function of the lateral geniculate body, which serves as a 'trunk' station relaying messages, including a large number of feedback messages, between different regions of the brain [19].

The potential benefits of using artificial neural networks thus extend beyond just the high computation rates provided by a very high level of parallelism. Different networks are characterized by particular configurations of the arrays of neurones, node characteristics, and learning algorithms. The learning algorithm performs the essential role of 'training' the network, by adjusting the weights to improve performance. This may use the correlation between the activities of different nodes in the same layer, which is the case in self-organizing networks, or it may take the form of gradient descent along a suitable cost function, usually measuring the difference between the desired behaviour of the network and its actual behaviour, which is known as supervised learning. Both of these network architectures are now discussed in detail for their role in the classification of binary images.

7.5 Kohonen networks

Self-learning networks have particular importance because they can act as 'optimal' vector quantizers. They provide useful descriptions of the input signal in terms of self-generated primitives, arranged to form an ordered map which has topological properties with a metric that is related to the similarity between the input signals.

The architecture of a Kohonen network [11] is described in Fig. 7.7. The operation of this network is illustrated now with reference to the problem of handwritten digit recognition. The set of data used to train the network is shown in Fig. 7.8 and a fresh test which may be used to assess the generalization abilities of a network in the performance of the classification task is shown in Fig. 7.9. These data represent samples that have been ideally digitized, scaled, and thinned.

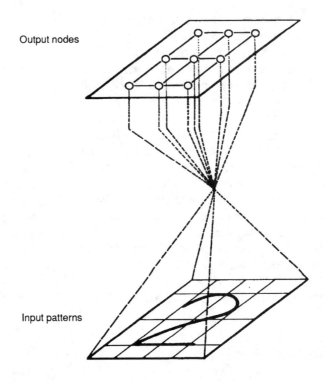

Figure 7.7 Architecture of a Kohonen network. The figure 2 represents a pattern present at the input nodes. Each of the laterally connected nodes in the output layer has a full set of weights reaching down to the input window.

The operation of this network on complete images is described first. Network training is based solely on the correlation between the excitations of neighbouring nodes, and therefore it self-organizes, without the need for any amount of external supervision. Training starts with a random set of weights, but after 500 presentations of the complete set of training images the weights have formed a topologically ordered array of templates of all the digits, shown in Fig. 7.10. The preferred digit for each node, that is to say the digit whose image in the training set causes the strongest activation of that node, is shown for every node in the network in Fig. 7.11. It is now possible to interrogate the network about the nodes which are most activated by each of the images in the test set. The labels of those nodes may provide a classification of the image, and clearly, images that closely resemble the 'templates' formed by the weight configurations will be correctly recognized, and some degree of robustness against distortion is expected. This is indeed the case, but this type of network is not naturally suited to the classifiction of whole images, and the recognition performance of 70% which it achieves on the test data, while reasonable given the operation of the algorithm, does not match the performance later for the perceptron algorithm.

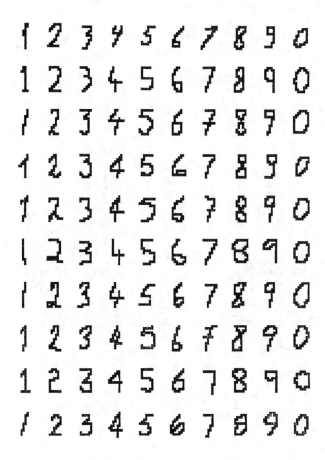

Figure 7.8 Training data for handwritten digit recognition.

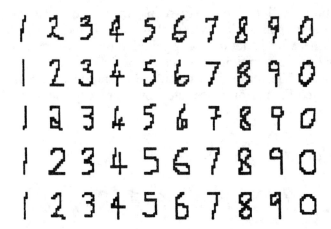

Figure 7.9 Test data for handwritten digit recognition.

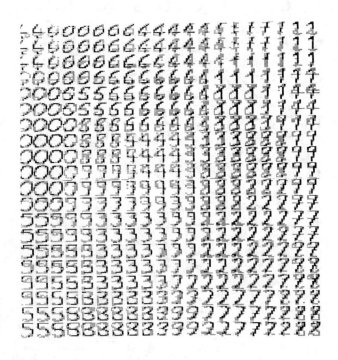

Figure 7.10 Topologically ordered array of templates of the digits 0, 1, ... , 9 generated by plotting the weights of each node of a Kohonen network trained on the digits in Figs 7.10–7.11.

```
6 4 5 7 9 4 8 9 5 7 3 6 3 3 2 9 4 0 3 1
2 9 7 2 6 7 4 3 5 7 1 0 0 5 1 0 8 1 5 8
5 9 1 9 8 6 3 6 9 4 4 4 2 6 2 8 9 3 9 1
2 3 0 4 3 0 1 3 4 2 6 3 1 2 4 4 0 5 3 3
6 9 2 3 0 0 4 5 1 1 2 3 9 1 2 4 3 3 6 3
6 2 3 9 7 6 9 7 9 3 4 0 3 7 9 8 3 3 3 7
5 1 1 7 0 3 0 8 0 0 4 1 1 1 3 9 8 5 4 3
3 2 7 3 4 3 2 6 1 6 7 6 1 1 5 7 6 6 9 5
4 6 8 5 0 9 7 6 8 6 0 1 8 6 5 6 1 4 8 4
5 7 4 7 4 6 8 1 3 4 9 0 8 4 5 7 7 0 9 4
9 7 9 1 4 0 2 4 3 2 7 1 1 1 7 7 4 0 2 5
1 4 3 1 9 1 1 3 7 0 7 2 7 9 8 1 2 5 8 0
4 0 7 2 0 3 3 8 4 3 3 1 6 7 0 0 2 3 6 6
2 1 1 4 6 4 4 3 9 9 4 0 4 4 3 4 3 6 7 6
3 5 1 7 9 1 8 7 6 3 3 7 0 3 2 9 2 1 3 1
5 0 2 6 0 2 3 6 0 6 8 3 6 3 9 3 0 6 7 7
7 6 5 4 3 9 6 3 3 4 4 5 8 4 9 3 4 5 0 7
2 7 8 9 6 4 0 7 2 6 7 6 7 4 4 0 3 3 4 6
6 4 1 1 2 2 8 8 0 7 4 6 7 2 3 1 7 9 7 3
7 2 7 3 1 4 7 0 6 7 4 7 9 9 6 3 2 3 0 5
```

```
4 4 4 4 4 4 4 4 8 8 8 8 8 8 0 0 0 0 0 0
4 4 4 4 4 4 4 4 8 8 8 8 8 8 0 0 0 0 0 0
4 4 4 4 4 4 4 4 8 8 8 8 8 8 0 0 0 0 0 0
4 4 4 4 4 4 4 4 8 8 8 8 8 0 0 0 0 0 0 0
4 4 4 4 4 4 4 4 8 8 8 8 8 8 8 8 0 0 0 0
1 1 1 1 1 1 5 8 8 8 8 8 8 8 8 9 9 9 9 9
1 1 1 1 1 1 5 5 5 5 5 5 5 5 9 9 9 9 9 9
1 1 1 1 1 1 5 5 5 5 5 5 5 5 9 9 9 9 9 9
1 1 1 1 1 1 5 5 5 5 5 5 5 5 9 9 9 9 9 9
1 1 1 1 1 1 5 5 5 5 5 5 5 5 9 9 9 9 9 9
1 1 1 1 1 1 5 5 5 5 5 5 5 5 9 9 9 9 9 9
1 1 1 1 2 2 2 5 5 5 5 5 5 5 9 9 9 9 9 9
2 2 2 2 2 2 2 5 5 5 5 5 5 5 9 9 9 9 9 9
2 2 2 2 2 2 2 5 5 5 5 5 5 5 5 5 9 9 9 9
2 2 2 2 2 2 2 2 6 6 6 6 5 5 5 5 3 3 3 3
2 2 2 2 2 2 2 6 6 6 6 6 6 6 3 3 3 3 3 3
7 2 2 2 2 2 6 6 6 6 6 6 6 6 3 3 3 3 3 3
7 7 7 7 2 2 6 6 6 6 6 6 6 6 3 3 3 3 3 3
7 7 7 7 7 2 6 6 6 6 6 6 6 6 3 3 3 3 3 3
7 7 7 7 7 6 6 6 6 6 6 6 6 6 3 3 3 3 3 3
```

Figure 7.11 Map of the preferred digits for the nodes of a neural network similar to that shown in Fig. 7.12. This is the digit corresponding to the pattern which causes the strongest excitation of that node.

A more interesting experiment results from reducing the size of the window which forms the input into the network, say to a square with a side of three pixels. The resulting weight configurations also after

500 iterations are shown in Fig. 7.12. This time, the network generates image primitives, some resembling bar and edge detectors, straight lined or curved. Other primitive features are more complex, and relate to line endings, T-junctions, angles, crossings and even the occurrence of empty areas in the image. These features can themselves be made the inputs to a second Kohonen network, whose weights are trained holding the weights in the first network fixed. The resulting cascade of two self-organized networks can then be interrogated in the classification problem in the same way as was done earlier, and we shall return to this later. However, the perceptron algorithm should be more appropriate for performing the final discrimination, which is discussed in the next section.

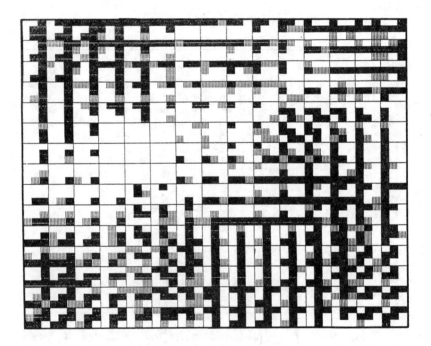

Figure 7.12 Weight map of a Kohonen network trained by scanning a window of size 3 × 3 through every position on the patterns in Fig. 7.10. This network develops detectors of elementary two-dimensional shapes. A similar experiment carried out on natural images would result in visual primitives describing Gabor-like receptive fields.

7.6 Back error propagation

This is the training algorithm for the multi-layered perceptron network, which consists of a layered structure, illustrated in Fig. 7.13. Neighbouring layers are usually fully connected, with no connection between nodes in the same layer. However, direct connections between the input and output nodes were also included, forming a single-layer perceptron in parallel with its multi-layered counterpart. The reason for this was to investigate the necessity for the hidden layer of nodes in this particular problem. The hidden nodes are expected to take over the main role in performing classification only when this goes beyond the capabilities of the outer single-layer network [20].

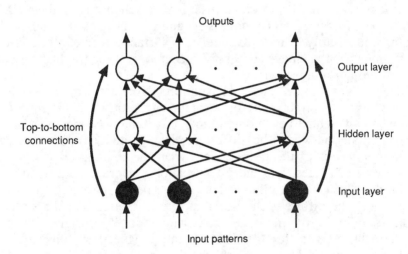

Figure 7.13 Extended architecture of the multi-layered perceptron.

Teaching now proceeds by comparing the current output of the network with the desired, or target, value for the excitation of each output node. The operation of this network therefore requires the action of an external supervisor supplying the 'answers' for the output excitations. It differs from the action of the previous network in another important respect, namely that the perceptron algorithm attempts to discriminate between the different classes of input patterns by partitioning the configuration using hyperplanes [12,13]. Therefore it uses the differences between patterns nominated to different classes, rather than using naturally occurring similarities to group patterns of the same kind.

In order to assess the optimal network topology for this particular classification task, preliminary tests were carried out varying the number of hidden nodes in the multi-layered perceptron, starting from a large number, 96. The result was a flat curve, showing a variation of only 2% in the generalization ability of the network when applied to the test data. The peak value was 78%, for 12 hidden nodes.

As a result of this, even a single layer perceptron is able to discriminate successfully between all the classes in the training set, achieving 78% success in generalizing to the test set. Albeit an improvement upon the Kohonen network, which also has just one layer of weights, on account of the much smaller number of independent parameters (970 for the single-layer perceptron instead of 36 400), this performance is still very poor. The reason for this is that it is much harder to create useful representations of the images with the supervised algorithm, as it ignores any natural order in the data, and simply forces its decision surfaces to lie along those directions which achieve successful recognition in the training set with the minimum required effort.

The action of the back propagation algorithm can be seen by inspecting the weight patterns created during training. Figure 7.14 shows the weights to each output node as (a) the network just starts to discriminate between the different classes, and (b) after several hundred sweeps of the training set, when the training error is nil to five decimal places, and the classification performance has, in fact, degraded from its optimum value. The role of the weight maps in separating the different classes is apparent. Notice that the patterns corresponding to the numerals are not immediately recognizable, and in fact the weights for the digits 6 and 7 have their 'on-weights', represented in black, particularly poorly distributed.

Figure 7.15 shows weight maps near optimum training, after only 200 sweeps, in (a), as well as the templates obtained by simply averaging the 100 data patterns, in (b). The main effect of continuing training beyond the optimum point is to give too much weight to a small number of discriminating patterns. The effect is small in this example, although still sufficient to reduce the performance of the network in generalization. When the action of the perceptron filter is regarded as a mathematical mapping between input and output patterns, this effect is known as over-fitting. Whichever way this is seen, the obvious consequence is that the relatively few discriminating pixels are wrongly regarded as representing the pattern classes.

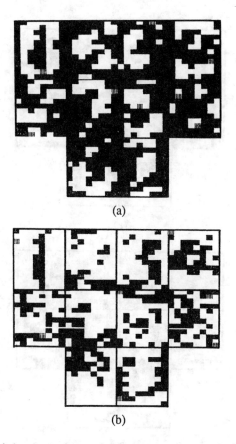

(a)

(b)

Figure 7.14 Weight maps for a single-layer perceptron at (a) early stages during training, and (b) overtrained. Dark, grey and clear represent weights that are positive, within 1% of zero, and negative, respectively.

In order to carry out, with back-propagation, the considerable amount of pre-processing that is necessary for more difficult classification tasks, such as the recognition of handwritten digits with a large number of samples collected from live mail, it is necessary to constrain the weights and thus limit the number of independent variables during training [21]. The careful design of the network in this case is the subject of Chapter 10.

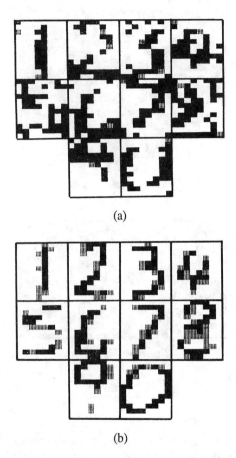

(a)

(b)

Figure 7.15 (a) Weight map for an optimally trained network as above. (b) Templates derived by averaging the 100 training patterns; dark, grey and clear denote values that are over, within 1% of, and equal to 0.5, respectively.

7.7 Feature extraction

We continue the traditional approach of using a pre-filter as a front-end to the multi-layered perceptron. To achieve this with a small number of image primitives, representations of the same sets of handwritten digits as used during the previous experiments, were created using a zoning technique, illustrated in Fig. 7.16. A small set of features based on the visual primitives generated by the Kohonen network was used to form a reduced representation of the digits simply by flagging the features present in each of the four overlapping quadrants. The pattern thus generated for each image has 72 binary elements, one to represent the presence (1), or absence (0), of one feature anywhere inside of one quadrant.

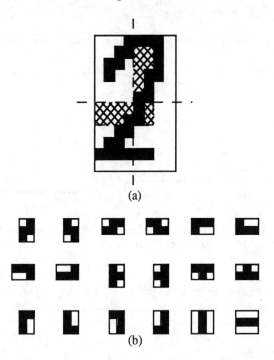

(a)

(b)

Figure 7.16 Representation of the zoning technique used for coding the images of handwritten digits as a front-end to a perceptron network.

When a single-layer perceptron was trained using image representations rather than pixel maps, the generalization performance of the network jumped to 96% on the test data (48/50 patterns). It is interesting to note that this network can also overtrain, therefore a test sample should generally be used to determine the optimum point of training by back error propagation. A curve showing the effect of training error upon generalization performance is shown in Fig. 7.17.

The performance of the classification algorithm was therefore substantially dependent upon the introduction of knowledge about the domain of application, whether by constraining the network during training or by automatic pre-processing, for instance using self-organized networks. There are other ways of further enhancing the generalization abilities of the network, such as using the hidden layers to push the input data through a bottleneck, forcing better representations to be generated. However, it is unlikely that any such simple technique would, by itself, raise the generalization ability of the network quite as substantially.

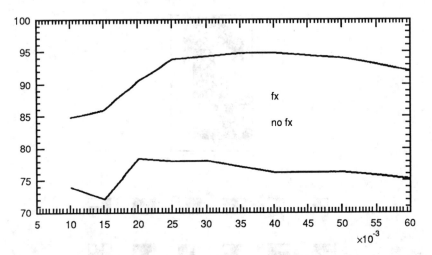

Figure 7.17 Success in generalization vs. training error, expressed as the root mean square training output error averaged over all output nodes and training patterns; fx denotes the use of feature extraction.

7.8 Comparison with statistical classifiers

It is appropriate now to compare the performance of the perceptron algorithm against conventional statistical classifiers.

The first, and simplest, technique chosen was straight nearest neighbour pattern matching. The average templates in Fig. 7.15(b) were appropriate for this purpose, since it is easily shown that the average of a class of patterns minimizes the sum of the Euclidean distances to those patterns. The results obtained in this way, and also for a linear Widrow-Hoff classifier and nearest neighbour classifiers and Parzen classifiers are shown in Table 7.2.

In this example, where a 'good' set of data can be linearly separated by the non-linear single-layer perceptron, the performance of this classifier has been shown to match or supersede that of all alternative algorithms that were tried. Yet the greatest increase in performance results from integrating domain knowledge via appropriate data conditioning. In the case of handwritten numeral classification, the pre-conditioning can also be derived with neural tools.

Table 7.2 Neural vs. conventional classifiers (Success rates in generalization, in %).

Classifier	Pixel map	Feature map
Pattern matching	76	92
Widrow-Hoff	70	92
Nearest neighbour	78 (k=2,3)	90 (k=5)
Parzen	80 (σ=2.7)	90 (σ=2.7)
Kohonen network	70	86
Single-layer perceptron	78	96

7.9 Overview of applications and conclusion

Artificial neural networks have, over the last two years, yielded promising results in the solution of practical problems in computer vision, and the range of problems tackled, as well as the quality of the solutions provided, is likely to grow.

Application areas related to practical problems are mentioned in the concluding chapter. They include visual inspection for industrial quality assurance, facial feature identification and location, filtering noise, satellite image compression, and several other examples described in later chapters of this book. More advanced areas where further theoretical progress is likely to develop include:

- image segmentation [7,22] and restoration [23,24]
- shape from shading [25,26] and surface interpolation [27]
- motion detection [28–30]
- stereo [31,32]
- colour compensation [33,34]
- automatic target recognition [35].

Overall, artificial neural computation has certainly already provided computer vision with analysis tools of considerable power [36–38], often readily able to match or better the performance of established methods. They offer simple and powerful solutions to problems, mainly in low-level vision, that are difficult to solve using conventional computing methods and artificial intelligence techniques. Resolutions of the main difficulties associated with neural-based computing, namely scaling to large-size networks, speed of training, and the requirement for more complex architectures with feedback, are all progressively materializing.

In computer vision, these techniques are likely to become permanent residents in the tool-kits of the design engineer as much as the theoretical researcher, and the current effort to develop suitable hardware for direct implementation points towards early benefits to be gained in real-world applications.

Acknowledgements

I would like to thank J. K. Leung, S. Kirwin and J. Athanassiadis for carrying out some of the simulations as part of their Masters projects. I am also grateful to M. Bedworth of the Royal Signals and Radar Establishment for kindly testing the character recognition data using conventional statistical classifiers.

References

1. Barrow, H.G. Learning receptive fields. *Int. Joint Conf. on Neural Networks*, San Diego, Volume IV, 115-121 (1987).

2. Marr, D. and Hildreth, E. Theory of Edge Detection. *Proc. R. Soc. London B*, **207**, 187-217 (1980).

3. Lisboa, P.J.G. Gabor filters for image classification. In Linggard, R. and Nightingale, C. (eds.) *Vision, Speech and Natural Language*, Chapman and Hall, London (in press).

4. Wilson, R. and Knutsson, H. Uncertainty and inference in the visual system. *IEEE Trans. Syst. Man and Cybern.*, **SMC-13**, $\underline{2}$, 305-312 (1988).

5. Turner, M.R. Texture discrimination by Gabor functions. *Biol. Cybern.*, **55**, 71-82 (1986).

6. Jacobson, L.D. and Wechsler, H. Joint spatial/spatial-frequency representation. *Signal Processing*, **14**, 37-68 (1988).

7. Bovik, A.C., Clark, M. and Geisler, W.S. Multichannel texture analysis using localized spatial filters. *IEEE Trans. Pattern Anal. Machine Intell.*, **PAMI-ll**, 7, 674-693 (1989).

8. Trivedi, M.M. and Rosenfeld, A. On making computers "see". *IEEE Trans. Syst. Man and Cybern.*, **SMC-19**, 6, 1333-1334 (1989).

9. Daugman, J.G. Complete discrete 2-D Gabor transforms by neural networks for image analysis and compression. *IEEE Trans. Acoust. Speech and Signal Proc.*, **ASSP-36**, 7, 1169-1179 (1988).

10. McCulloch, W.S. and Pitts, W.H. A logical calculus of ideas immanent in nervous activity. *Bull. Math. Phys.*, **5**, 115, 115-133 (1943).

11. Kohonen, T. *Self-Organisation and Associative Memory*, 2nd edn, Springer-Verlag, Berlin and Heidelberg (1988).

12. Lippmann, R.P. An introduction to computing with neural nets. *IEEE ASSP Mag.*, **4**, 2, 4-22 (1987).

13. Duda, R.O. and Hart, P.E. *Pattern Classification and Scene Analysis*, Wiley, New York (1973).

14. Grossberg, S., Mingolla, E. and Todorovic, D. A neural network architecture for preattentive vision. *IEEE Trans. Biomed. Eng.*, **BE-36**, 1, 65-84 (1989).

15. Bischel, M. and Seitz, P. Minimum class entropy: a maximum information approach to layered networks. *Neural Networks*, **2**, 133-141 (1989).

16. Reid, M.B., Spirkovska, L. and Ochoa, E. Rapid training of higher-order neural networks for invariant pattern recognition. *Int. Joint Conf. on Neural Networks*, Washington, DC, Volume I, 689-692 (1989).

17. Khotanzad, A. and Hong, Y.H. Invariant image recognition by Zernike moments. *IEEE Trans. Pattern Anal. Machine Intell.* **PAMI-12**, 5, 489-497 (1990).

18. Seibert, M. and Waxman, A. Spreading activiation layers, visual saccades, and invariant representations for neural pattern recognition systems. *Neural Networks*, **2**, 9-27 (1989).

19. Harth, E, Unnikrishnan, K.P. and Pandua, A.S. The inversion of sensory processing by feedback pathways: a model of visual cognitive functions. *Science*, **237**, 184-187 (1987).

20. Lisboa, P.J.G. and Perantonis, S.J. Convergence of recursive associative memories obtained using the multi-layered perceptron. *J. Phys.A.: Math. Gen.*, **23**, 4039-4053 (1990).

21. Fukushima, K. A neural network for visual pattern recognition. *IEEE Computer*, **21**, 3, 65-75 (1988).

22. Wilson, R. and Span, M. *Image Segmentation and Uncertainty*, Research Studies Press, Wiley, Chichester (1988).

23. Zhou, Y.T., Chellappa, R., Vaid, A. and Jenkins, B.K. Image restoration using a neural network. *IEEE Trans. Acoust. Speech and Sig. Proc.*, **ASSP-36**, 7, 1141-1151 (1988).

24. Bedini, L. and Tonazzini, A. neural network use in maximum entropy image restoration. *Image and Vision Computing*, **8**, 2, 108-114 (1990).

25. Lekhy, S.R. and Sejnowski, T.J. Network model of shape-from shading: neural function arises from both receptive and protective fields. *Nature*, **333**, 452-454 (1988).

26. Rimey, R., Gouin, P., Scofield, C. and Reilly, D.L. Real-time 3-D object classification using a learning system. *Proc. SPIE, Intel. Robots and Computer Vision*, **726**, 552-557 (1986).

27. Koch, C., Marroquim, J. and Yuille, A. Analogue "neuronal" networks in early vision. *Proc. Nat. Acad. Sci. USA*, **83**, 4263-4267, (1986).

28. Koch, C. Computing motion in the presence of discontinuities – algorithm and analogue networks. In Eckmiller, R. and von der Marlsburg, C. (eds.). *Neural Computers*, Springer-Verlag, New York (1988).

29. Bullthoff, H., Little, J. and Poggio, T. A parallel algorithm for real-time computation of optical flow. *Nature*, **337**, 549-553 (1989).

30. Lawton, T.B. Outputs of paired Gabor filters summed across background frame of reference predict the direction of movement. *IEEE Trans. Biomed. Eng.*, **BE-36**, 1, 130-139 (1989).

31. Mahowald, M.A. and Delbruck, T. Cooperative stereo matching using static and dynamic image features. In Mead, C. and Ismail, M. (eds.). *Analog VLSI Implementation of Neural Sustems*, Kluwer Academic, Boston, MA, 213-238 (1989).

32. Zhou, Y.T. and Chellappa, R. Neural network algorithms for motion stereo. *Int. Joint Conf. Neural Networks, II*, IEEE, Piscatway, NJ, 251-258 (1989).

33. Hulbert, A.C. and Poggio, T.A. Synthesizing a color algorithm from examples. *Science*, **239**, 482-485 (1988).

34. Hulbert, A. and Poggio, V. A network for image segmentation using color. In Touretsy, D.S. (ed.). *Advances in Neural Information Processing Systems, I*, Morgan-Kaufmann, San Mateo, CA, 297-304 (1989).

35. Roth, M.W. Survey of neural network technology for automatic target recognition. *IEEE Trans. Syst. Man and Cybern.*, **SMC-l**, 1, 28-43 (1989).

36. Poggio, T., Torre, V. and Koch, C. Computational vision and regularization theory. *Nature*, **317**, 314-319 (1985).

37. Nasrabadi, N.M. and Feng, Y. Vector quantization of images based upon the Kohonen self-organizing feature maps. *IEEE Int. Conf. Neural Networks, I*, 101-108 (1988).

38. Roth, M.W. Neural-network technology and its applications. *Heuristics*, **2**, 1, 46-62 (1989).

8

Image labelling with a neural network

W. A. Wright
British Aerospace, England

8.1 Summary

The lack of contextual integrity in region labelling schemes for segmented visual images has been a long-standing problem in computer vision. In the past it has been common to adopt some form of relaxation scheme, such as relaxation labelling, to remove both labelling ambiguities and labellings which, usually, are obviously contextually incorrect. So far no general region labelling system has been found.

A neural network has now been applied to the above problem. A simple multi-layer perceptron, trained on the relative positions of, and the unary features pertaining to, a set of regions obtained from image segmentations has been shown to be capable of finding roads in natural scenes.

8.2 Introduction

The correct labelling of segmented images has been a difficult and generally unsolved problem in computer vision for many years (see [1,2]). Most labelling systems at the moment rely upon obtaining a tentative initial set of labels for the regions in a segmented image and then applying contextual knowledge to try and resolve the labelling ambiguities that inevitably occur. The tentative labelling schemes, such as Euclidean distance or K nearest neighbour clustering for example [3,4], usually act by comparing a measure of the unary features of a region (features internal only to the region) against the features of typical region types derived from a training set. The results from this method are quite often ambiguous: a region may have several possible labels. To try and rectify these ambiguities the contextual significance of a region's label with respect to the labels of the neighbouring regions is used. Schemes such as relaxation, or probabilistic relaxation labelling [5,6] use such contextual knowledge. Although these schemes work well with edge data in real images [7] and region segmentations of artificial images [2] they are found to be less robust with region segmentations of real imagery. This is because it proves exceptionally difficult to produce a complete and general set of rules to describe the contextual relationships between labelled regions for a real image [8].

Learning mechanisms such as those put forward by Michalski *et al.* [9] and Quinlan [10] could be used to generate a suitable set of contextual rules directly from examples of region data. However, apart from a few exceptions, such as those given in references [11,12], very little work has been carried out in computer vision using these methods.

An alternative method may be to use a neural network. The neural method proposed by Hopfield and Tank [13] has been used to optimize the tentative labellings of the regions present in an image [14]. However, the method only considers artificial images, and does not find the contextual rules relating regions in the image itself. The method, therefore, has the same drawbacks as the relaxation methods mentioned above. Other neural network methods which are capable of being trained could be more useful. Such a network is the multi-layered perceptron [15]. This has been shown to be robust against uncertain data [16] and able to extract the contextual relationships from real training data [17]. In fact recent work, related to the work presented here [18], has shown that a multi-layered perceptron is capable of forming a set of contextual relationships between the labelled regions in a segmented image by training it on correctly labelled images. Further, Sejnowski's and Rosenberg's [17] work shows that a network does not necessarily require a tentative labelling of the features present in the input data to be able to form contextual relationships. Unlike the conventional labelling methods, therefore, it should be possible to design a neural network implementation which only uses contextual and statistical features that are obtained directly from an image, and does not require any initial region labelling at all. This chapter describes the preliminary results of a study into the possibility of using such a neural network to label the regions obtained from real images of natural outdoor scenes, by first training it on such scenes.

8.3 Network

The type of network used in this implementation is known as the multi-layered perceptron [15]. To try and keep this chapter as brief as possible it has been assumed that the reader has a limited knowledge of the principles behind these ideas. However, for completeness, a limited description of this type of network is given here.

The multi-layered perceptron (MLP), as the name suggests, consists of layers of simple non-linear processing units. These units are highly connected and 'threshold', usually with a sigma function, the sum of the unit's inputs to give an output. Each unit in a layer is connected to the units in layers adjacent to that layer via a weighted link (see Figs 8.1 and 8.2).

The network feeds-forward signals from its previous layer, via the non-linear function, to the next layer. The weights on the links together with the non-linear function on the unit allow non-linear relationships to be encoded between the network's layers and therefore between its input and output.

A set of weights for a given problem may be learnt by training the network, on known examples, with an algorithm known as back error propagation [15]. Back error propagation is a gradient descent algorithm. The algorithm allows the weights on the network to be altered in proportion to an error generated by taking the Euclidean distance of the network's actual output, for a given output, from what is considered to be the true output of the network for that input. How the network is tailored to the particular labelling problem discussed here is explained in the next section. A more complete description of the ideas behind neural networks may be found in Rumelhart and McClelland [19].

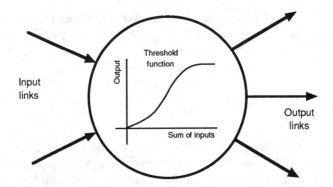

Figure 8.1 Typical neural element with a sigma function threshold.

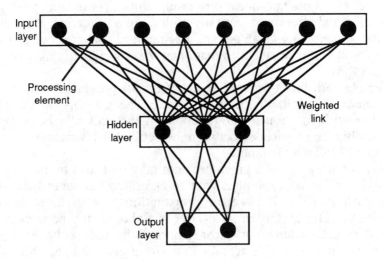

Figure 8.2 Schematic diagram of a three-layered MLP.

8.4 Implementation

To ease the amount of computation during this initial study the network was only required to look for one type of region, i.e. 'roads'. Although this is a simplification the implementation is still relevant for other types of region such as fields or vehicles for instance. The implementation, therefore, differs from that of Pomerleau [20] which is tailored solely for the detection of roads.

A three-layer multi-layer perceptron [15] was designed, as described below, to act on a region segmentation of an image and output a description (a label) of the regions in the image. The aim was to label every region (correctly) as road or not-road. A typical example of an image and its associated region segmentation is given in Figs 8.3 and 8.4. The segmentation was obtained by processing the image with a region-based segmentation algorithm, *coalesce*, designed at British Aerospace [21]. However, in principle any other reasonably efficient segmentation algorithm could have been used.

Figure 8.3 Test image.

The region features in the segmented image were presented to the network on a region by region basis. The network was configured to allow this to happen as follows:

Layer 1: 89 input units. 80 of these units coded the position and statistical features, as described below, of up to eight regions adjacent to the region to be classified (the central region). The features from the eight adjacent regions allowed contextual information about the central region to be presented in a local manner. The remaining nine units coded the central region's unary features, also described below.

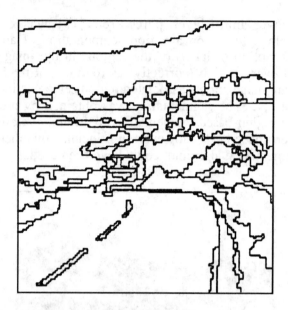

Figure 8.4 Segmentation of the test image.

Layer 2: 16 hidden units (eight and four hidden units were also tried for this implementation). Although the network converged with the smaller configurations the weight set obtained was not as good as that found with the 16 hidden unit configuration. With a much larger number of hidden units (e.g. 30) the network did not converge.

Layer 3: Two output units. This allowed the coding of road [1,0] and not-road [0,1] for the central region label.

The position of each adjacent region relative to the central region was found by taking the angle measured clockwise from the positive Y-axis to the line joining the centroids of both regions. Each angle was given to the network as one of eight grey codes, taking up four elements of the input for each region, see Table 8.1.

Grey codes were used because the code is cyclic and therefore has no discontinuity at 360 degrees. The grey code angle [0,0,0,0] for the central region was also given for completeness. The remaining six input elements for each adjacent region coded the features:

Table 8.1 Grey coding for angles between region centroids.

Angle	Code			
338 – 22	1	0	0	0
23 – 67	1	1	0	0
68 – 112	0	1	0	0
113 – 157	0	1	1	0
158 – 202	0	0	1	0
203 – 247	0	0	1	1
248 – 292	0	0	0	1
293 – 337	1	0	0	1

1. mean grey level: this value was normalized by dividing the value by the maximum grey level value of 255,
2. standard deviation of the grey levels inside the region: this value was normalized in the same way as for 1,
3. homogeneity of the grey levels (see [22]),
4. relative area of the region: this is the ratio of the region area with respect to the area of the whole image, in pixels,
5. compactness of the region, $\frac{4\pi \times area}{(perimeter\ of\ region)^2}$,
6. adjacent-perimeter length: this is the ratio of the perimeter common to the adjacent region and the central region with respect to the perimeter of the central region. This value was not given for the central region.

As is pointed out, some of the above values were normalized. This ensured that all the values presented to the network were bounded on the unit interval and, thus, no artificial bias was introduced into the initial stages of training as this would slow the network's convergence to its final configuration.

All the above features and angles were presented to the network as an 89-element long string. The first nine elements of the string held five central region statistics, in the order given above, together with its angle code. The next 80 units, divided into 8 × 10 blocks, contained the statistics and angle codes for the eight adjacent regions. When more than eight adjacent regions were present, the eight with the largest adjacent-perimeter were taken. For regions with fewer than eight neighbours, null codings (zeros) were given for the unoccupied inputs. The ordering of the adjacent-region statistics in the input was determined by the adjacent-perimeter length. The features for the region with the largest adjacent-perimeter were placed closest to the central region's features and so on.

The choice of only using up to eight regions is, to a certain extent, an arbitrary one. A region can have anything from between 1 to ≈100 adjacent regions. However, one finds that the regions polarize between those that are highly connected (on average ≈40 adjacent regions), and those that have a low connectivity (on average ≈4). If the input were extended to allow for a large number of adjacent regions the training of the network would become too computationally expensive. Eight adjacent regions were taken as a compromise since it allows all the adjacent regions to be taken into account for the regions with a low connectivity, and allows the network to realize that the region possibly has a high connectivity (i.e. when more than seven adjacent regions are present).

The way that the adjacent-region information has been selected and presented to the network obviously encodes a certain degree of prior information about the type of region that the network is trying to label. This is also true about the selection of the other region features used in this particular example. This type of information may be termed extrinsic, that is, the information given to the network by the operator's choice of feature rather than the information present in that data which may be termed intrinsic. Extrinsic information may be likened to what is termed 'background information' in the field of artificial intelligence. The amount of extrinsic information given to the network is important since too large an amount can overconstrain the network. Under these circumstances the operator restricts the problem for which the network was designed, reducing the ability of the network to generalize. It is also found, in these situations, that the more simple statistical clustering algorithms, such as K nearest neighbour, can be used on the data instead of the type of adaptive network discussed here [23]. This problem in relation to this network is discussed further in section 8.5 below.

The network was trained on the features described above using back error propagation [15]. The training data was obtained from the segmentations of 36 images of differing outdoor scenes obtained from the Alvey database produced for the MMI 007 project. To allow the training to take place the true identities of the regions contained in these segmented images were obtained by hand labelling the segmentations prior to training. This gave ≈250 examples of road regions. In addition ≈250 not-road regions, evenly sampled from the most frequent types of region present in the segmented images, were also taken as counter-examples. The order that the regions were presented to the network was randomized to prevent any bias being introduced into the training. The weights on the network's links were updated after each presentation of a region and its associated neighbours' features. This continued until the total error over the training set, generated by the network, converged, i.e. became stable. Typically for this network, to produce a small error, this took 2000 iterations (one iteration being the application and weight update of all the vectors in the training data).

8.5 Results

Once an adequate convergence on the training data was obtained, the network's weight configuration was tested on:

Test data: region data which had been used to form the road/not-road data but had been removed and therefore not used to train the network.

A test image: a complete image which had not been used to form the road/not-road data (see Fig. 8.3). This image, therefore, was not used to train the network.

The performance of the network was determined by comparing the output of the network against the true output or label. These results are shown in Table 8.2 for the test data, and Table 8.3 for the test image. The assigned label was found by taking the label with the closest Euclidean distance to the networks output.

The action of the network on the test image reflects its performance on the test data (see Tables 8.2 and 8.3). Close inspection of these results suggests that this implementation is able to use contextual information; Fig. 8.5 demonstrates this. The white lines in the road, and the gravel sides of the road, as desired, are labelled as road just as is the main piece of tarmac. Although some of the regions are labelled incorrectly there is some suggestion that the network is stable against uncertain data as it was able to cope with the poor segmentation between the vehicle and the road.

Table 8.2 Best guess estimates (%) for road detection network on the test data.

True label	Assigned label Road	Not-road	Freq.
Road	66.70	33.30	48
Not-road	17.30	88.70	52

Table 8.3 Best guess estimates (%) for road detection network for the test image.

True label	Assigned label Road	Not-road	Freq.
Road	82.60	17.40	23
Not-road	33.00	67.00	97

Figure 8.5 Segmentation of the test image with the regions labelled by the neural network as road displayed in black.

The weights generated by the learning mechanism can, in some cases, be interpreted as rules which describe how the network differentiated between road and not-road regions. The number of rules that have been determined is very limited at the moment but they mainly mirror those rules that experienced workers in the area regard as important. However, in some cases, the network appears to have highlighted new relationships which were not originally thought to be significant. For example, compactness is shown to be an important signature when looking for roads, whereas the central region's mean Gray level does not appear to be significant. Further examination of the weights suggests that the network only considers the first five adjacent neighbours to be important. All the weights corresponding to the inputs for the three adjacent neighbours with the smaller adjacent perimeter were almost zero. Since eight neighbours were considered, this suggests that the restriction of only taking a maximum of eight neighbours has not overconstrained the training of the network. This is also supported by the fact that the performance of this network is markedly better than the best performance of a K nearest neighbour clustering scheme on the same data, the results of which are given in Fig. 8.6.

Figure 8.6 K nearest neighbour labelling (K=6).

Further inspection of the weights also suggests that the network has formed contextual relationships between the data; rules such as:

> A central region that has a small homogeneous region with a small adjacent perimeter to the left of it, and has a region to the right which is not homogeneous, is road-like,

are evident in the weights. This rule may be interpreted as finding the edge of the road. The ability of the network to generate contextual rules is encouraging and implies that such networks could be used to generate rules for more conventional systems. However, these results are tentative and still require further work.

Lastly, these results suggest that a more compact network implementation may be possible with an input reduced to only those features that the weights suggest have a significant influence, and a reduced number of hidden units. Analysis of the weights suggests that three of the hidden units are superfluous; all the weight values to and from these units are practically zero.

8.6 Conclusion

The results presented in this article are limited and by no means conclusive. Nevertheless, they do indicate that neural networks may provide a useful tool for analysis in computer vision. Furthermore if these results can be shown to be more general than they suggest, then these systems may provide an alternative and useful region classification system. However, much work still remains to be done before a definite answer can be given as to the extent to which neural network implementations may be said to 'solve' the image labelling problem.

Acknowledgements

The author would like to thank: A. Page for his invaluable help in carrying out the image segmentations that were essential for this work; A. Murton for the routines used to display the results; the members of the Research Initiative in Pattern recognition for their helpful comments on this work; and P. Greenway for reading the manuscript.

References

1. Fischler, M. and Firschein, 0. (eds.). *Readings in Computer Vision*, Morgan Kaufmann, San Mateo, CA (1987).

2. Ballard, D. and Brown, C. *Computer Vision*, Prentice-Hall, Englewood Cliffs, NJ (1982).

3. Fukunaga, K. *Introduction to Statistical Pattern Recognition*, Academic Press, New York (1972).

4. Fu, J. *Syntactic Methods in Pattern Recognition*, Academic Press, New York, (1974).

5. Haralick, R. and Shapiro, L. The consistent labelling problem: part 1. *IEEE Trans. Pattern Anal. Machine Intell.*, **PAMI**, 2, 173-184 (1979).

6. Kittler, J., Illingworth, J. and Mallesh, V. A study of optimisation approaches to probabilistic relaxation labelling on a 3-node 2-label problem. *Proc. of the 3rd Alvey Vision Conference*, 311-318, Sept. (1987).

7. Geman, S. and Geman, D. Stochastic relaxation, Gibbs distributions, and the Bayesian restoration of images. *IEEE Trans. Pattern Anal. Machine Intell.*, **PAMI-6**, 6, 721-741 (1984).

8. Kittler, J. Private communication (1989).

9. Michalski, R., Carbonell, J. and Mitchell, T. *Machine Learning An Artificial Intelligence Approach*, Tioga (1983).

10. Quinlan, J. Learning from noisy data. *Proc. of the Int. Mach. Learning Workshop*, University of Illinois, 58-64 (1983).

11. Hutber, D. and Sims, P. Use of machine learning to generate rules. *Proc. of the 3rd Alvey Vision Conference*, 27, Sept. (1987).

12. Parsons, T. Disordered databases and ordered explanations. *Proc. of the 4th Alvey Vision Conference*, Sept. (1988).

13. Hopfield, J. and Tank, D. Neural computation of decisions in optimization problems. *Biol. Cyb.*, 2, 141-152 (1985).

14. Jamison, T. and Schalkoff, R. Image labelling: a neural network approach. *Image and Vision Computing*, 6, 4, 203-214 (1988).

15. Rumelhart, D., Hinton, G. and Williams, R. Learning representations by back propagation of errors. *Nature*, **323**, 533-536, Oct. (1986).

16. Valiant, L. A theory of the learnable. *Comm. of the ACM*, **27** (1984).

17. Sejnowski, T. and Rosenberg, C. Parallel network that learns to pronounce English text. *Complex Systems*, **1**, 145-168 (1987).

18. Wright, W. and Bounds, D. *Contextual Image Analysis With a Neural Network*. Tech. Rep. RIPR REP/1000/48/89, Research Initiative in Pattern Recognition (1989).

19. Rumelhart, D. and McClelland, J. *Parallel Distributed Processing: Explorations in the Microstructure of Cognition*, Volume 1, Bradford Books, MIT Press, Cambridge, MA (1986).

20. Pomerleau, D. An autonomous land vehicle in a neural network. *IEEE Conf. on Neural Inf. Proc. Systems: Natural and Synthetic*, Denver, Dec. (1988).

21. Page, A. *Segmentation Algorithms*. Tech. Rep. AOI/TR/BASR/880201, Sowerby Research Centre, British Aerospace, Bristol (1988).

22. Haralick, R., Shanmugam, K. and Distein, I. Textual features for image classification. *IEEE Trans. Syst. Man and Cybern.*, **SMC-3**, 620 (1973).

23. Bounds, D., Lloyd, P. and Matthew, B. A *Comparison of Neural Network and Other Pattern Recognition Approaches to the Diagnosis of Low Back Disorders*. Tech. Rep., Research Initiative in Pattern Recognition, RIPRREP/1000/54/89 (1989).

9

Object recognition with optimum neural networks

M. Bichsel and P. Seitz
Paul Scherrer Institute, Switzerland

9.1 Summary

Many classification tasks in image processing, especially the recognition of objects, are still essentially unsolved problems. Neural networks might represent a general solution for these classifying problems, provided they can be constructed optimally for advantageous performance/complexity ratios. By interpreting feedforward neural networks as multi-stage encoders in the framework of Shannon's information theory it is possible to judge the performance of single neurones and complete networks with a given problem.

Using these results a new learning algorithm for feedforward networks is developed, making it possible to design neural networks with optimum performance. It is demonstrated that this algorithm works as claimed in practical applications: two image processing problems were selected, both considered to be difficult, and optimum neural networks for their solution are constructed. The first problem is the shift-invariant recognition of symmetry axes in binary patterns. The second problem is the recognition of human faces in arbitrary, natural scenes. In both cases, reliable recognition results are obtained. These results are discussed in a more general framework of image processing, making the trade-offs in traditional image processing and neurocomputing more apparent.

9.2 Introduction

The wide field of image processing, although sometimes called 'image science', is often still more an art rather than a science. After three decades of work, no generally accepted framework for machine vision has been put forward and proved its concept in practical problems. Especially in applications where the problem is the robust recognition of objects in complex natural scenes, biological neural networks still out-perform any computer vision algorithm by far. This realization has recently led to the hope that artificial neural networks might be a panacea for any kind of difficult recognition problem for which solutions are known so that such a network could be trained with them. Moreover, neural networks are well suited for parallel hardware implementation because of the simplicity and repetition of the processing elements.

As is often the case, the problem to be solved is really a classification problem, i.e. one has to sort input patterns into (usually only a few) different classes. For this reason layered feedforward networks are preferred instead of the older 'autoassociative' Hopfield networks with feedback [1]. Many different types of neural networks have been proposed in recent years, each providing a different trade-off in memory, computation, training time, and adaptation requirements [2]. It has been shown that feedforward networks can solve any classification problem with no more than three layers [3,4]. For this reason feedforward networks with three layers are inherently the fastest general neural network solution to a given problem. Once a set of weights has been learned, such a network may be realized with one resistor per weight and one amplifier per neurone. Between input and output the signals therefore have to pass, at most, three amplifiers.

A neural network which is 'learning with a teacher' (supervised learning) has to adapt its parameters (weights and thresholds) according to a specific learning rule in order to obtain the correct input-output relation for a given training set of input patterns with known classification. One of the major problems in neurocomputing is still the development of efficient training algorithms. Back-propagation, the most popular and most frequently applied training algorithm for feedforward networks has its known drawbacks, see for example reference [4]. Convergence to a stable state may be very slow and the training algorithm is not guaranteed to converge to a global optimum.

Another fundamental problem in neurocomputing is the absence of a method with which the performance of a neural network – trained with any learning algorithm – can be judged in a given application. Such a tool would make it much easier to answer the question of 'reasonable' sizes for neural networks for a given task, i.e. how many nodes are really necessary, and how should they be distributed in the different network layers? For applications in image processing, where massive amounts of data have to be processed, it is crucial that the processing networks can be realized in sizes that make it possible to carry out the computations in reasonable time. It is therefore necessary to have a measure with which the performance of a neural network can be judged and also optimized.

In the following section, such a performance measure for general feedforward neural networks is developed.

9.3 Measuring the information flow in neural networks: the conditional class entropy

In a first step we will restrict ourselves to hard limiter activation functions, according to the McCulloch–Pitts model [5]. In this way the powerful concepts of Shannon's information theory can be applied directly to neural networks by interpreting them as multi-stage encoders [6].

A neurone with a hard-limiter activation function shows a binary output. The output of a neurone changes from an off-state to an on-state if the weighted sum of all incoming synapses (weights) exceeds a given threshold. Thus a binary pattern of outputs, which we choose to interpret as a code in the sense of Shannon [7], is produced in each layer (Fig. 9.1). For this reason the network may be interpreted as a multi-stage encoder that transforms an input pattern to a corresponding code in each layer. The transformation between codes in succeeding layers is determined by the parameters of the corresponding neurones, i.e. the weights and thresholds. This unconventional view of a neural network allows us to apply the powerful concepts of information theory developed by Shannon almost half a century ago.

The network has the task of filtering out the information concerning the class of the input patterns and to transmit this information with the smallest possible loss through the hidden layers to the output layer. Note especially that information that is lost

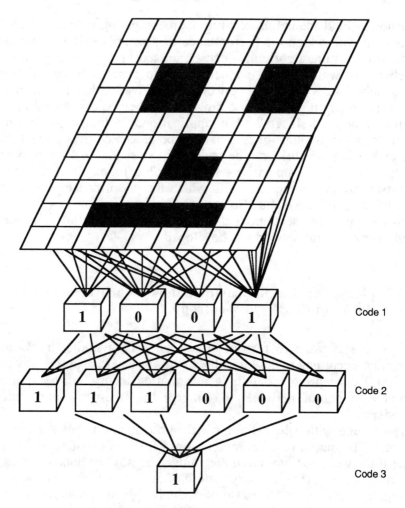

Figure 9.1 A feedforward network with a hard-limiter activation function may be interpreted as a multi-stage encoder.

between two succeeding layers may not be recovered in any further layer and will therefore also be missing at the output. The second goal is to concentrate the class information in as few neurones as possible in order to obtain good generalization capabilities of the network with a small number of training patterns.

How much information about the class of the input patterns is transmitted in a particular layer is determined by the statistics of the codewords appearing in this layer in response to the input patterns. If a certain codeword only appears in response to input patterns belonging to one particular class then the full information about the class of the input pattern is provided by this codeword. No information concerning the class of the corresponding input patterns is missing. If, on the other hand, several input patterns belonging to different classes c result in the same codeword (or pattern) p in the layer under consideration then the missing class information or class entropy S_{class}(codeword=p) for this particular codeword is according to Shannon's formula [7]:

$$S_{class}(\text{pattern}=p) = \sum_{c=1,N_c} P_{cp}\log_2(P_{cp}) \qquad (9.1)$$

using the conditional probabilities $P_{cp} = P$(class=c | pattern=p) that an input pattern from class c was presented to the network, given the observed pattern p in the considered layer. N_c is the number of different classes.

The class information contained in all the possible codewords of a particular layer is calculated by weighting the class entropy S_{class}(codeword=p) of every codeword with the probability $P(p)$ that this codeword appears. This weighted sum is called conditional class entropy (CCE) S_{cond} in accordance with Shannon's terminology:

$$S_{cond} = \sum_{p=1,N_p} P(p) \sum_{c=1,N_c} P_{cp}\log_2(P_{cp}). \qquad (9.2)$$

Here N_p is the number of possible output patterns in the layer under consideration. In practical applications the probabilities are calculated using the frequency interpretation of probabilities [8].

The probability $P(p)$ for the pattern p is estimated by

$$P(p) = \frac{N(p)}{N_{total}} \qquad (9.3)$$

where $N(p)$ is the number of occurrences of the pattern p in the layer (hidden or output) when all the input patterns are presented to the network. N_{total} is the total number of input patterns.

In the same way the joint probability $P(\text{class}=c \text{ and pattern}=p)$ can be estimated, describing the simultaneous occurrence of pattern p in the layer under examination and the input pattern belonging to class c:

$$P(\text{class}=c \text{ and pattern}=p) = \frac{N(\text{class}=c \text{ and pattern}=p)}{N_{\text{total}}}. \quad (9.4)$$

Here $N(\text{class}=c \text{ and pattern}=p)$ is the number of occurrences of the pattern p in a layer for all input patterns belonging to class c.

The conditional probability $Pcp = P(\text{class}=c \mid \text{pattern}=p)$ that an input pattern from class c was presented to the network, given the observation of the pattern p in the layer under examination, can now be determined:

$$Pcp = \frac{P(\text{class}=c \text{ and pattern}=p)}{P(p)}$$

$$= \frac{N(\text{class}=c \text{ and pattern}=p)}{N(p)}. \quad (9.5)$$

Information theory has thus provided us in a unique manner with the ability to measure the relevance of the outputs of the neurones in a layer. The optimum neural network is constructed by selecting parameters resulting in maximum class information (minimum CCE). In contrast to conventional neural network techniques, we can not only judge the performance of a net as a whole, but are also able to calculate the contribution to the overall performance for single neurones or groups of neurones in intermediate layers.

Due to the fact that a layer may be judged without any reference to parameters in the succeeding layers the network may be constructed layer by layer. The number of neurones in a particular layer is determined by choosing the minimum number of neurones that transmit the class information without (or with negligible) loss.

The idea of treating neural networks in the context of information theory is not completely new. Linsker [9] has demonstrated that Hebbian learning tends to conserve information from the input layer to further layers. Gardner [10] characterized a learning network as a conditional probability computer. As we want to emphasize, however, in most problems we are not interested in the complete information of the input patterns, as it was used for example by Gardner [10] and

Linsker [9], but rather we want to separate this information from the information concerning the class of these patterns. Therefore the conditional entropy with respect to the class of the input pattern (CCE) is a much better performance measure than the conditional entropy with respect to the whole information content in the input patterns and it follows that Hebbian learning is not, in general, optimum.

In summary, the presented principle of minimum CCE determines connections that transmit maximum information about the class of the input patterns and concentrate this information in as few neurones as possible.

9.4 Extension to general sigmoid activation functions

Hard-limiter activation functions may be generalized to more general sigmoid activation functions by assuming that the output of a neurone is not a deterministic but a probabilistic function of a given input pattern. This input pattern can result now in arbitrary bit patterns (codewords), but the probability that a neurone in a particular layer is in its on-state (firing) becomes a sigmoid function of the weighted sum of its inputs in accordance to natural nerve cells.

We assume that the probability that a neurone fires is not determined by the firing of other neurones in the same layer. The probability for a particular codeword to appear is thus the product of the probabilities for the individual bit values.

This generalization has the advantage that a small variation in the input also results in a small variation of the CCE in contrast to the hard-limiter case.

9.5 A teaching algorithm for the construction of optimum neural networks: minimizing conditional class entropy

The CCE represents a general information measure with which the performance of single neurones or complete neural networks can be judged in a given application. It is therefore obvious that this information measure can be used for a training algorithm that optimizes the performance of a neural network: simply adapt the network's parameters in a suitable fashion, so that the CCE is minimized, i.e. the information flow through the network is maximized. We have to find the global minimum of a function in many dimensions where each parameter of the network, e.g. a threshold or a weight, corresponds to one dimension.

No finite time method can guarantee that a global minimum of an arbitrary function can be found. For this work we are using a simulated annealing technique [11–13]. Simulated annealing is an efficient optimization method in many dimensions. On a random walk in the space spanned by the network parameters it allows the crossing of function variations on a scale given by an artificial parameter called temperature. If the calculated CCE at a new location is lower than at the previous location then this step is accepted, otherwise the step is only accepted with probability $e^{-\Delta CCE/T}$ where T denotes an annealing parameter (physically the 'temperature' of the annealing process) which has to be lowered slowly. Lowering the temperature corresponds to searching for good solutions on a smaller scale. By starting at a high temperature and then cooling slowly, a better solution is generally found than with conventional optimization techniques such as the conjugate gradient method.

The efficiency of the simulated annealing algorithm critically depends on a good choice of the random walk step size. The step size should be adapted in order to obtain an *expected* function difference of the order of the current annealing temperature. For this step size the probability that the current step will be accepted is approximately 1/2. If the steps are chosen much smaller, then most of the steps will be accepted. Hence the random walk can be described as a diffusion process with only a small drift towards smaller function values. A lot of function values have to be calculated without much effect on the random walk – thus much computing time is wasted. If on the other hand much bigger steps are chosen, then most of the steps will be rejected, also resulting in a waste of computer time. Note that the argument outlined above contains the reasonable implicit assumption that the function shows bigger variations on a large scale than on a small scale.

To achieve a probability of the order of 1/2 that a step is accepted, we carry a statistic of the function variation for the last few successful steps. If this variation is smaller (bigger) than the temperature the step size will be enlarged (reduced).

Only one parameter (i.e. a connection strength or a threshold) is varied at a time. Combined with an update strategy this results in a saving of computing time because a lot of intermediate results in the CCE calculation are constant in a single step and do not need to be recalculated. Nevertheless, any point in the parameter space is in general reachable also with this strategy.

A difficulty, related to our specific problem, stems from the fact that the function (CCE) values tend towards a global maximum for unreasonable, i.e. very large, parameter values. For unreasonable parameter values we achieve a maximum class uncertainty because then the network output will be independent of the input and hence contain no useful information. Using the CCE directly as the function to be optimized would allow the random walk to leave the region of interest with a vanishing chance of ever returning (Fig. 9.2(a)). This problem was solved by noting that if the parameters of a particular neurone are varied then the CCE cannot exceed the value $\bar{S}_{max}$ that would be calculated if this neurone were not present at all. This insight can be used to construct a new energy function (see Fig. 9.2(b)), having approximately the same shape near the minimum but tending to infinity in the previously flat energy region:

$$E = \bar{S} + \varepsilon \cdot \frac{1}{\bar{S}_{max} - \bar{S}} \qquad (9.6)$$

with a suitably chosen ε, small compared with the global CCE (denoted by $\bar{S}$) variation.

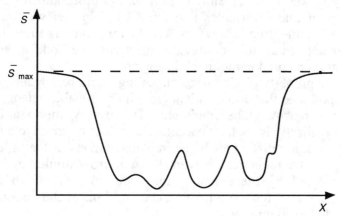

Figure 9.2 (a) Typical conditional class entropy (CCE) on a straight line through the multi-dimensional space of weights and thresholds. Far away from the minimum the CCE $\bar{S}$ tends towards the upper boundary $\bar{S}_{max}$. Thus if the CCE is optimized directly with a random walk of simulated annealing at finite temperature then the random walk will escape from the interesting region and will not return.

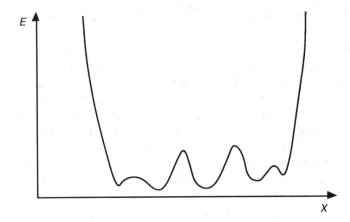

Figure 9.2 (b) The function being optimized is changed to $E = \overline{S} + \varepsilon \cdot (\overline{S}_{max} - \overline{S})^{-1}$ with ε small compared with the global CCE variation. Now the random walk is confined to the interesting region but the new function has the shape of the CCE function near a global minimum.

No variation algorithm can guarantee that the global minimum of a function is found in finite time; the method of simulated annealing, however, offers the possibility of escaping local minima. This property makes it a well-suited optimization procedure for complex functions of many variables like our CCE. In fact we found that simulated annealing shows much faster convergence for our applications than the conjugate gradient method, a standard optimization method in multiple dimensions.

Another property of simulated annealing could be advantageous: it is more probable that a local minimum with reasonable extent is found than a very narrow global minimum. This is very important because physical realizations contain inaccuracies (values digitized to a few bits only, electronic noise in analogue implementations or the failure of a neurone in the redundant network). A narrow minimum is much more affected by these inaccuracies and might lead to inferior performance than the more tolerant choice of parameters indicated by an extended local minimum.

The learning rule developed above is the only one that extracts all the information contained in the training set and does not add any spurious information based on artificial additional assumptions. If any other teaching method should result in better performance of the trained network then this would signify that additional information concerning the nature of the particular problem was included in this learning rule implicitly. Any additional information concerning the nature of a problem should therefore be included explicitly either in the training set or in the network parameters directly. With this explicit inclusion of information, the presented algorithm will out-perform any other algorithm.

This optimality property of networks trained with the described algorithm is very important for applications in image processing where huge amounts of data have to be treated. In the following two sections, two practical image processing problems are considered, and optimum neural networks for their solutions are developed using the methods described above.

9.6 Shift-invariant classification of symmetry axes in binary patterns

Based on experience with traditional image processing algorithms, it is often considered obvious that the only way of achieving shift-invariance in object recognition is to implement (usually small-sized) processing windows and to slide them over the image to be analysed.

The problem and its solution with optimum neural networks presented here demonstrates that this is not necessarily always true. It is possible to construct neural networks that develop the property of being truly shift-invariant, without ever being explicitly told to behave this way. The problem with which we would like to illustrate this surprising capability is the classification of mirror symmetry axes in binary images, where the axes of symmetry are allowed to translate. A similar problem has been studied by Sejnowski *et al.* [14] and they consider it to be a difficult test case for a neural network.

The patterns whose classification we wanted to teach our network consisted of 10×10 arrays of randomly generated binary images which were symmetrical with respect to one of three symmetry axes as shown in Fig. 9.3. This axis was either horizontal, vertical or diagonal and was aligned with pixel boundaries. Vertical and horizontal boundary conditions were such that the images exhibited toroidal topology. The resulting patterns can be interpreted as 10×10 sub-arrays of a periodic pattern with period 10 and being mirror-symmetrical along one of three symmetry axes at any position.

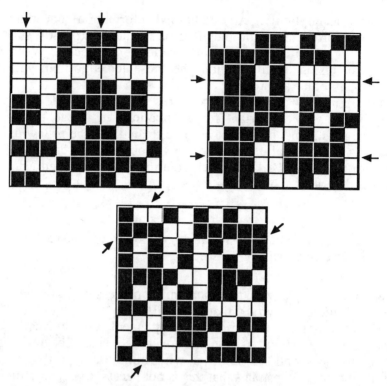

Figure 9.3 Examples of input patterns for the 10 × 10 mirror symmetry problem with periodicity such that the array has the topology of a torus. The light squares represent input values 1, the dark ones represent value 0. The symmetry axes lie vertical in the first, horizontal in the second and diagonal in the third pattern. Because of the implicit periodicity every pattern shows two parallel symmetry axes.

A set of 8000 randomly generated patterns was used to train the network. We proceeded as described in section 9.5 by adding new neurones and optimizing the neurone weights with respect to the CCE. The successful emergence of a network solving the shift-invariant symmetry classification problem can be illustrated by inspecting the two-dimensional pattern of weights to a neurone: Sejnowski *et al.* [14] showed that, in order to recognize a particular symmetry axis, this pattern of weights should be antisymmetric with respect to the particular symmetry axis at any translated position of this axis. Our training algorithm actually generated such patterns, for which an example is shown in Fig. 9.4. Hence our training algorithm is able to reveal the hidden invariance of a problem.

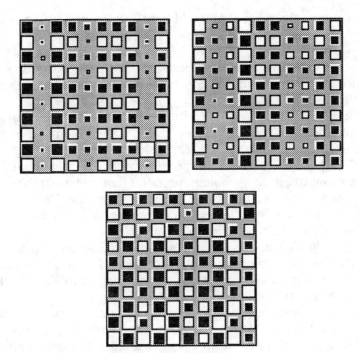

Figure 9.4 Representation of the weights found by the maximum information algorithm for the 10 × 10 mirror symmetry problem. The 10 × 10 array of weights from the input units to three hidden units is shown. Positive weights are represented as weight squares and negative weights as black squares. The area of the squares is proportional to the magnitude of the corresponding weights. Every unit has its weights antisymmetric with respect to all positions of the symmetry axes of one single class, leading to an invariant output for all members of that class.

9.7 Detection of human faces

One of the astonishing properties of the human visual system is the ease with which it can recognize the presence of human faces in very complex scenes, and even under the most adverse conditions. For this reason we selected this problem for demonstrating the capabilities and limitations of neural networks with a difficult object recognition task in an uncontrolled environment. In this example the recognition must be performed robustly because human faces may differ in a lot of ways (head orientation, size, hair style, illumination, emotion, etc.).

Many practical applications could benefit from such a face-detector, beyond the obvious applications in access-control systems:

1. Elevator control. Counting the number of persons waiting in the individual floors would help to serve the elevator passengers better.
2. Photograph printers. Most of today's photographs are produced automatically by photograph printers. The automatic exposure control however does not distinguish between interesting objects and background. Therefore the faces of human beings, the most interesting parts of a photograph, are often under-exposed, over-exposed or the colour balance is inappropriate ('plaster head' effect). An automatic detection of human faces on the negatives would eliminate these errors.
3. Television viewer polling. The presence of human beings in front of the television screen could be more reliably detected based on an automatic face-recognition system than with the traditional keypad indicator.
4. Monitoring systems. Most automatic burglar detectors are in fact motion detectors. They give alarm for any moving object, e.g. a cat or a dog. A face detector could exclude such false alarms and could even be combined with an automatic camera taking a picture of the burglar to identify him afterwards.

Psychologist's studies revealed that the most important region in a face is the region containing the eyes [15–17]. Therefore this part of a face was used to detect faces.

A network was taught to work as a detector of eye pairs, i.e. to assign one of two class numbers to an arbitrary pattern (eye pair or not an eye pair). The eye pair training set contained 100 patterns of size 11h by 4v pixels, each pattern showing an eye pair in low resolution. The training set for 'no eye pairs' contained 400 patterns showing an arbitrary pattern of the same size.

Instead of using the grey values of the image directly (or spatially filtered versions of it, for example Laplacians) it was decided to pre-process the images and to generate maps of local orientations. The decision was based on biological evidence that in natural visual pathways similar operations are carried out [18], and on work reported in the field of image processing, in which the use of local orientation led to a very robust algorithm for object recognition [19]. Local orientation may be calculated in many different ways [20]. We chose the most simple way by calculating a local normalized gradient:

$$\vec{g}(i,j) = \frac{\vec{\nabla}f}{\sqrt{|\vec{\nabla}f|^2 + n^2}} \qquad (9.7)$$

where the Gray value gradient $\vec{\nabla}f$ is estimated with a 2 by 2 Roberts operator. The parameter n is an estimate of the noise and in our application $n = 10$ was used. This first pre-processing step is illustrated in Fig. 9.5. Each normalized gradient vector is represented by its two vector components, thus resulting in 10h by 3v pairs of input signals, or 60 signal lines with associated neurone weights in total.

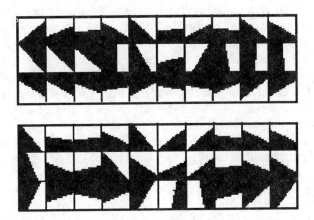

Figure 9.5 Two training patterns for a network detecting eye pairs represented as an array of local orientations. Each square in a 10h by 3v array contains an oriented black to white transition describing the local orientation that is provided by the normalized gradient vector. The two components of each vector are fed into a pair of input units.

The network was designed to contain four neurones in the first hidden layer. A threshold logic output function (Lippmann [4]) of the form

$$\text{output} = \begin{cases} 1 & \text{if activation} > \text{threshold} + \frac{\sigma}{2} \\ 0 & \text{if activation} < \text{threshold} - \frac{\sigma}{2} \\ \dfrac{\text{activation} - \text{threshold}}{\sigma} + \frac{1}{2} & \text{else} \end{cases}$$

was chosen, corresponding to the probabilistic interpretation described above. The parameter σ determines the steepness of the sigmoid function at the threshold and was chosen to be $\sigma = 2$. The shape of the sigmoid function is not critical. Due to this fact, a function was chosen which is fast to calculate.

First the four-neurone input layer of the network was trained for optimum performance with the algorithm described above. Adding neurones in the second layer and training again for optimum performance showed a surprising result: the performance of the neural network as measured with the CCE remained essentially the same as determined with the first neurone in the second layer.

The reason for this particularly simple optimal network structure can be explained by analysing the distribution of the four hidden neurone outputs for the training patterns: the response of these four neurones to an input pattern lies within a four-dimensional hypercube. Monitoring the responses to input patterns belonging to one of the two classes (face/no face) it was seen that these responses formed a cluster in one of the corners of the hypercube (Fig. 9.6). As Fig. 9.6 shows, the two clustered distributions can well be separated by a single hyperplane. This explains the fact that only one additional neurone is needed.

The resulting eye pair detector network was tested on a newspaper picture of a marathon containing a number of heads with all the difficulties mentioned above. Since the training was carried out with faces from a completely different picture, none of the faces in the marathon scene was included in the training set. To test the network a window was scanned over the image. For each window position the window content was presented to the network. The corresponding image region was classified according to the network output of the eye pair detector.

The neural network eye pair detector performed surprisingly well in this complex scene it had never seen before. Only 0.06% of the pixels were classified erroneously (false-positive) as the location of a human eye pair and 90% of the human eye pairs were correctly identified (Fig. 9.7). Note that the wrongly classified image regions actually resemble eye pairs – the surrounding image region does not contain enough additional elements of a face (hair, nose, mouth, ears, chin, etc.) to make the presence of a face probable for a human observer. Hence a logical extension of this procedure to detect faces even more reliably is to use several neural networks, trained to react on the different parts of a human face, and then deduce from the geometrical arrangement of the face components if the presence of a face is probable at this position.

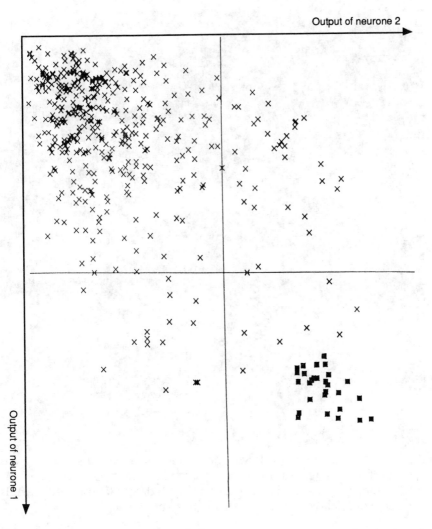

Figure 9.6 Outputs of two neurones responding to eye pairs (squares) and no eye pairs (crosses). Note that these outputs form a single cluster of points for each of the two classes.

Figure 9.7 Test of a trained eye pair detector on a natural scene that was not used for training. All the detected eye pairs are marked with a cross. 90% of the eye pairs are identified correctly and only 0.06% of the pixels are erroneously classified as eye pairs in this busy scene.

9.8 Conclusion

We have shown in two examples that a network, trained optimally with the minimum class entropy algorithm, is able to generalize from a training set to unknown patterns. Because the training algorithm was derived on the basis of information theory we know that in a general case there is no selection of the network's parameters performing better than the one determined with the presented method.

Any other training algorithm will produce parameters biasing the network towards a special set of solutions, and it will only result in good solutions for the subset of problems for which this bias is justified because of additional constraints contained implicitly in this subset of problems.

The underlying problem with the construction of neural networks is to select an architecture of the network (a certain number of neurones and their distribution in the different layers) so that the network does not just store the training patterns, without abstracting the common traits of the input patterns. On the other hand if the network is too small then the level of abstraction desired cannot be reached, i.e. the network is not able to extract the common traits of the training patterns.

It is concluded that these common traits will be represented in the network solution found by the minimum class entropy algorithm if there are enough training samples to reveal the problem's essential features. The number of training patterns required to reveal these features may grow, in the worst case, proportionally with the volume spanned by the input parameters, i.e. it may grow exponentially with the number of input parameters. Thus the number of training samples and the time required to construct the corresponding network may quickly become prohibitive.

Of course, the considerations outlined here apply to all kinds of neural network classifiers and to all the training algorithms, also to the one presented in this work. An important conclusion is that with the CCE algorithm reported here, it is possible to construct the optimum neural network classifier for a given problem. It does not mean that this neural network is also the best possible classifier algorithm for the given problem: it is possible that there exists a very simple algorithmic solution to the problem, albeit not a neural network type of computation. The experience reported by other researchers in the field (see for example [2]) indicates that neural networks are indeed not always the best classifier solutions to a problem. The early enthusiasm of researchers who expected neural networks – together with a mysterious learning rule and a few training examples – to be the universal problem solver is not justified.

Although it is true that a neural network can in principle calculate anything, for example an FFT [21], the authors of this work doubt this 'pure-neurocomputing' approach to a problem. Our practical experience stresses the point of analysing a problem and applying the human intelligence to reveal common traits, so that they can be used a priori for the construction of pre-processing algorithms. This investigation and understanding of a problem can serve to decrease substantially the number of free parameters in a network, and it will therefore increase the network's chances of finding a practical classifying strategy that can be computed in reasonable time. Lippmann [4] has given a geometrical interpretation of feedforward neural networks as systems that partition the space of input data with planes. An appropriate pre-processing of the raw input data, allowing one to work with more general surfaces than planes, may substantially reduce the number of neurones needed to solve a given task, thus reducing the number of training samples needed and the training time. This point is illustrated for example in the selection of local orientation as the basic image features in the eye pair recognition problem, with which we obtained significantly better results than with the pure or spatially filtered grey-level images.

In conclusion, this work reports on the conditional class entropy, a measure derived from Shannon's information theory, with which the performance of any feedforward network or part of it can be measured. A training algorithm based on the CCE is – in principle – capable of adapting a network's parameters so that the network will show optimum performance in a given problem. Practical experience indicates that these optimum neural networks are not necessarily the optimum solutions to a problem (in terms of performance, complexity, cost, time, storage size, etc.) but that careful analysis of a problem may lead to a conventional pre-processing algorithm, substantially enhancing an additional classifer neural network's performance.

References

1. Hopfield, J.J. Neural networks and physical systems with emergent collective computational abilities. *Proc. Natl. Acad. Sci. USA*, **79**, 2554-2558 (1982).

2. Lippmann, P. Pattern classification using neural networks. *IEEE Comm. Mag.*, **27**, 11, 47-64, Dec. (1989).

3. Duda, R.O. and Hart, P.E. *Pattern Classification and Scene Analysis*, Wiley, New York (1973).

4. Lippmann, P. An introduction to computing with neural nets. *IEEE ASSP Mag.*, **4**, 4-22 (1987).

5. McCulloch, W.S. and Pitts, W A logical calculus of the ideas immanent in nervous activity. *Bull. of Math. Bioph.*, **5**, 115-133 (1943).

6. Bichsel, M. and Seitz, P. Minimum class entropy: a maximum information approach to layered networks. *Neural Networks*, **2**, 133-141 (1989).

7. Shannon, C.E. A mathematical theory of communication. *The Bell System Tech. J.*, **27**, 379-423 and 623-656 (1948).

8. Papoulis, A. *Probability, Random Variables and Stochastic Processes*, McGraw-Hill, New York (1964).

9. Linsker, R. Self-organization in a perceptual neural network. *Computer*, **21**, 105-117 (1988).

10. Gardner, S.B. Application of neural network algorithms and architectures to correlation/tracking and identification. In J.S. Denker (ed.). *Neural Networks for Computing*, American Institute of Physics, New York, 153-157 (1986).

11. Kirkpatrick, S., Gelatt Jr., C.D. and Vecchi, M.P. Optimization by simulated annealing. *Science*, **220**, 671 (1983).

12. Vanderbilt, D. and Louie, S.G. A Monte Carlo simulated annealing approach to optimization over continuous variables. *J. of Comp. Phys.*, **56**, 259-271 (1984).

13. Corana, A., Marchesi, M., Martini, C. and Ridella, S. Minimizing multimodel functions of continuous variables with the "simulated annealing" algorithm. *ACM Trans. on Math. Soft.*, **51**, 262-280 (1987).

14. Sejnowski, T.J., Kienker, P.K. and Hinton, G.E. Learning symmetry groups with hidden units: beyond the perceptron. *Physica,* **22D**, 260-275 (1986).

15. Goldstein, A.J., Harmon, L.D. and Lesk, A.B. Identification of human faces. *Proc. of the IEEE*, **59**, 5 (1971).

16. Haig, N.D. Exploring recognition with interchanged facial features. *Perception*, **15**, 3, 235-247 (1986).

17. Haig, N.D. – (1983b). High-resolution facial feature saliency mapping. *Perception*, **15**, 4, 373-386 (1986).

18. Hubel, D. Eye, *Brain and Vision*, Scientific American Library, New York (1988).

19. Seitz, P. The robust recognition of object primitives using local axes of symmetry. *Signal Proc.*, **18**, 1, 89-108 (1989).

20. Seitz, P. Using local orientational information as image primitive for robust object recognition. *SPIE Proc. on Visual Comm. and Image Proc. IV*, **1199**, 1630-1638 (1989).

21. Hecht-Nielsen, R. Neurocomputing: picking the human brain. *IEEE Spectrum*, **25**, 3, 36-41 (1988).

10

Handwritten digit recognition with a back-propagation network*

Y. Le Cun, B. Boser, J. S. Denker, D. Henderson, R. E. Howard,
W. Hubbard and L. D. Jackel
AT & T Bell Laboratories, USA

10.1 Summary

We present an application of back-propagation networks to handwritten digit recognition. Minimum pre-processing of the data was required, but the architecture of the network was highly constrained and specifically designed for the task. The input of the network consists of normalized images of isolated digits. The method has 1% error rate and about a 9% reject rate on zipcode digits provided by the US Postal Service.

10.2 Introduction

The main point of this paper is to show that large back-propagation (BP) networks can be applied to real image-recognition problems without a large, complex pre-processing stage requiring detailed engineering. Unlike most previous work on the subject [1], the learning network is directly fed with images, rather than feature vectors, thus demonstrating the ability of BP networks to deal with large amounts of low-level information.

---

* This paper was previously published in Touretzky, D.S. (ed.). *Advances in Neural Information Processing Systems, Volume 2*, Morgan Kaufman, San Mateo, CA, 396-404 (1990).

Previous work performed on simple digit images [2] showed that the architecture of the network strongly influences the network's generalization ability. Good generalization can only be obtained by designing a network architecture that contains a certain amount of a priori knowledge about the problem. The basic design principle is to minimize the number of free parameters that must be determined by the learning algorithm, without overly reducing the computational power of the network. This principle increases the probability of correct generalization because it results in a specialized network architecture that has a reduced entropy [2–5]. On the other hand, some effort must be devoted to designing appropriate constraints into the architecture.

10.3 Zipcode recognition

The handwritten digit-recognition application was chosen because it is a relatively simple machine vision task: the input consists of black or white pixels, the digits are usually well-separated from the background, and there are only ten output categories. Yet the problem deals with objects in a real two-dimensional space and the mapping from image space to category space has both considerable regularity and considerable complexity. The problem has added attraction because it is of great practical value.

The database used to train and test the network is a superset of the one used in the work previously reported [1]. We emphasize that the method of solution reported here relies more heavily on automatic learning, and much less on hand-designed pre-processing.

The database consists of 9298 segmented numerals digitized from handwritten zipcodes that appeared on real US Mail passing through the Buffalo, New York, post office. Examples of such images are shown in Fig. 10.1. The digits were written by many different people, using a great variety of sizes, writing styles and instruments, with widely varying levels of care. This was supplemented by a set of 3349 printed digits coming from 35 different fonts. The training set consisted of 7291 handwritten digits plus 2549 printed digits. The remaining 2007 handwritten and 700 printed digits were used as the test set. The printed fonts in the test set were different from the printed fonts in the training set. One important feature of this database, which is a common feature to all real-world databases, is that both the training set and the testing set contain numerous examples that are ambiguous, unclassifiable, or even misclassified.

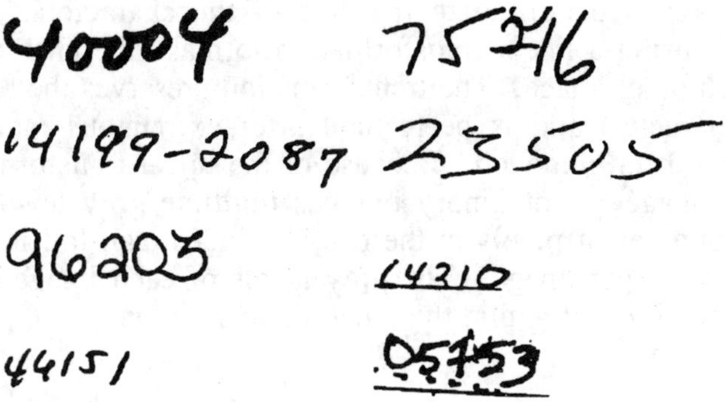

Figure 10.1 Examples of original zipcodes from the testing set.

10.4 Pre-processing

Acquisition, binarization, location of the zipcode, and preliminary segmentation were performed by Postal Service contractors [6]. Some of these steps constitute very hard tasks in themselves. The segmentation (separating each digit from its neighbours) would be a relatively simple task if we could assume that a character is contiguous and is disconnected from its neighbours, but neither of these assumptions holds in practice. Many ambiguous characters in the data base are the result of mis-segmentation (especially broken 5's) as can be seen on Fig. 10.2.

```
1410119134857268032264141
8663597202992997225100467
0130844115910106154061036
3110641110304752620077799
66891203478855713147279554
60601+730187112991089970 9
8401097075973319720155190
5510755182551828143580109
43178753416554605546035460
55182551085030475204394 01
```

Figure 10.2 Examples of normalized digits from the testing set.

At this point, the size of a digit varies but is typically around 40 by 60 pixels. Since the input of a back-propagation network is fixed size, it is necessary to normalize the size of the characters. This was performed using a linear transformation to make the characters fit in a 16 by 16 pixel image. The transformation preserves the aspect ratio of the character, and is performed after extraneous marks in the image have been removed. Because of the linear transformation, the resulting image is not binary but has multiple grey levels, since a variable number of pixels in the original image can fall into a given pixel in the target image. The grey levels of each image are scaled and translated to fall within the range –1 to 1.

10.5 The network

The remainder of the recognition is entirely performed by a multi-layer network. All of the connections in the network are adaptive, although heavily constrained, and are trained using back-propagation. This is in contrast with earlier work [1], where the first few layers of connections were hand-chosen constants. The input of the network is a 16 by 16 normalized image and the output is composed of 10 units: one per class. When a pattern belonging to class i is presented, the desired output is +1 for the ith output unit, and –1 for the other output units.

A fully connected network with enough discriminative power for the task would have far too many parameters to be able to generalize correctly. Therefore a restricted connection scheme must be devised, guided by our prior knowledge about shape recognition. There are well-known advantages to performing shape recognition by detecting and combining local features. We have required our network to do this by constraining the connections in the first few layers to be local. In addition, if a feature detector is useful on one part of the image, it is likely to be useful on other parts of the image as well. One reason for this is that the salient features of a distorted character might be displaced slightly from their position in a typical character. One solution to this problem is to scan the input image with a single neurone that has a local receptive field, and store the states of this neurone in corresponding locations in a layer called a feature map (see Fig. 10.3).

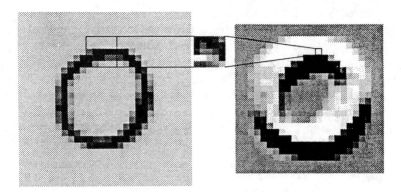

Figure 10.3 Input image (left), weight vector (centre), and resulting feature map (right). The feature map is obtained by scanning the input image with a single neurone that has a local receptive field, as indicated. White represents −1, black represents +1.

This operation is equivalent to a convolution with a small size kernel, followed by a squashing function. The process can be performed in parallel by implementing the feature map as a plane of neurones whose weight vectors are constrained to be equal. That is, units in a feature map are constrained to perform the same operation on different parts of the image. An interesting side-effect of this weight sharing technique, already described in [7], is to reduce the number of free parameters by a large amount, since a large number of units share the same weights. In addition, a certain level of shift invariance is present in the system: shifting the input will shift the result on the feature map, but will leave it unchanged otherwise. In practice, it will be necessary to have multiple feature maps, extracting different features from the same image.

The idea of local, convolutional feature maps can be applied to subsequent hidden layers as well, to extract features of increasing complexity and abstraction. Interestingly, higher-level features require less precise coding of their location. Reduced precision is actually advantageous, since a slight distortion or translation of the input will have reduced effect on the representation. Thus, each feature extraction in our network is followed by an additional layer which performs a local averaging and a subsampling, reducing the resolution of the feature map. This layer introduces a certain level of invariance to distortions and translations. A functional module of our network consists of a layer of shared-weight feature maps followed by an averaging/subsampling layer. This is reminiscent of the Neocognitron architecture [8], with the notable difference that we use backprop (rather than unsupervised learning) which we feel is more appropriate to this sort of classification problem.

The network architecture, represented in Fig. 10.4, is a direct extension of the ones described in [2,9]. The network has four hidden layers respectively named H1, H2, H3, and H4. Layers H1 and H3 are shared-weights feature extractors, while H2 and H4 are averaging/subsampling layers.

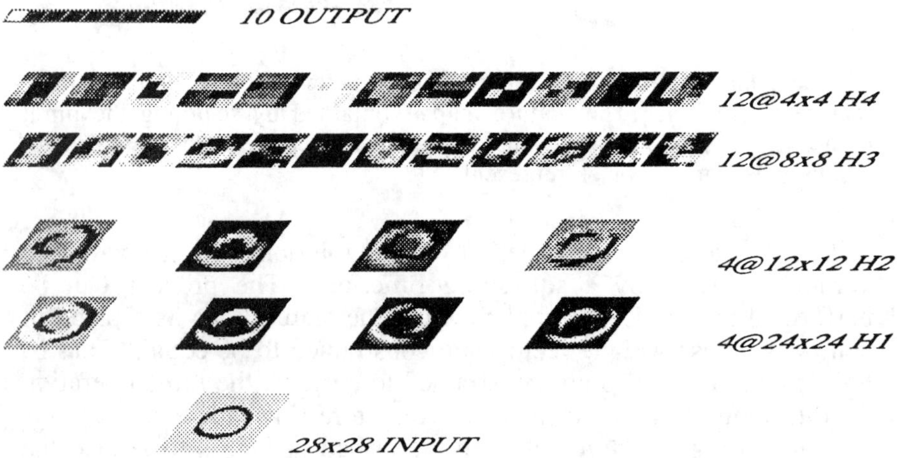

Figure 10.4 Network architecture with five layers of fully adaptive connections.

Although the size of the active part of the input is 16 by 16, the actual input is a 28 by 28 plane to avoid problems when a kernel overlaps a boundary. H1 is composed of four groups of 576 units arranged as four independent 24 by 24 feature maps. These four feature maps will be designated by H1.1, H1.2, H1.3 and H1.4. Each unit in a feature map takes its input from a 5 by 5 neighbourhood on the input plane. As described above, corresponding connections on each unit in a given feature map are constrained to have the same weight. In other words, all of the 576 units in H1.1 use the same set of 26 weights (including the bias). Of course, units in another map (say H1.4) share another set of 26 weights.

Layer H2 is the averaging/subsampling layer. It is composed of four planes of size 12 by 12. Each unit in one of these planes takes inputs on four units on the corresponding plane in H1. Receptive fields do not overlap. All the weights are constrained to be equal, even within a single unit. Therefore, H2 performs a local averaging and a 2 to 1 subsampling of H1 in each direction.

Layer H3 is composed of 12 feature maps. Each feature map contains 64 units arranged in an 8 by 8 plane. As before, these feature maps will be designated as H2.1, H2.2 ... H2.12. The connection scheme betwen H2 and H3 is quite similar to the one between the input and H1, but slightly more complicated because H3 has multiple 2-D maps. Each unit receptive field is composed of one or two 5 by 5 neighbourhoods centred around units that are at identical positions within each H2 maps. Of course, all units in a given map are constrained to have identical weight vectors. The maps in H2 on which a map in H3 takes its inputs are chosen according to a scheme described on Table 10.1. According to this scheme, the network is composed of two almost independent modules. Layer H4 plays the same role as layer H2; it is composed of 12 groups of 16 units arranged in 4 by 4 planes.

Table 10.1 Connections between H2 and H3.

	1	2	3	4	5	6	7	8	9	10	11	12
1	X	X	X		X	X						
2		X	X	X	X	X						
3							X	X	X		X	X
4								X	X	X	X	X

The output layer has 10 units and is fully connected to H4. In summary, the network has 4635 units, 98 442 connections, and 2578 independent parameters. This architecture was derived using the Optimal Brain Damage technique [10] starting from a previous architecture [9] that had four times more free parameters.

10.6 Results

After 30 training passes the error rate on training set (7291 handwritten plus 2549 printed digits) was 1.1% and the MSE was 0.017. On the whole test set (2007 handwritten plus 700 printed characters) the error rate was 3.4% and the MSE was 0.024. All the classification errors occurred on handwritten characters.

In a realistic application, the user is not so much interested in the raw error rate as in the number of rejections necessary to reach a given level of accuracy. In our case, we measured the percentage of test patterns that must be rejected in order to get 1% error rate. Our rejection criterion was based on three conditions: the activity level of the most active output unit should by larger than a given threshold t_1 the activity level of the second most active unit should be smaller than a given threshold t_2 and finally, the difference between the activity levels of these two units should be larger than a given threshold t_d. The best percentage of rejections on the complete test set was 5.7% for 1% error. On the handwritten set only, the result was 9% rejections for 1% error. It should be emphasized that the rejection thresholds were obtained using performance measures on the test set. About half the substitution errors in the testing set were due to faulty segmentation, and an additional quarter were due to erroneous assignment of the desired category. Some of the remaining images were ambiguous even to humans, and in a few cases the network misclassified the image for no discernible reason.

Even though a second-order version of back-propagation was used, it is interesting to note that the learning takes only 30 passes through the training set. We think this can be attributed to the large amount of redundancy present in real data. A complete training session (30 passes through the training set plus test) takes about three days on a SUN SPARCstation 1 using the SN2 connectionist simulator [11].

After successful training, the network was implemented on a commercial Digital Signal Processor board containing an AT&T DSP-32C general purpose DSP chip with a peak performance of 12.5 million multiply-add operations per second on 32-bit floating point numbers. The DSP operates as a coprocessor in a PC connected to a video camera. The PC performs the digitization, binarization and segmentation of the image, while the DSP performs the size-normalization and the classification. The overall throughput of the digit recognizer including image acquisition is 10 to 12 classifications per second and is limited mainly by the normalization step. On normalized digits, the DSP performs more than 30 classifications per second.

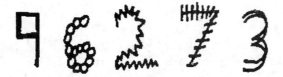

Figure 10.5 Atypical data. The network classifies these correctly, even though they are quite unlike anything in the training set.

10.7 Conclusion

Back-propagation learning was successfully applied to a large, real-world task. Our results appear to be at the state-of-the-art in handwritten digit recognition. The network had many connections but relatively few free parameters. The network architecture and the constraints on the weights were designed to incorporate geometric knowledge about the task into the system. Because of its architecture, the network could be trained on a low-level representation of data that had minimal pre-processing (as opposed to elaborate feature extraction). Because of the redundant nature of the data and because of the constraints imposed on the network, the learning time was relatively short considering the size of the training set. Scaling properties were far better than one would expect just from extrapolating results of back-propagation on smaller, artificial problems. Preliminary results on alphanumeric characters show that the method can be directly extended to larger tasks.

The final network of connections and weights obtained by back-propagation learning was readily implementable on commercial digital signal processing hardware. Throughput rates, from camera to classified image, of more than ten digits per second were obtained.

Acknowledgements

We thank the US Postal Service and its contractors for providing us with the zipcode database. We thank Henry Baird for useful discussions and for providing the printed-font database.

References

1. Denker, J.S., Gardner, W.R., Graf, H.P., Henderson, D., Howard, R.E., Hubbard, W., Jackel, L.D., Baird, H.S. and Guyon, I. Neural network recognizer for handwritten zip code digits. In Touretzky, D. (ed.). *Neural Information Processing Systems*, Volume 1, 323-331, Morgan Kaufman, Denver, (1988).

2. Le Cun, Y. Generalization and network design strategies. In Pfeifer, R., Schreter, Z., Fogelman, F. and Steels, L. (eds.). *Connectionism in Perspective*, Elsevier, Zurich (1989).

3. Denker, J., Schwartz, D., Wittner, B., Solla, S.A., Howard, R., Jackel, L. and Hopfield, J. Large automatic learning, rule extraction and generalization. *Complex Systems*, 1, 877-922 (1987).

4. Patarnello, S. and Carnevali, P. Learning networks of neurons with Boolean logic. *Europh. Lett.*, 4, 4, 503-508 (1987).

5. Tishby, N., Levin, E. and Solla, S.A. Consistent inference of probabilities in layered networks: predictions and generalization. *Proc. of the Int. Joint Conf. on Neural Networks*, Washington, DC (1989).

6. Wang, C.H. and Srihari, S.N. A framework for object recognition in a visually complex environment and its application to locating address blocks on mail pieces. *Int. J. of Comp. Vis.*, 2, 125 (1988).

7. Rumelhart, D.E., Hinton, G.E and Williams, R.J. Learning internal representations by error propagation. In Rumelhart, D.E. and McClelland, J.L. *Parallel Distributed Processing: Explorations in the Microstructure of Cognition*, Volume 1, 318-362, Bradford Books, Cambridge, MA (1986).

8. Fukushima, K. and Miyake, S. Neocognitron: a new algorithm for pattern recognition tolerant of deformations and shifts in position. *Patt. Rec.*, 15, 455-469 (1982).

9. Le Cun, Y., Boser, B., Denker, J.S., Henderson, D., Howard, R.E., Hubbard, W. and Jackel, L.D. Back-propagation applied to handwritten zipcode recognition. *Neural Computation*, 1, 4 (1990).

10. Le Cun, Y., Denker, J.S., Solla, S., Howard, R.E. and Jackel, L.D. Optimal brain damage. In Touretzky, D. (ed.). *Neural Information Processing Systems*, Volume 2, Morgan Kaufman, Denver (1989).

11. Bottou, L.Y. and Le Cun, Y. *SN2: A Simulator for Connectionist Models*, Neuristique SA, Paris, France (1989).

11

Higher-order neural networks for invariant pattern recognition

S. J. Perantonis
University of Liverpool, England

11.1 Summary

The implementation of different types of neural networks for the recognition of patterns irrespective of their position, orientation and size is discussed. The networks studied include the Hopfield model and the autoassociating layered perceptron, high-order networks and layered networks used as classifiers of features extracted by the method of moments. The relative strengths and weaknesses of the different approaches are pointed out and illustrated through digit recognition applications.

11.2 Introduction

The aim of invariant pattern recognition research is to develop flexible systems which can recognize images irrespective of their position, orientation and size. In addition, these systems should ideally exhibit some degree of tolerance to mild shape variation, distortion and corruption by noise. Recent developments in the area of neural network research have led to a multitude of new ideas and approaches to pattern recognition in general (for a comprehensive review of the literature, see reference [1]). In this paper we present some neural network-based approaches to the problem of invariant pattern recognition in particular.

A class of neural network models for invariant pattern recognition comprises associative memory models, in which the nominated patterns occupy minima of appropriately defined energy or cost functions. In these models, the network dynamics during the pattern recollection phase play an important role in associating transformed versions of the nominated patterns to the original versions on which the networks have been trained. In this paper we shall show that even simple autoassociating neural network models, such as the Hopfield network and the perceptron, can exhibit some ability for invariant pattern recognition with a suitable retrieval algorithm. We shall implement these models for recognizing digits irrespective of their position and orientation and point out some of the difficulties related to the approach, as well as methods of overcoming these difficulties.

Other neural network-based approaches to invariant pattern recognition involve constraining the synaptic weights to achieve invariant output, or extracting invariant features from the images which are then classified using a neural network classifier. These approaches are often equivalent, as we illustrate in the case of neural networks of high order. We introduce a method of controlling the number of weights in a network of the third order designed for translation, rotation and scaling invariant recognition. The method leads to the construction of networks with a relatively small number of weights which are tolerant to the shape distortion. We also compare the performance of our third-order network to that of a network which processes invariant features extracted by the method of moments.

11.3 Invariant 'dynamical' associative memories

In the Hopfield network [2] the energy function

$$\xi = -\frac{1}{2} \sum_{i,j} w_{ij} \, s_i s_j \qquad (11.1)$$

acquires locally minimal values for the spin configurations corresponding to the stored patterns. Here s_i are the inputs of the network nodes and w_{ij} are the synaptic weights, which are adjusted using the Hebb rule [2] to reinforce the storage of a number P of bit patterns T^β ($\beta=1,2,...,P$) nominated for memorization. The recollection process then consists of an attempt to minimize the energy so that the nominated patterns can be retrieved. In particular, the usual iterative recollection algorithm

$$s_i \rightarrow \text{sgn}(\Sigma_j \, w_{ij} s_j) \qquad\qquad (11.2)$$

is an energy minimization process which retrieves the nominated patterns from corrupted or incomplete versions, provided that they are stored with sufficient basins of attraction.

There has been some interest in generalizations of the Hopfield model which can serve as invariant associative memories, whereby the nominated patterns can be retrieved from corrupted versions even when these have undergone coordinate transformations, notably translations, rotations and scaling transformations. In these models, the nominated patterns occupy the minima of an appropriately defined energy function and transformed versions of the nominated patterns fall within the basins of attraction surrounding these minima, so that an appropriate energy minimization algorithm can regenerate a nominated pattern from these versions.

In particular, Bienenstock and von der Malsburg [3,4] and Kree and Zippelius [5] have proposed models in which the problem of pattern recognition is formalized as a problem of labelled graph matching. These authors use neural networks whose synaptic weights depend on a superposition of the nominated graphs and define Hamiltonians (energy functions), the minimization of which leads in principle to the 'correct' nominated graph. A simpler approach has been introduced by Dotsenko [6] who has proposed using the energy function of the Hopfield model and attempting minimization in two stages. In the first stage (stage A), a transformed (shifted, rotated or scaled) and corrupted version s of one of the nominated patterns T^β is presented to the network and minimization of the energy function is attempted using only transformed (shifted, rotated or scaled) versions of this pattern. It is proposed that under this process the pattern s will be gradually transformed until it reaches the location (or orientation, or size) of the nominated pattern T^β. Once this has been achieved, the usual recollection algorithm of equation (11.2) will produce the nominated pattern itself (stage B). Dotsenko has also described how these two stages can be combined using a single model very similar to the original Hopfield model.

In the following sections we study the capability of the Hopfield model as a system for translation and rotation-invariant recognition. To this end, we adopt Dotsenko's suggestions, but keep the two stages in the recollection process separate, so that we can point out some of the problems related to the approach. To overcome some of the difficulties which we encounter in studying the invariant associative memory properties of the Hopfield model, we propose using a feedforward network (perceptron) trained by gradient descent as an invariant associative memory, with an appropriately defined cost function which we attempt to minimize in stage A of the recollection process. We illustrate our arguments by implementing both the Hopfield network and the perceptron in experiments using numerals as the nominated patterns. Finally, we suggest that the size and shape of the basins of attraction for stage A of the recollection process can be improved by 'smoothing' or 'fuzzing' the images presented to the networks as input and provide an algorithm for achieving this.

11.4 Invariant associative memory properties of the Hopfield network and the autoassociating perceptron

Restriction of the available phase space of the spin variables s_i to the states which are transformed versions of the state presented to the network in stage A of pattern recollection reduces the problem to the minimization of the Hopfield energy with respect to a few parameters (say the Cartesian coordinates x, y for translation and an angle for rotation). If the system has been trained using the Hebb rule [2], the energy of a state vector s presented to the network as input can be written as

$$\xi = -N^2 \sum_{\beta} \left(\frac{1}{N} \sum_{i} T_i^{\beta} s_i^{\beta}\right)^2 = -N^2 \sum_{\beta} [\mathcal{M}^{\beta}(s)]^2 \tag{11.3}$$

where $\mathcal{M}^{\beta}(s)$ is the overlap between the pattern s and the nominated pattern T^{β}. Let us first consider the storage of just one pattern by the system. For a pattern of finite correlation length, for which most of the active pixels are concentrated around a 'centre of mass' point, the overlap between the pattern itself and successive versions of it translated by a vector $r_0 = (x_0, y_0)$ has its maximum at $r_0 = 0$ (and therefore the energy has a minimum at this point) and it is reasonable to expect it to decrease (and the energy to increase) progressively as we move away from the point $r_0 = 0$ in the direction opposite to that of the gradient in a region round $r_0 = 0$ [6]. Thus a basin of attraction is formed around $r_0 = 0$. It is then hoped that mild corruption of the image will not significantly alter the shape of the basin of attraction, so that if a corrupted and translated version of the stored image is proposed to the network, a corrupted (but not translated) version of the stored image itself can be reached in stage A before the image is cleaned up from distortion or noise by the recollection algorithm of equation (11.2) in stage B. Similar considerations can be made for the rotation of patterns.

Approximate symmetries, or similarities in shape between an image and a transformed version of it, limit the range of the basins of attraction. If such symmetries or similarities exist, the overlap between an image and certain of its transformed versions is high and additional minima are created preventing the energy minimization process from finding the desired minimum. In practical problems, discrete-step minimization algorithms, whereby patterns are moved in successive steps towards directions in the x,y plane and changes in pattern orientation v, for which the energy decreases, can be used to reach the desired minima [7].

Turning to the problem of storing more than one pattern, we note that the energy function is expressed as a sum of squares of overlaps between the current state vector and each of the nominated state vectors (equation (11.3)). As has been pointed out by Dotsenko [6], it is desirable that throughout stage A of the recollection algorithm the state vectors of the network have a finite overlap with a certain nominated pattern T^β and a comparatively small overlap with the other nominated patterns, so that attraction will take place. This is a stringent constraint on the topological features of the patterns which can be recognized by the system. Alternatively, adequate basins of attraction for translation and rotation-invariant recognition can be formed, provided that the system is trained using versions of the nominated patterns at approximately the same position (say at the centre of the screen) and orientation. A good example of patterns which can be taught in this way is provided by a set of numerals ranging from '0' to '9' (Fig. 11.1).

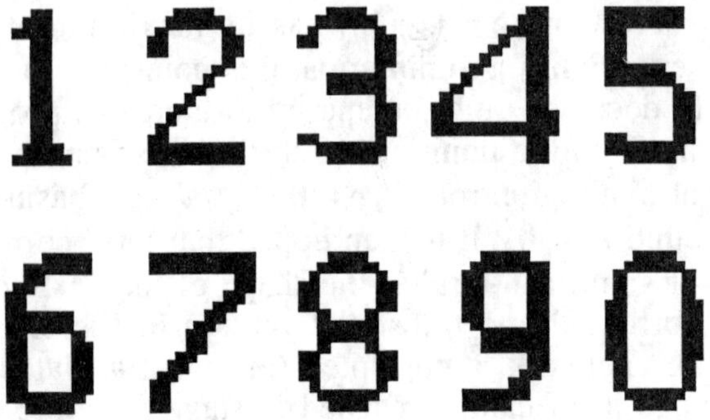

Figure 11.1 Patterns representing digits from '0' to '9' used as the nominated state vectors for training the Hopfield network and the perceptron.

The process of locating the 'correct' minimum during stage A of the recollection algorithm can then be described as follows: in a first step, the individual features of each pattern are ignored by the system, which attempts to reach the general area of the screen where the nominated patterns were located and to match the general orientation of these patterns. Once this has been achieved, the individual features of each pattern come into effect and the system is driven towards the minimum in energy which corresponds to the correct pattern. Thus the topological structure of the nominated patterns and a degree of similarity in the structure of different nominated patterns is essential for the success of stage A of the recollection process.

Unfortunately, this means that the nominated patterns must be correlated and it is well known that the storage capacity of the Hopfield model for correlated patterns is small [8]. This problem can be resolved by using – instead of the Hopfield network – a perceptron with an equal number of input and output nodes which is trained through gradient back-propagation (GBP) [9,10] as an autoassociative memory [11–13]. An appropriate cost function which can replace the energy function of the Hopfield model during stage A of the recollection process is equal to the sum of the squares of the differences between the outputs of the network and the corresponding input values.

$$E_r = \sum_i (O_i - S_i)^2. \tag{11.4}$$

The nominated patterns correspond to global minima of E_r. The advantage of the perceptron relative to the Hopfield model is that during the training process the input nominated patterns are very strongly correlated to the outputs of the network, so that there is no interference from 'noise' from other patterns at the location of the minimum of E_r, and hopefully, in a region in (x,y,υ) around this location. The retrieval of the nominated patterns from transformed and corrupted versions is once more achieved in two stages: in stage A, minimization of E_r is attempted in the space of transformed versions of the input pattern, while in stage B a recursive recollection algorithm involving feedback of the network output into its input [11,12] is activated to clean the image of any noise or distortion.

11.5 Digit recognition using the Hopfield network and the autoassociating perceptron

Ten nominated patterns representing digits ranging from '0' to '9' on a 20 by 20 pixel screen are shown in Fig. 11.1. These are used to train a Hopfield network using the Hebb rule and a perceptron with one or two layers of nodes using the cost function of equation (11.4) and the GBP algorithm. The ability of the networks to recognize translated, rotated and noisy versions of the ten nominated digits is subsequently tested. Periodic boundary conditions are used with respect to translation.

For the Hopfield model, typical energy landscapes for stage A are shown in Fig. 11.2.

It is evident that basins of attraction of some extension around the minimum are formed. However, the minimum is in some cases displaced relative to the desired position (corresponding to the location or orientation of the nominated pattern) due to the interference of other nominated patterns (Fig. 11.2(b)). Notice also the additional unwanted minima which are formed due to approximate symmetries and interference. We test the ability of the model to reach the position of the nominated patterns when initialized with versions of these patterns translated in the x and y directions by a number of pixels chosen with uniform random distribution in the regions $\{-6,6\}$ and $\{-4,4\}$ respectively. This corresponds to translations for which the whole image remains on the screen (without use of the boundary conditions). The experiment is repeated for images rotated through angles with uniform random distribution in the range $\{-2\pi/5,2\pi/5\}$.

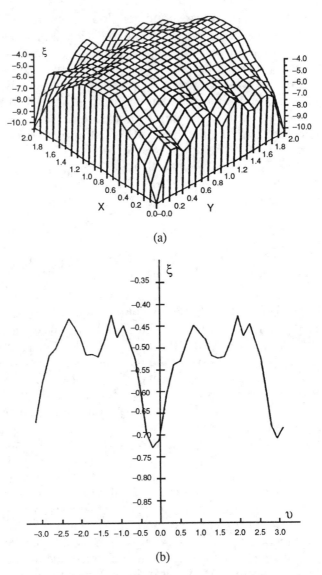

(a)

(b)

Figure 11.2 Typical energy landscapes for transformed versions of nominated patterns for the Hopfield network. (a) Energy landscape for translated versions of the nominated pattern representing the digit '5'. Periodic boundary conditions are used, so that the location of the nominated pattern corresponds to the four corners of the grid. (b) The energy as a function of the angle of rotation υ for successive rotations of a version of the digit '7' initially rotated by $2\pi/5$ with respect to the nominated pattern. The location of the nominated pattern corresponds to $\upsilon = 0$.

The results, shown in Table 11.1, show partial recollection success, but confirm that in some cases either the minimum is displaced from the position of the nominated pattern or the size of the basins of attraction is inadequate. Moreover, we find that the nominated patterns are very highly correlated, so that they are unstable with respect to stage B: even when stage A transforms the input patterns correctly, stage B often leads to spurious states which are admixtures of the nominated states [8].

Table 11.1 Success rate for the recollection of translated or rotated versions of the digits in Fig. 11.1 by the Hopfield network and of translated, rotated and noisy versions of these digits by the autoassociating SLP. The range of the shift and rotation parameters over which recollection is attempted is given in the text.

Hopfield network (stage A)		
Noise	*Success rate*	
(pixels)	*Translation*	*Rotation*
0	76	52

SLP (stages A and B)			
Noise	*Success rate*		
(pixels)	*Translation*	*Rotation*	*Combined*
0	90	93	54
10	88	86	44
20	78	84	40
40	69	81	34

A single-layered perceptron (SLP), on the other hand, exhibits better performance than the Hopfield model with respect to similar pattern retrieval tasks. Typical cost function landscapes for stage A are shown in Fig. 11.3.

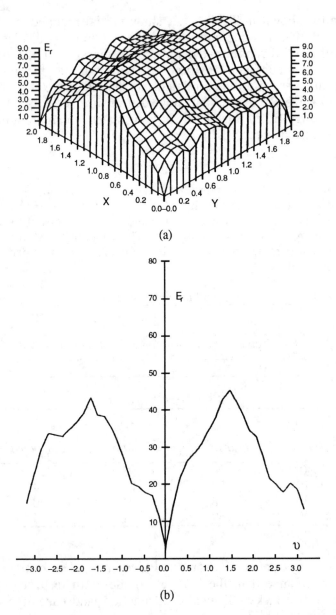

(a)

(b)

Figure 11.3 Typical cost function landscapes for (a) translated and (b) rotated versions of nominated patterns stored by the SLP. The digits '5' and '7' are used as in Fig. 11.2.

Basins of attraction look similar to those of the Hopfield model, but are in general more extended, especially for the retrieval of rotated patterns. Moreover, patterns correctly transformed in stage A of the recollection process are easily associated to one of the nominated patterns in stage B. Success rates for the retrieval of translated and/or rotated versions of the nominated patterns by the SLP after the completion of stages A and B of the recollection process are also shown in Table 11.1. Satisfactory results are obtained for separate translation and rotation (respective success rates of 90% and 93%), although the ability for retrieval of patterns both translated and rotated is relatively poor (success rate of 54%). Results for retrieval from translated and/or versions of the nominated patterns, to which noise has been superimposed by reversing a number of pixels on the screen are also presented in Table 11.1. These results indicate that the basins of attraction around the minimum are not destroyed when corrupted images are presented to the network, although their size is gradually reduced as the amount of noise increases.

No appreciable improvement in performance was recorded when a multi-layered perceptron (MLP) was used instead of a single-layered one. Thus, the only advantage of the MLP over the SLP remains its superior capacity of retrieval in stage B of the recollection algorithm [11], although this is not reflected in these experiments due to the small number of nominated states, with which the SLP is perfectly capable of coping.

11.6 The role of image fuzzing in improving the basins of attraction

The basins of attraction around the minimum for stage A of the recollection process can be improved if the nominated patterns are represented by functions of the coordinates which change gradually, rather than abruptly, as we move from a pixel to its nearest neighbours. An image represented by a binary state vector can be converted into a smooth image – without loss of its essential features by which it can be distinguished from other images – through a fuzzing algorithm. Fuzzy images would then be used to train a neural network as an invariant associative memory. During the recollection phase, an image proposed to the network should be converted into a fuzzy image and then subjected to stages A and B of an energy or cost function minimization algorithm. For example, Fuchs and Haken [14] have proposed representing an image by a truncated series expansion in a complete set of orthonormal functions. They have illustrated the technique using a neural network with analogue nodes and a truncated expansion in spherical harmonics for the purpose of recognizing a rotated image. Similarly, a truncated Fourier expansion can be used for the recognition of translated images. In both cases the appropriate expansion is selected, so that fuzzing will produce an image of the same shape irrespective of the orientation (for rotation-invariant memory) or the position (for translation-invariant memory) of the original image. This 'image-centred' fuzzing is essential so that a transformed version of a nominated pattern which is presented to the network for recall will resemble – after being properly transformed during stage A of the recollection algorithm – the original fuzzed image on which the network has been trained.

Such 'image-centred' fuzzing cannot be achieved by expansion in Fourier modes or spherical harmonics when combined translations and rotations of images are considered. A fuzzing technique which can be used for combined translations and rotations involves adding to the value of each pixel i a multiple of the values of all pixels which are situated in a circle of radius r_c with its centre at $r(i)=(x(i),y(i))$. Under this fuzzing algorithm a pattern s is fuzzed to produce a new pattern s' as follows:

$$s'_i = J \left(s_i + \xi \sum_{\substack{j \in c(i) \\ j \neq i}} F(|r(j) - r(i)|) \, s_i\right). \tag{11.5}$$

Here ξ is a constant and F is a function of the distance from the centre of the circle. The fuzzing procedure can be carried out iteratively a number of times N_F using the same algorithm, until a smooth enough image is obtained. The normalization factor J ensures that no overflow occurs during this process. Similar fuzzing techniques are used in field theory for constructing smooth operators on a lattice [15–17]. In Fig. 11.4 we show the effect of successive fuzzing operations on the image representing the digit '5' using $\xi = 0.02$, $F(r) = 1/r$ (with r measured in lattice spacings), different fuzzing levels N_F and circles of radius $r_c = 2$ (measured in units of the distance between adjacent pixels).

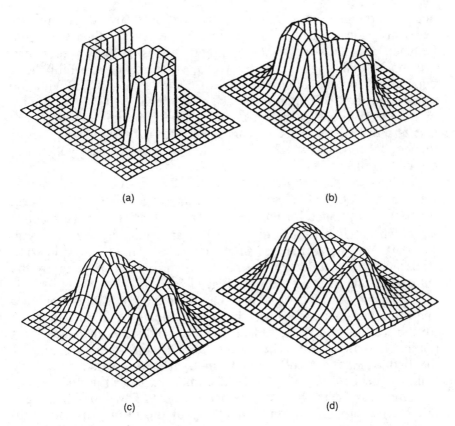

(a)

(b)

(c)

(d)

Figure 11.4 The pattern representing the digit '5' and 'fuzzy' versions of this pattern corresponding to different values of the fuzzing level N_F are shown. The values $\xi = 0.02$ and $r_c = 2$ are used. (a) $N_F = 0$ (original pattern). (b) $N_F = 5$. (c) $N_F = 10$. (d) $N_F = 15$.

This fuzzing technique satisfies the condition of shape invariance under translations. Shape invariance under rotations is only approximate for small values of r_c, because of the coarseness of the screen grid. However, with $r_c \geq 2$ we find that shape invariance under rotations is adequately restored and good results for the recognition of rotated images can be obtained.

We have used fuzzy versions of the digits in Fig. 11.1 to train an SLP for autoassociation and carry out stage A of the recollection process. Unfortunately, stage B cannot be carried out using the same network, because the pixel values of the fuzzed patterns are not close to the saturation values of the logistic activation function of the network nodes and the nominated patterns are therefore not necessarily locally stable [11]. However, the fuzzing algorithm could be used for networks with analogue nodes [14,18] which can accomplish both stages A and B. We do not study this possibility here, but complement the autoassociating SLP with a second SLP with 400 input nodes and 10 output nodes which is trained by GBP to produce output equal to one at the ith output node for the ith fuzzed pattern and zero otherwise. This network is used for carrying out stage B of the recollection process after stage A has been completed by the auto-associating SLP.

We have considered different values of r_c, ξ and N_F. For $r_c = 2$, we find that for $\xi = 0.02$ and for N_F in the range 5–10 we can obtain the best performance for recall. For N_F greater than 10, the features by which patterns can be distinguished are gradually lost (see Fig. 11.4(d)) and performance deteriorates. Typical cost function landscapes for recollection of translated and rotated patterns by the autoassociating SLP are shown in Fig. 11.5.

The basins of attraction around the minimum are always smoother and often more extended than the corresponding basins of attraction for the SLP trained with unfuzzed patterns and some unwanted local minima are eliminated. The success rate of the system consisting of the two SLPs for recollection from translated, rotated and noisy patterns is shown in Table 11.2. The improvement in performance – in comparison with the performance of the SLP without fuzzing – reflects the broadening and smoothing of the basins of attraction. Moreover, the system is now able to cope more effectively with noisy versions of the nominated patterns. However, despite the marked improvement, the system still encounters difficulties in coping with the task of recalling patterns which are both translated and rotated.

Table 11.2 Success rate for the recollection of translated, rotated and noisy versions of the digits in Fig. 11.1 by SLPs using fuzzy images as discussed in the text.

Noise	Success rate		
(pixels)	Translation	Rotation	Combined
0	100	97	70
10	100	94	66
20	100	93	60
40	96	90	52

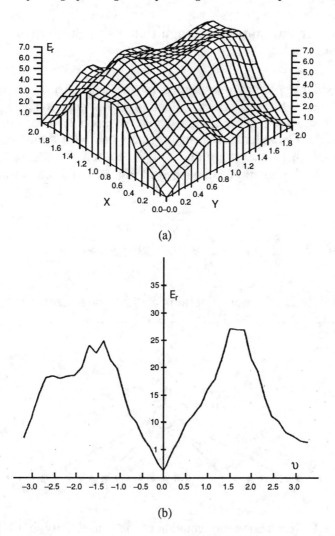

(a)

(b)

Figure 11.5 Typical cost function landscapes for (a) translated and (b) rotated versions of fuzzy nominated patterns stored by the SLP. The patterns representing the digits '5' and '7' are used here as in Figs 11.2 and 11.3. The fuzzing parameters are $r_c = 2$, $\xi = 0.02$ and $N_F = 5$.

11.7 Invariant pattern recognition using high-order networks

We consider a pattern represented by the values s_i of its pixels $i = 1,2,...,N$, on an N-pixel screen. Each pixel i is regarded as a point on a regular square grid or lattice whose position is determined by a vector $r(i)$. Consider now a natural network with a single layer of weights which processes products of the form $s_{i_1}s_{i_2}...s_{i_p}$ (network of order p). In the notation established in Fig. 11.6, the output of a node j is of the form

$$O_j(s) = f(\sum_{i_1} \sum_{i_2} \cdots \sum_{i_p} w_{i_1 i_2 \cdots i_p j} s_{i_1} s_{i_2} \cdots s_{i_p}) \tag{11.6}$$

where f is the activation function for the formal neurones (we shall use the logistic function $f(x) = 1/[1+\exp(-x)]$).

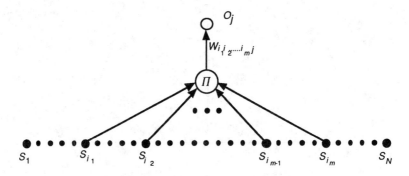

Figure 11.6 Schematic representation of the connectivity in a high-order network with one layer of weights.

Let ξ be a group of coordinate transformations realizable on the pixel lattice, under which we wish O_j to be invariant. An example is the group of translations by vectors whose components are multiples of the spacing between pixels. It can be shown [19] that O_j will be invariant under the action of all elements in ξ if the weights of the network are chosen according to the equation

$$w_{i_1 i_2 \cdots i_p j} = w_{k_1 k_2 \cdots k_p j} \tag{11.7}$$

provided that there exists an element of ξ through which $r(i_m)$ and $r(k_m)$ are related for all $m = 1,2,...,p$. Thus the desired invariance is built into the architecture of the network through the imposition of appropriate constraints on the synaptic weights.

For linear coordinate transformations, equation (11.7) means that in order to ensure invariance, we must set $w_{i_1 i_2 \cdots i_p j} = w_{k_1 k_2 \cdots k_p j}$ whenever the relative coordinates of any pair (i_a, i_b) $(a,b = 1,...,p)$ can be obtained from the relative coordinates of the corresponding pair (k_a, k_b) through a transformation in ξ. For example, to obtain a second-order network which produces output invariant under translation by lattice vectors, we must set equal to each other weights $w_{i_1 i_2 j}$ and $w_{k_1 k_2 j}$ for which the line segments $i_1 i_2$ and $k_1 k_2$ can be transformed to one another through such a translation, i.e. weights for which these segments are equal in length and parallel to each other (Fig. 11.7(a)).

Note that this procedure for building invariance under a group of transformations into the network architecture, assigns p-tuples of points in the plane to equivalence classes ζ_h, $h = 1,2,...$ defined by the classification rule of equation (11.7). We can thus substitute the notation $w_{i_1 i_2 \cdots i_p j}$ for the weights with the notation w_{hj} where h is a collective index corresponding to the class ζ_h. The output of a node in the top layer of the high-order network can now be written as

$$O_j = f\left(\sum W_{hj(i_1,...,i_p) \in \zeta_h} s_{i_1} s_{i_2} ... s_{i_p}\right) \tag{11.8}$$

so that we are effectively dealing with a single-layered feedforward network (perceptron) with weights w_{hj} and effective inputs:

$$I_h = \sum_{(i_1,...,i_p) \in \zeta_h} s_{i_1} s_{i_2} ... s_{i_p} \tag{11.9}$$

representing the invariant features of the images which the network is called upon to classify. Bias terms clearly do not affect the invariance

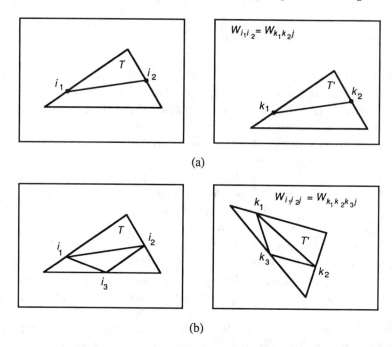

(a)

(b)

Figure 11.7 Rules for constructing high-order networks for invariant pattern recognition. In all cases the triangle T represents an image which the network is called upon to recognize. (a) Translation invariant recognition by a second-order network: for the parallel and equal segments i_1i_2 and k_1k_2 the weights $w_{i_1j_2j}$ and $w_{k_1k_2j}$ are set equal to each other. (b) Translation, rotation and scale invariant recognition by a third-order network: for the similar triangles $i_1i_2i_3$ and $k_1k_2k_3$ the weights $w_{i_1j_2i_3j}$ and $w_{k_1k_2k_3j}$ are set equal to each other. The effective inputs of the network must be normalized as discussed in the text.

properties of the network, nor do subsequent layers of weights. In this way, the network architecture is the same as that of multi-layered first-order feedforward networks, widely studied elsewhere, and additional programming tasks are confined to the determination of the equivalence classes and to the calculation of the effective inputs I_h from s. The network is thus implemented in a feature extractor-classifier mode.

It is evident that exact transformations corresponding to translation by arbitrary vectors r_0, rotation by arbitrary angles υ and scaling by arbitrary factors ρ are not realizable on a square lattice, because under these transformations a lattice point does not necessarily transform on to another lattice point. However, we can use schemes involving the lattice points closest to the continuum transform. It should be noted that such 'lattice transformations' do not necessarily form a group, but rather have the mathematical structure of a 'loop' [20], so that the above considerations are not directly applicable. For example, neighbouring lattice points may be mapped on to the same lattice point under a lattice scaling transformation which is thus non-invertible. We can nevertheless utilize some of the main points in the discussion above to build networks which ensure approximate invariance under translation, scaling and rotation.

Recognition of translated, rotated and scaled patterns can be achieved using a third-order network. Output approximately invariant to all three transformations can be obtained if any two weights $w_{i_1 i_2 i_3 j}$ and $w_{k_1 k_2 k_3 j}$ are set equal whenever the triangles with vertices at i_1, i_2, i_3 and k_1, k_2, k_3 respectively can be transformed into each other by a combined translation, scaling and rotation [19,21]. This means that the two triangles must be similar to each other with their equal angles encountered in the same order when the perimeters of the triangles are transversed in a counterclockwise manner (Fig. 11.7(b)). In addition, the effective inputs of the network must be normalized to a standard Euclidean length, in order to compensate for a multiplicative factor ρ^6 brought about by scaling transformations [19].

Second-order networks with outputs invariant under translation have been implemented for associative memory [22] and pattern recognition [23] applications. In addition, a second-order neural network with automatic translation and scaling invariance able to recognize the characters T and C irrespective of position and size with 100% accuracy was presented in reference [21]. In this work we concentrate on invariance under translations, rotations and scaling transformations simultaneously. We shall thus implement a third-order network, suitably augmented by a method for the reduction of the number of weights which we discuss forthwith.

A problem inherent in high-order networks is the combinatorial increase of the number of weights with the order of the network. Indeed, this was the reason why Minsky and Papert dismissed high-order networks as impractical in the 1960s [24]. Building invariances into a third-order network by assigning similar triangles to the same equivalence class leads to a reduction of the number of weights – or, equivalently, of the number N_I of effective inputs. However, this classification scheme does not allow the user to vary the number of effective inputs or the size of the network independently of the number of pixels on the screen. Even on relatively coarse screens, the scheme leads to a large number of effective inputs and weights. Moreover, it is very sensitive to the mild distortions that a triangle defined on the screen can suffer if subjected to an approximate lattice rotation or scaling transformation. This is clearly not a satisfactory situation. What is needed is a classification scheme which can lead to a relatively small number of invariant features controllable independently of the screen resolution and which is relatively insensitive to the distortion of images brought about through lattice coordinate transformations.

A simple scheme adopted here involves classifying 'approximately similar' triangles into the same equivalence class. 'Approximately similar' triangles will be characterized by the same value of their two smallest angles within a finite tolerance ω. More specifically, let us consider the set of all triangles which can be defined on the screen and denote their angles by α, β, γ with $\alpha \leq \beta \leq \gamma$. The set ζ_1 of triangles for which α and β are encountered in immediate succession and in that order when the triangle is transversed in a counterclockwise manner must be considered separately from the set ζ_2 consisting of the inverted images of these triangles, if we do not want to impose additional inversion invariance on our system. The following relations are obeyed by α and β

$$\alpha \leq \beta, \ 0 \leq \alpha \leq \pi/3, \ 0 \leq \beta < \pi/2, \ 0 \leq \beta + \alpha/2 \leq \pi/2. \tag{11.10}$$

We choose an angular tolerance ω so that $W = \pi/(3\omega)$ and $Q = \pi/(2\omega)$ are integers, and partition the sets of possible values of α and β into bins defined by

$$(k-1)\omega \leq \alpha < k\omega, \ (l-1)\omega \leq \beta \leq l\omega, \ 1 \leq k \leq W, \ 1 \leq l \leq Q \tag{11.11}$$

Finally, we assign all triangles whose angles satisfy relations (11.11) for given values of k and l to the same equivalence class.

This classification scheme is illustrated in Fig. 11.8 for $\omega = \pi/2$ and for the triangles belonging to ζ_1.

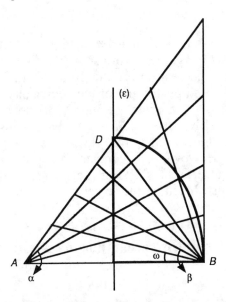

Figure 11.8 Schematic representation of the partitioning of the set of triangles defined on the screen into classes of approximately similar triangles for the purpose of invariant pattern recognition using a third-order network.

The segment *AB* represents the side of the triangle *ABC* adjacent to the smallest and next smallest angles α and β. The lines emerging from points *A* and *B* define the boundaries of the bins in which the range of α and β is partitioned. The intersections of these lines define triangular and quadrilateral regions, so that all triangles in a given region are classified in the same equivalence class. Note that relations (11.10) must be obeyed, so that non-empty classes correspond only to regions in the area bounded by the bold line in Fig. 11.8 which consists of the segment *AB*, its perpendicular bisector (ε) and the arc *BD* of the circle with its centre at *A* corresponding to an angle of $\pi/3$.

It can be shown [19] that the number of effective inputs of the network, which is equal to the number of non-empty equivalence classes, is given by the equation

$$N_I = \frac{2Q(Q + 2)}{3} = \frac{\pi(4\pi + \pi)}{6\omega^2}.$$

(11.12)

Finally, we note that as ω increases and N_I decreases, the average area of the regions in Fig. 11.8 corresponding to each class increases. Consequently, it becomes more unlikely that mild distortions of the shape of a triangle will push it out of the equivalence class to which it originally belongs. The effective inputs of the network therefore become less sensitive to mild image distortions, including the distortions brought about by lattice scaling and rotation transformations. However, this conclusion applies only to structured distortion which affects the shape of the image. It does not apply to noise randomly distributed on the screen.

11.8 Invariant pattern recognition by the method of moments

In selecting a suitable invariant pattern recognition system with which to compare the performance of our third-order network, we decided to make use of a system utilizing the so called Zernike moments – suitably normalized – as the invariant features and a (possibly multilayered) feedforward neural network as the classifier.

Moments and invariant functions of moments have been extensively used for invariant feature extraction in a wide range of two- and three-dimensional pattern recognition applications (see [25–31] and references cited in [31]). Pattern recognition results from moment-based methods compare well with the results of other popular invariant feature extraction schemes, e.g. Fourier descriptor analysis [29]. Of the various types of moments defined in the literature (regular, Zernike, pseudo-Zernike, Legendre, rotational and complex moments), Zernike and pseudo-Zernike moments have been shown to be superior to the others in terms of their insensitivity to image noise, information content and ability of faithful image representation [31]. Moreover, a scheme of image representation using Zernike moments was studied by Khotanzad and Hong [30] and shown to yield superior results to other moment-based methods in an invariant character-recognition task. We therefore adopt this scheme as our bais for comparison with invariant third-order neural networks.

The scheme involves the use of the moduli of the Zernike moments of images as invariant features. These quantities are invariant under rotation only, so that the image has to be initially normalized to compensate for the effects of translation and scaling. This is done using low-order regular moments. The Zernike moments are characterized by their order n and multiplicity m. From the point of view of pattern recognition it is useful to approximate the image by using a finite number of Zernike moments, with order less than or equal to n^*. The value of n^* can be chosen so that a substantial proportion of the image (say 90%) can be reconstructed using these moments. Details of the formalism of Zernike moments and their application to pattern recognition can be found in references [19] and [30].

As regards the choice of classifier, it is by now established that multi-layered neural networks are able to match, and often improve upon the performance of conventional classifiers [1] in a large number of applications, including invariant character recognition via the method of moments [32]. Moreover, the use of a common neural network architecture facilitates the comparison between the two approaches (high-order networks versus moments) to the problem of invariant pattern recognition addressed in this paper.

In short, the scheme for invariant pattern classification referred to in this section involves the following steps:

1. adjustment of all images for translation and scaling using low-order regular moments.
2. calculation of the moduli of Zernike moments for the adjusted images which are used as invariant features representing the original images.
3. classification of the images by inputting the invariant features to a (possibly multi-layered) feedforward network with an adjustable number of hidden nodes and a number of output nodes equal to the total number of classes to which the images belong.

11.9 Digit recognition using third-order networks and Zernike moment classifiers

We have implemented the following types of networks to recognize images representing typed and handwritten digits '0' to '8'* (Figs 11.9 and 11.11) on a $N = 20^2$ pixel screen.

---

*No image is included to represent '9', which can obviously be obtained from '6' by rotation.

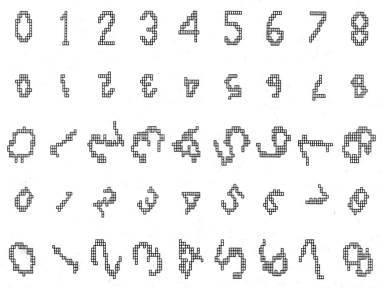

Figure 11.9 A set of typed numerals used to train TONs and ZFCs. All digits are rotated and scaled versions of those shown in the first row.

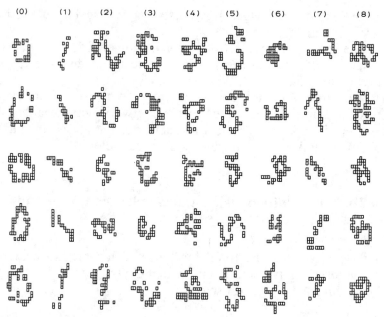

Figure 11.10 Scaled, rotated and locally distorted versions of the digits in the first row of Fig. 11.9 correctly recognized by a third-order network with 32 effective inputs and 40 hidden nodes.

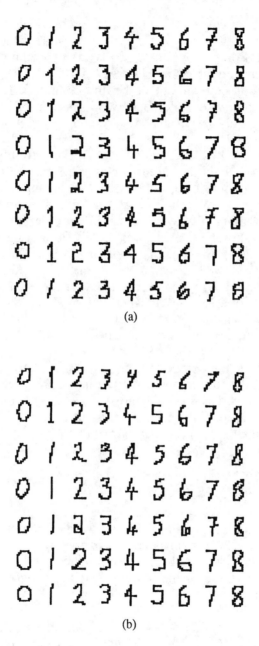

(a)

(b)

Figure 11.11 Two sets of handwritten numerals. The digits in (a) as well as four rotated and scaled versions for each digit are used for training TONs and ZFCs. (b) The digits in (b) as well as arbitrarily rotated and scaled versions of these digits are used for testing.

1. Third-order networks (TONs) for a range of values of the angular tolerance ω (from $\pi/144$ to the highest possible value of $\pi/6$). We consider networks with one or two layers of weights and 9 output nodes corresponding to the 9 classes ('0'–'8'), which are trained to produce output equal to one at the ith output node for the ith digit and zero otherwise. These networks are implemented in the feature extractor-classifier mode (see above) and trained by GBP.

2. First-order feedforward networks with a variable number of hidden nodes which are used as classifiers for the moduli of the Zernike moments of the nominated images appropriately scaled and translated. We shall refer to these networks as Zernike feature classifiers (ZFCs). The maximum order n^* of the Zernike moments is chosen so that approximately 90% of the image can be reconstructed using moments of order $n \leq n^*$. Thus, values of n^* in the range 9 to 12 (which is the maximum number used by Khotanzad and Hong [30] in an experiment involving typed characters of the Roman alphabet) are studied. This corresponds to networks with 28 and 47 inputs [19]. As before, the networks have nine output nodes and are trained by GBP.

We have carried out extensive simulations involving the set of typed numerals to study and compare the ability of the networks to cope with transformed, distorted and noisy images. A more restricted number of simulations has been carried out to test the ability of the networks to recognize handwritten numerals.

11.9.1 *Invariant recognition of typed digits*

A set of typed digits ranging from '0' to '8' represented by binary input on a 20 by 20 screen is shown in the first row of Fig. 11.9. These images are scaled and rotated to produce five different versions per image. The range of the scaling factor is between 0.7 and 1.3. The 45 resulting images, which are shown in Fig. 11.9, are used for training TONs and ZFCs.

Translation by arbitrary vectors leaves both the effective inputs of the TON and the Zernike features invariant, so that both TONs and ZFCs exhibit 100% success rate in recognizing translated patterns. Therefore, only lattice scaling transformations and rotations need be considered in testing these networks. We test the ability of the networks to correctly recognize separately or simultaneously scaled and rotated versions of the typed digits for arbitrary scaling factors between 0.7 and 1.3 and for arbitrary angles of rotation between 0 and 2π.

A look at the scaled and rotated images in Fig. 11.9 will convince the reader that rotating and especially scaling images on a 20 by 20 grid introduces a substantial amount of distortion. As a result, both the effective inputs of the TON and the inputs of the ZFC are only approximately invariant under these transformations. A measure of the sensitivity of these features to rotation and scaling on the grid is the ratio of the standard deviation σ over the mean μ of the value of each of these features for a large sample of rotated and scaled images. We find that the average σ/μ increases sharply with the number N_I of effective inputs of the TON [19]. It is thus verified that the effective inputs are less sensitive to rotation and scaling for larger values of the angular tolerance ω. Moreover, for the smaller values of N_I, the effective inputs of TONs are less sensitive to the transformations than the Zernike features for a range of values of n^*. Provided that these TONs can adequately separate the patterns, they should be expected to exhibit better performance than ZFCs.

In Table 11.3 we list the success rates for recognition of scales, rotated and both scaled and rotated versions of the nine digits by TONs with different values of ω. For one-layered networks, as ω increases starting from $\omega = \pi/144$, the success rate increases, with the network reaching its optimal performance in the region $\omega = \pi/36$ to $\pi/12$ corresponding to 112–32 effective inputs. The optimal performance corresponds to perfect or nearly perfect recollection of images separately scaled and rotated and to a success rate of 96% for images subjected to both transformations. It follows that a relatively small number of effective inputs corresponding to relatively large values of ω constitutes an adequate set of features for efficient invariant pattern recognition. Only for the largest possible value of $\omega = \pi/6$ do we find that the one-layered TON cannot be trained successfully, indicating that the resulting 10 effective inputs cannot be separated by linear decision boundaries. We have also investigated the effect on performance of adding a hidden layer with a variable number M of nodes (in the range 5–80) and find that this can lead to a marginal improvement in performance, corresponding to 97% maximum accuracy for both transformations (Table 11.3).

Table 11.3 Performance of TONs for the recognition of rotated and/or scaled versions of the nine typed digits. Different values of ω are used. Additional translation of the digits does not alter recognition performance.

		One-layered		
			Success Rate	
ω/π	N_I	*Rotation*	*Scaling*	*Combined*
1/144	3552	85	87	81
1/72	912	91	91	88
1/36	240	97	98	93
1/24	112	97	100	96
1/18	66	99	100	95
1/12	32	99	98	96
Best two-layered: 40 hidden nodes				
1/12	32	100	100	97

In Table 11.4 we show the success rate for recognition of rotated and/or scaled patterns by ZFCs. Optimal performance is achieved for n^* in the range 11–12. With a two-layered network, we can achieve a maximum recognition accuracy of 91% for both transformations. It is thus evident that TONs with a relatively small N_I exhibit performance superior to that of the optimum ZFC.

Table 11.4 The success rate for recognition of scaled and/or rotated versions of the typed digits by ZFCs.

		One-layered		
	Number of moments		*Success Rate*	
n^*		*Rotation*	*Scaling*	*Combined*
12	47	94	94	85
11	40	95	94	89
10	34	92	90	84
9	28	86	88	78
Best two-layered: 40 hidden nodes				
12	47	93	95	91

We have also tested the ability of TONs and ZFCs to recognize transformed patterns, which are in addition locally distorted by shifting some of the active pixels to one of their four nearest neighbours. We find that TONs with a relatively small N_I perform substantially better in this task than TONs with a large number of inputs and also the use of ZFCs. Adding a hidden layer to the flat TON leads to improved performance. Fig. 11.10 shows some of the distorted and transformed patterns a network with $N_I = 32$ and $\omega = \pi/6$ has been able to classify correctly.

However, for images scaled, rotated and subjected to noise randomly distributed on the screen similar success rates are obtained by TONs irrespective of the value of N_I. TONs appear to be generally less noise-tolerant than ZFCs although both can tolerate relatively small amounts of noise (not more than 3% of the number of pixels in the screen) [19], especially when compared with layered networks used as non-invariant associative memories [11] and pattern recognition systems [33,34].

11.9.2   *Invariant recognition of handwritten digits*

The set of handwritten digits shown in Fig. 11.11 (the same set as used in Chapter 7) is split into two subsets, one of which is used for training TONs and ZFCs (Fig. 11.11(a)) while the other is used for testing (Fig. 11.11(b)). As before, each digit is presented to the networks in five differently oriented and scaled versions (including the version shown in Fig. 11.11(a)), for a total number of 360 states in the training set. The networks are tested in their ability to recognize versions of the digits in Fig. 11.11(a) rotated by arbitrary angles and scaled by factors between 0.8 and 1.2. Moreover, they are tested in their ability to recognize the digits in Fig. 11.11(b), on which they have not been trained (but which are approximately of the same size and orientation as those in Fig. 11.11(a)), as well as scaled and/or rotated versions of these digits.

In the typed numeral recognition tests described so far, where a database consisting of 45 digits was used for training TONs, it has become apparent that two-layered TONs show only marginal improvement in performance compared to one-layered networks. However, it has also become clear that to ensure efficient invariant recognition, networks with a large number of effective inputs have to be abandoned in favour of smaller networks. The option of including hidden nodes in the network architecture has to be retained as the means of ensuring adequate capacity to deal with large amounts of data in the training set. Moreover, our strategy of using relatively few effective inputs abandons the principle whereby the strength of high-order networks in dealing with tasks for which the formation of non-linear decision boundaries is required, lies in their sideways expansion to include enough 'image-enhancing' terms [35–37]. The option of including a second layer of nodes to deal with these problems must therefore be retained.

Our handwritten digit recognition experiments provide a good illustration of these points. We find it impossible to train successfully flat TONs with a relatively small number of nodes (in the range 32–112) on the 360-image training set. Although more extended flat networks can cope with the task, their performance is poor compared with the performance of two-layered networks with a relatively small number of effective inputs. Typical results are shown in Table 11.5, where the performances of a flat network with $N_I = 912$ and of a two-layered network with $N_I = 66$ and 40 hidden nodes are compared. Although the second network has approximately twice as many weights as the first one, it exhibits inferior recognition rates.

Table 11.5 Success rates for recognition of handwritten digits by TONs and ZFCs are shown with respect to rotated (a), scaled (b) and both rotated and scaled (c) versions of the digits in the training set of Fig. 11.11(a) as well as with respect to the digits in the testing set of Fig. 11.11(b) (d) and with rotated (e), scaled (f) and both rotated and scaled (g) versions of these digits.

	Training set			Test set			
	rot.	*scal.*	*rot.* +*scal.*	*original*	*rot.*	*scal.*	*rot.* +*scal.*
Type of network	(a)	(b)	(c)	(d)	(e)	(f)	(g)
TON, $N_I = 66, M = 40$	93	97	91	90	82	83	80
TON, $N_I = 912, M = 0$	82	93	77	78	71	74	66
ZFC, $n^* = 11, M = 40$	89	89	79	71	68	72	63

The performance of the TON with $N_I = 66$ and 40 hidden nodes also compares favourably with the performance of the ZFC (a typical result is also shown in Table 11.5). The 90% recognition rate for the digits of Fig. 11.11(b), on which the network has not been trained, is also superior to the recognition rate of 78% of feedforward networks to which the pixel representations of the digits are presented as input without any feature extraction [33,34].

11.10 Conclusion

In this paper we have studied various methods of implementing neural networks for invariant pattern recognition.

We have shown that invariant recollection of patterns can be achieved by Hopfield networks and autoassociating feedforward networks (perceptrons), provided that it is attempted in two stages, the first of which serves to transform the proposed pattern, while the second serves to clean the transformed pattern from the noise or distortion present and to associate it to one of the nominated patterns. We have argued that the method is more likely to succeed for topologically structured and correlated nominated patterns, the storage of which can be achieved more effectively by the perceptron than by the Hopfield network. We have demonstrated through typed digit recognition experiments that the perceptron is indeed more successful than the Hopfield network in retrieving the nominated patterns from translated and/or rotated versions thereof. We have also discussed the role of image fuzzing in improving the size and shape of the basins of attraction for the first stage of the recollection process and in enhancing performance.

Our results show that these neural networks, when trained to auto-associate, can retrieve the nominated patterns from transformed versions under certain conditions, even though they have not been trained using transformed patterns. This serves as a good illustration of the capability of neural networks for generalization, and might be of some interest in practical applications. However, pattern recollection is restricted to patterns of a certain topological structure and the method is not very successful when recognition of patterns subjected to more than one transformation is considered. Moreover, successful invariant retrieval is limited by the existence of spurious minima of the energy or cost function landscape, even when fuzzing techniques are employed to restrict the number of these minima. Similar limitations are reported for other neural network models implemented as invariant associative memories, in which the network dynamics play an important role in achieving recollection (cf. the work of Bienenstock and von der Malsburg [3,4] and Coolen and Kuijk [38].

By contrast, high-order networks, whose weights are constrained to produce output approximately invariant under affine transformations, do not suffer from these drawbacks and achieve efficient invariant classification and recognition, even when combinations of different transformations are considered. Using our method of partitioning the set of triangles in the image plane into classes of approximately similar triangles we have constructed economical third-order networks with a relatively small number of weights which exhibit improved recognition performance compared to larger structures. The improvement is evident in recognizing transformed (translated, scaled and rotated) as well as locally distorted patterns. Thus implemented, third-order networks are superior to the use of moments followed by a conventional neural network classifier in invariant typed and handwritten digit recognition tasks including recognition of distorted digits.

Given these encouraging results, we feel that the high-order network approach to invariant pattern recognition deserves further attention. For example, further research is possible towards optimal ways of defining the boundaries between the equivalence classes of approximately similar triangles in order to minimize the sensitivity of third-order networks to distortion. The networks should also be tested on larger databases.

References

1. Lippmann, R.P. Pattern classification using neural networks. *IEEE Comm. Mag.*, 47-64, Nov. (1989).

2. Hopfield, J.J. Neural networks and physical systems with emergent collective computational abilities. *Proc. Natl. Acad. Sci. USA*, **79**, 2554-2558 (1982).

3. Bienenstock, E. and von der Malsburg, C. A neural network for the retrieval of superimposed connection patterns. *Europhys. Lett.*, **3**, 1243-1249 (1987).

4. Bienenstock, E. and von der Malsburg, C. A neural network for invariant pattern recognition. *Europhys. Lett.*, **4**, 121-126 (1987).

5. Kree, R. and Zippelius, A. Recognition of topological features of graphs and images in neural networks. *J. Phys. A: Math. Gen.*, **21**, L813-L818 (1988).

6. Dotsenko, V.S. Neural networks: translation-, rotation- and scale invariant pattern recognition. *J. Phys. A: Math. Gen.*, **21**, L783-L787 (1988).

7. Perantonis, S.J. *Neural Network Applications to Associative Memory and Pattern Recognition Problems*. M.Sc. thesis, Department of Computer Science, Liverpool University (1990).

8. Wallace, D.J. Neural network models: a physicist's primer. In Kenway, R.D. and Pawley, G.S. (eds.) *Computational Physics (Proc. of the SUSSP Summer School)*, 168-211 (1987).

9. Rumelhart, D.E., Hinton, G.E. and Williams, R.J. Learning internal representations by error propagation. In Rumelhart, D.E. and McClelland, J.L. (eds.). *Parallel Distributed Processing: Explorations in the Microstructure of Cognition*, Volume 1, MIT Press, Cambridge, MA, 318-362 (1986).

10. Rumelhart, D.E., Hinton, G.E. and Williams, R.J. Learning representations by back-propagating errors. *Nature*, **323**, 533-536 (1986).

11. Lisboa, P.J.G. and Perantonis, S.J. Convergence of recursive associative memories obtained using the multilayered perceptron. *J. Phys. A: Math. Gen.*, **23**, 4039-4053 (1990).

12. Fogelman Soulie, F., Gallinari, P., Le Cun, Y. and Thiria, S. Evaluation of network architectures on test learning tasks. *IEEE 1st Int. Conf. on Neural Networks*, Volume 2, 653-660 (1987).

13. Fogelman Soulie, F., Gallinari, P., Le Cun, Y. and Thiria, S. Automata networks and artificial intelligence. In Fogelman Soulie, F., Robert, Y. and Tsuente. M. (eds.). *Automata Networks in Computer Science, Theory and Applications*, Manchester University Press, Manchester, 133-186 (1987).

14. Fuchs, A. and Haken, H. Pattern recognition and associative memory as dynamical processes in nonlinear systems. *IEEE 1st Int. Conf. on Neural Networks*, Volume 1, 217-224 (1987).

15. Albanese, M. *et al.* (APE collaboration). Glueball masses and string tension in lattice QCD. *Phys. Lett.*, **B192**, 163-169 (1987).

16. Perantonis, S.J. and Michael, C. Static potentials from pure SU(2) lattice gauge theory. *Nucl. Phys.*, **B326**, 544-556 (1989).

17. Perantonis, S.J. and Michael, C. Static potentials and hybrid mesons from pure SU(3) lattice gauge theory. *Nucl. Phys.*, **B** (in press).

18. Hopfield, J.J. Neurons with graded response have collective computational properties like those of two-state neurons. *Proc. Natl. Acad. Sci. USA*, **81**, 3088-3092 (1984).

19. Perantonis, S.J. and Lisboa, P.J.G. Invariant pattern recognition using high-order neural networks and moment classifiers. *IEEE Trans. Neural Networks* (in press).

20. Lisboa, P.J.G. and Michael, C. Lattices in group manifolds: applications to lattice gauge theory. *Nucl. Phys.*, **B210 [FS6]**, 15-28 (1982).

21. Reid, M.B., Spirkovska, L. and Ochoa, E. Rapid training of higher-order neural networks for invariant pattern recognition. *IJCNN Int. Conf. on Neural Networks*, Washington, DC, Volume 1, 689-692 (1989).

22. Maxwell, T., Giles, C.L., Lee, Y.C., and Chen, H.H. Nonlinear dynamics of artificial neural system. *AIP Conf. Proc.*, **151**, 299-304 (1986).

23. Chen, H.H., Lee, Y.C., Sun, G.Z., Lee, H.Y., Maxwell, T. and Giles, C.L. High order correlation model for associative memory. *AIP Conf. Proc.*, **151**, 86-99 (1986).

24. Minsky, M. and Papert, S. *Perceptrons*, MIT Press, Cambridge, MA (1969).

25. Hu, M.E. Visual pattern recognition by moment invariants. *IRE Trans. Inform. Theory*, **IT-8**, 179-187 (1962).

26. Dudani, B.A., Breeding, K.J. and McGhee, R.B. Aircraft identification by moment invariants. *IEEE Trans. on Computers*, **C-26**, 39-46 (1977).

27. Reddi, S.S. Radial and angular moment invariants for image identification. *IEEE Trans. Pattern Anal. Machine Intell.*, **PAMI-3**, 2, 240-242 (1981).

28. Abu-Mostafa, Y.S. and Psaltis, D. Image normalization by complex moments. *IEEE Trans. Pattern Anal. Machine Intell.*, **PAMI-7**, 1, 46-55 (1985).

29. Reeves, A.P., Prokop, R.J., Andrews, S.E. and Kuhl, F.P. Three-dimensional shape analysis using moments and Fourier descriptors. *IEEE Trans. Pattern Anal. Machine Intell.*, **PAMI-10**, 6, 937-943 (1988).

30. Khotanzad, A. and Hong, Y.H. Invariant image recognition by Zernike moments. *IEEE Trans. Pattern Anal. Machine Intell.*, **PAMI-12**, 5, 489-497 (1990).

31. Teh, C.H. and Chin, R.T. On image analysis by the method of moments. *IEEE Trans. Pattern Anal. Machine Intell.*, **PAMI-10**, 4, 496-513 (1988).

32. Khotanzad, A. and Lu, J.H. Distortion invariant character recognition by a multi-layer perceptron and back-propagation learning. *IEEE 2nd Int. Conf. on Neural Networks*, 625-631 (1988).

33. Leung, J.K.O. *Experimental Study on Neural Net Recognition of Handwritten Numerals*. M.Sc. thesis, Liverpool University (1988).

34. Lisboa, P.J.G. Single layer perceptron for the recognition of hand written digits. *Int. J. of Neural Networks* (in press).

35. Giles, C. L. and Maxwell, T. Learning invariance, and generalization in high order neural networks. *Applied Optics*, **26**, 4972-4978 (1987).

36. Pao, Y. H. *Adaptive Pattern Recognition and Neural Networks*, Addison-Wesley, New York (1989).

37. Sobajic, D. *Neural Nets for Control of Power Systems*. Ph.D. thesis, Department of Computer Science, Case Western Reserve University, Cleveland, Ohio (1988).

38. Coolen, A. C. C. and Kuijk, F. W. A learning mechanism for invariant pattern recognition in neural networks. *Neural Networks*, **2**, 6, 495-506 (1989).

12

The bionic retina and beyond

J. G. Taylor
King's College, London, England

12.1 Summary

The structure and mode of action of early visual processing is discussed, with particular reference to modelling leading to engineering devices. Both the retina and visual cortex in vertebrates are considered. In the former, an analysis of the silicon retina of Mead and Mahowald is shown to lead to both a mathematically tractable model of the outer plexiform layer and a detailed description of ganglion cell output. In the latter, the equivalent electrical circuit needed to obtain a Gabor-function type of receptive field for simple cells in storate cortex is determined.

12.2 Introduction

Visual or optical processing is a very active field with many exciting new ideas and developments. One of these has been in the use of neural nets in what may be regarded as the classical manner, where the neural net may be of Hopfield–Kohonen or similar well-known form [1]. However successful such approaches may be to the problem of vision they do not seem to make any use of the very efficient solution to that problem that has been achieved over the millions of years by living species. Both invertebrates and vertebrates have evolved, by the well-known process of 'survival of the fittest', various neural nets which allow the animal to function efficiently in its environment. Both the retina and the later layers of neurones, such as the primary and associative cortex in mammals, have been evolved to form a remarkable vision machine. Even if we could understand the working of only parts of that machine it should be possible to duplicate them in hardware. Standard neural networks could then be used to fill in the gaps in the processing chain to give what might be expected to be a much more successful device. That method of approach has already been started for auditory processing, where the initial processing of the cochlea has been modelled for that purpose [2]. A similar study has been going on for quite some time in vision, as described for example in [3]. The purpose of this paper is to describe current work following this approach [4]. It will be seen that such an approach may allow a number of problems to be attacked at once, particularly:

1. the problem of vision from a neurophysiological perspective, a problem of considerable interest to neural science.
2. development of the most suitable mathematics to study the processing problem, i.e. efficient representations of images prior to higher-level processing.
3. consideration of ways in which a hardware implementation of the system can be achieved, and last but not least,
4. to determine how improvement on the processing in living systems can be obtained.

Understanding of the neuro-physiology of vision has proved difficult to obtain. There is still not complete knowledge of the wiring diagram of cells involved at the various stages, nor is the mode of action of a single visual cortical cell yet completely understood [5]. However, progress is being made in these various areas, and the time will come when the detailed models of the visual cortex presently being slowly constructed will be successful.

In spite of the difficulties noted above it can be argued that such possibly premature modelling is worth attempting if one may thereby discover the principles on which the various parts of the system work. However, it will be necessary to attempt a considerable degree of realism in the model if it can give such a level of insight. Neurones have very complex processes occurring at various levels – multiple chemical messengers at synaptic gaps, non-linear interactions between post-synaptic potentials, discontinuous nerve impulses, at least half a dozen different sorts of synapses (besides the usual axo-dendritic ones) and numerous others. The levels of modelling that are inherent in conventional neural network approaches, as described in other chapters in this book, leave out all such subtleties and may not be realistic enough. It is thus appropriate to consider the possibility that new paradigms for neural network research must be developed. I have termed such an approach 'towards more realistic neural networks' elsewhere [6]. It has lead to a new approach to the stochastic features of synaptic information transmission, for example encompassing the spin-glass approach [7], after physical models of the randomly distributed constituents of glass-like materials – which are theoretically well understood.

Where better to begin than at the beginning, the retina? This is already processing visual information at a high level, especially in lower vertebrates. Thus motion detection is achieved in, say, the pigeon eye; it does not appear to arise in our own. The nature of retinal processing is considered in the next section. That is followed by an analysis of various transformations that are performed on the retinal output by the primary visual cortex. The final section discusses the manner in which the knowledge gained from this approach may be applied in the design of electronic visual devices.

12.3 The retina

Much has been understood about the retinae of a wide range of animals and about the principles underlying the processing of visual information which it performs. There are, however, considerable differences in detail between different animal species. For this reason, a certain amount of simplification will be used here, to avoid missing the wood for the trees. In particular only the vertebrate eye will be considered in any detail; there are differences in principle between that and the invertebrate eye, with its usually compound structure. In vertebrates, the retina lies at the back of the more or less spherical eye, comprising several layers of excitable cells. The outermost layer consists of the photo-receptors, these being the rods and the cones. The former are used for low levels of illumination, the latter for brighter light and also for colour vision. These cells form a mosaic on the outside of the retina; light travels through two other layers of cells to reach them. These layers are called, respectively, the inner and the outer plexiform layers. They are composed of cells whose outgrowths (dendrites for receiving and axons for sending information) are parallel to the surface of the eye. The cells in the outer plexiform layer are called horizontal cells, those in the inner layer are the amacrine cells.

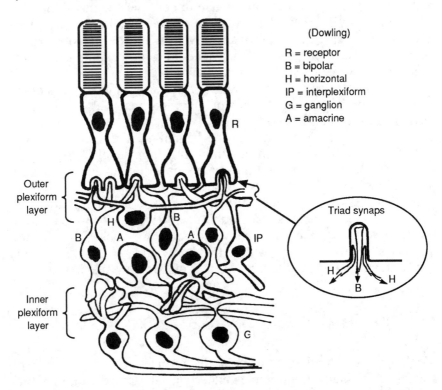

Figure 12.1 A schematized version of the retina, showing the two layers (outer and inner plexiform). The receptors R are rods or cones. H denotes horizontal cells, B bipolar, IP interplexiform cells, A amacrine and G ganglion cells (loosely taken from Dowling J. *The Retina*, 2nd edn., Belknap Press of Harvard University Press, MA (1987)).

In all, then, the retina is composed of an outermost sheet of receptors (the rods and cones), an adjacent sheet (the outer plexiform layer) of horizontal cells, and a further sheet of amacrine cells (the inner plexiform layer). The outer and inner plexiform layers are connected by a set of cells at right angles to the two layers; these cells are called bipolar (from the fact that they have two ends). Finally, the inner plexiform layer feeds into the final or output cells of the retina; these are called the ganglion cells. The flow chart in the retina is as follows:

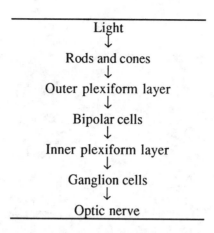

There are of the order of a hundred million rods and cones in the retina of a monkey, yet only about a million ganglion cells to transmit its output to the optic nerve. This is a reduction of the throughput by two orders of magnitude. Yet the output from the ganglion cells appears to contain the same amount of information as the image that reaches the eye. Moreover, there is a large amount of processing still to be performed on the retinal output by the monkey's visual cortex. It is thus of great interest to work out exactly what the retinal transformation is composed of, and what its function is.

One way to discover that is to shine light of various forms on to the retina and measure the ganglion cell output directly. The net result has been expressed in terms of the receptive field (RF) of the cell, which is defined by the region in visual space that causes a response in the ganglion cell under investigation. Experiments since the 1950s have revealed that there are in general two sorts of RFs (say for the cat). One class of ganglion cell, the so-called X cell, has a circular receptive field with a central circular disc surrounded by an annulus. The cell will increase its firing rate if a spot of light is shone on the central region, whilst it will turn off completely if the spot is shone on the surround. Such a cell is termed an on-centre off-surround cell, or an ON-cell for short. There is also the opposite sort of response, with an increase in the cell response if the surround is illuminated and a decrease if the centre is on. Such a cell is termed an off-centre on-surround (or OFF-cell). The response of these two sorts of cell persist as long as the input illumination is on. There are also cells with a transient response to incident illumination, these being called Y-cells. They are also of the ON or OFF kinds, but now with larger RFs.

Ganglion cells: on β (*X*)   on α (*Y*)

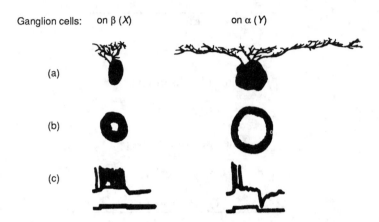

(a)

(b)

(c)

Figure 12.2 A schematic view of (a) dendritic and cell body sizes, (b) receptive field sizes (for ON-centre, OFF-surround) and (c) tonic versus phasic responses, for the β or *X* and α or *Y* ganglion cells.

This description solely in terms of RFs clearly leaves to one side the temporal response, other than the gross difference between transient and persistent response. Thus one can analyse the response pattern of the ganglion cell when periodically modulated light is shone on the retina; a similar question may be raised concerning the response to spatially modulated incident light. More generally what is the transfer function of the retinal ganglion cells to a spatio-temporally varying pattern of light?

Some aspects of this will be considered shortly, but it is valid at this point to ask what knowledge about the retina will be of value from an engineering design point of view. Suppose the complete transfer function of the retina were known for each cell. How would that help one design an effective early processor for a vision system? One would have to know how the later parts of the system used the output of the device. That is something we will have to turn to in the next section. The other question that we will have to answer is how the device can be constructed: what is its wiring diagram? In fact the answer to this latter question is still far from complete; the wiring diagram of the retina of a typical vertebrate is not yet completely known, so that some guesswork is needed to suggest what might be a correct structure for the retina.

The phrase 'wiring diagram' in this context is not as simple as it appears. It was already noted in the previous section that there are numerous complexities of neural activity, beyond that of which cell sends information to which other cell. Thus the nature of the synapse is decidedly non-trivial, as is the manner of action of the various cells. In order to consider these complexities in a little detail it would seem best to follow the order of information processing as given by the flow chart above.

The initial step is that of photon absorption by rhodopsin in the rods and cones. This causes the rhodopsin molecules to be activated, which leads, by a cascade of molecular activations, to the closing of bionic channel gates in the junctional wall between the photo-receptor and the cells in the outer plexiform layer. Such closure leads to a change in the membrane potential of the latter. Thus transduction occurs from light energy into electrical energy. This transformation is a very senstive one, with response being obtainable to only one or two photons at once. The sensitivity is limited by the thermal noise in the rods and cones, and animals functioning at a lower body temperature have a more sensitive response to the lower levels of illumination [8].

The change of photo-receptor membrane potential is transmitted, by means of a chemical synapse (one at which the electrical pulse causes release of a certain chemical into the synaptic cleft, which then leads to a change of the membrane potential of the post-synaptic membrane) into a similar change of the horizontal and bipolar cell membranes. The horizontal cells are themselves all connected through electrical synapses, in which there is a direct transfer of electrical energy, without any chemical intermediary. This leads to the outer plexiform layer acting as a resistive sheet, in which each horizontal cell is connected through resistors (the electrical synapses) to several nearest neighbouring similar cells. These cells also possess a capacitive membrane surface, which gives the cells the ability to store charge up to the time-constant of the membrane, of the order of tens of milliseconds. This allows memory of the local illumination to be stored and also a lateral spread of the input to more distant areas of the retina (as determined by the conductances between the cells).

For a given connectivity between the horizontal cells it is possible to write down the equations describing the response of these cells to an arbitrarily varying input in both space and time [4]. These equations may be solved by computer simulation. Alternatively the outer plexiform layer may be approximated as a continuous sheet, when the resulting equations reduce to a linear system of second order in space and first order in time. The transfer function may then be obtained in analytic form by means of Laplace or Fourier methods [4].

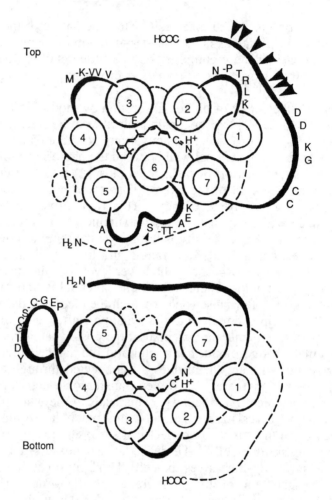

Figure 12.3 Artist's view of the rhodopsin molecule as seen from the cytoplasm (top) and from the extracellular side or intradiscal space (bottom). The amino acid residues in the loop or terminal segments that have been conserved in vertebrate and Drosophilia opsins are indicated with one letter symbols. Black arrows mark potential phosphorylation sites (serines and threonines). Absorption of light by a rhodopsin molecule starts a chain reaction of molecular dissociation during which nervous electrical activity in retinal cells is initiated. Variants of the products of this chemical process later recombine to regenerate rhodopsin. (From Baehr, W. and Applebury, M.L. Exploring visual transduction with recombinant DNA techniques. *Trends in Neuroscience*, **9**, 5, 198-203 (1986).)

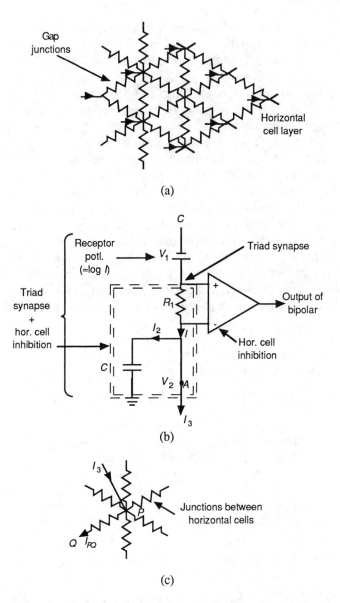

Figure 12.4 (a) The hexagonal resistive network used to model the retinal horizontal cell layer; the resistances simulate the gap junctions; (b) the resistance-capacitance structure used to model the horizontal cell current injection into the resistive network of (a) and the bipolar cell output as the difference of the photo-cell input V, at C and the horizontal cell potential V_2 at P; (c) the details of the current injection into the resistive network.

The output of the outer plexiform layer is given by taking away from the input illumination, as transferred directly to the bipolar cells from the rods and cones, the horizontal cell activity. This is justified by the result of detailed examination of the wiring diagram, by the use of neuro-anatomical and neuro-physiological methods. In other words the horizontal cells act in an inhibitory manner on the bipolar cells. The transfer function of the net response can now be obtained in analytic form as above in the continuum limit. The results of this analysis compare well with the experimental features of the cells in, say, the mud-puppy retina. The response is composed of an initial one from direct transmission through the bipolar cells, with a later phase bringing in the inhibition from more distant regions of the retina by means of the horizontal cell layer. This latter signal corresponds to a mean level of illumination over the retina, and acts as a background level against which the on-going activity is to be compared. Such a subtractive process leads to an explanation of various psychophysical anomalies such as Mach bands, etc. In particular it also leads to extraction of changes of illumination, both in space and in time.

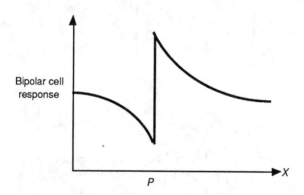

Figure 12.5 The bipolar cell response at an illuminated edge at *P*.

It is usually claimed that the inhibition provided by the horizontal cells in the vertebrate retina is similar to the so-called lateral inhibition in the invertebrate retina. That is not the case, as is shown in detail in [4]. In the vertebrate case, nearest neighbours augment the excitation at a given horizontal cell position. The inhibitory effect of the horizontal cell on its neighbouring bipolar cell leads to response similar in some ways to the invertebrate cell response. However, there is no comparison between the detailed ways in which the two types of retina are wired up. In the invertebrate there is a lateral plexus of connections between cells by which the lateral inhibition is achieved. This has no direct effect on the temporal properties in the way achieved by the capacitative features of the outer plexiform cell layer.

There are considerable differences between the inner plexiform layer in different animals. It possesses cells sensitive to motion in the case of lower vertebrates, such as the rabbit or pigeon. In the primate there are few cells with such properties, so that motion analysis must be performed in the cortex in the latter case. There appears to be greater use of the amacrine cells in the lower vertebrates, with bipolar cells connected to amacrines, which then connect to motion-sensitive ganglion cells as their main source of input. It has been suggested [9] that motion detection is achieved in this system, as in invertebrates such as the fly, by a veto action of one cell on to the output of another cell nearby. If the two cells are neighbours then they can be connected up to a further cell in such a way as to make the input to this latter cell depend crucially on the direction of motion of a moving spot of light. However, the manner in which a cell may become sensitive to motion over a small fraction of its RF, and with sensitivity that is the same over the whole RF is not presently understood.

It is usual to describe the RF of a retinal ganglion cell by means of suitably chosen parameters in a difference of two Gaussians (DOGs); in one dimension this would have the form

$$A.\exp(-x^2/a^2) - B.\exp(-x^2/b^2) \tag{12.1}$$

where a is the width of the positive central region in an ON-cell and b the inhibitory surround. An OFF-cell would have an overall minus sign multiplying equation (12.1). It is possible to obtain a response approximately equal to equation (12.1) by connecting the outputs of bipolar cells in a suitable manner to later ganglion cells. For the sustained X-cells with a small receptive field only a few nearby ON-bipolar cells need to be used to construct an ON-ganglion cell (and similarly for OFF-cells). The transient response, and larger RF of Y-cells may be constructed from the addition of many (in the hundreds) of bipolar cell responses. The larger RF is seen to arise from the addition of many bipolar cell responses, before the horizontal cell inhibition can enter. When this latter does arrive at the bipolar cells their response is reduced in total almost to zero. Given that the above connectivity succeeds in producing the correct static RF for the ganglion cells one would hope that it would lead to the correct response when there is temporal dependence. That will depend, however, on the detailed temporal responses of the amacrine and ganglion cells as well as the various synapses. In particular the latter between the bipolar and amacrine cells have an interesting reciprocal form. This may allow the synapses to act as time differentials on the input signal [10]. However, more analysis must be made of the possible modes of action of such synapses, especially their effects on various types of input signal [11]. It is necessary to include in the output function of the Y-cells a certain level of non-linearity, as is found in their response to modulated gratings [12]; this can be done.

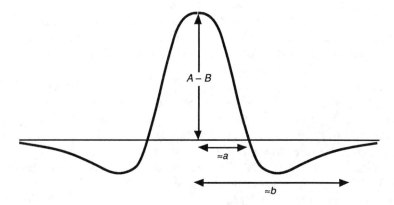

Figure 12.6 The Mexican hat of equation (12.1), corresponding to the output of an ON-ganglion cell, where $A > B$, $a < b$.

In all then it can be said that there is improvement of our understanding of the inner and outer plexiform layer response. It should be emphasized that the total activity in the retina is assumed to occur only by graded or continuous charges in the membrane potentials of the cells involved–receptors, horizontal, bipolar and amacrine. It is only at the ganglion cell level that there is nerve impulse production. This very likely occurs in order to preserve the information against possible degradation on transmission over considerable distances. It is of interest to consider the development of following devices to a bionic retina that are still using graded activity. We will return to that at the end.

12.4 The primary visual cortex

Information travels from the ganglion cells in the form of nerve impulses, and initally inputs to a centre in the thalamus called the lateral geniculate nucleus (LGN). There is some sharpening and modifying of information in the LGN, although the details of that have not been fully understood. We will turn our attention to the visual cortex, where an important feature occurs. It is found, by direct measurement of the response of a cortical cell when light is shone on to the retina, that the RF of a cortical cell may be classified as simple or complex (following the classic work of Hubel and Wiesel). The former RF is now that of an elongated ellipse, the latter RF is larger, but the complex cell now has motion sensitivity. The functional implications of this type of processing element and its relevance to image analysis are reviewed briefly in Chapter 7.

In the case of a simple cell the RF in both space and wave-number space, i.e. in Fourier space, is best described [13] by a two-dimensional Gabor function. In one-dimension this has the form of a Gaussian multiplied by a cosine or sine wave:

$$\exp(-x^2/a^2) \, . \, \sin(ux+b) \tag{12.2}$$

with an obvious extension to the two-dimensional case. Given this RF, what is the connectivity between ganglion cells and these cortical cells to result in such a Gabor function-type of RF (neglecting effects from the LGN)? That may be answered by using the DOG approximation to the RF of the retinal ganglion cell [4]. A sum of DOGs, with displaced centres, and modulated by a cosine or sine will lead to a difference of two Gabors:

$$\int dx_0 \, \exp(-x_0^2/c^2) \, . \, \cos(wx_0) \, [A \, \exp(-(x-x_0)^2/a^2)$$
$$- B \, \exp(-(x-x_0)^2/b^2] =$$
$$A \, \exp(-x^2/(a^2+c^2)) \, \cos[wx/(1+a^2/c^2)] -$$
$$B \, \exp(-x^2/(b^2+c^2)) \, \cos[wx/(1+b^2/c^2)]. \tag{12.3}$$

If $a,b \ll c$ then the right-hand side of equation (12.3) reduces approximately to:

$$(A-B) \, \exp(-x^2/c^2) \, \cos(wx). \tag{12.4}$$

It is the expression equation (12.4) which is the required Gabor function RF. Thus the correct response can roughly be achieved by summing the outputs of ganglion cells with RFs centres at x_0 over values of x_0 chosen with a Gaussian distribution of width c and modulated by a cosine of wavelength $2\pi/w$. This gives a direct physical interpretation of c as the range (in receptive field space) over which inputs to the simple cell feed, when that range is much larger than the range of the DOGs in the simple cells. The variable π/w can be considered as the distance, in receptive field space, over which inputs from ON X-cells are being summed (from $-\pi/2w$ to $\pi/2w$). The next range of x_0 ($\pi/2w < x < 3\pi/2w$) has contributions from OFF X-cells, and so on. The model predicts there to be a juxtaposition of ranges of ON and ranges of OFF X-cells in this interpretation of the modulation function $\cos(wx_0)$.

Complex cells may also be modelled in a similar manner, but now with half-wave rectification, as noted by Pollen *et al.* [14]. This leads to a complex cell response which depends on the energy of the incident light. Such a response is regarded as a possible mechanism for motion and for texture discrimination [14], and is clearly of interest.

It is not known in such detail how information is processed at higher levels in the visual cortex, although a great deal of effort is presently being expended on finding it out.

12.5 Bionic processing

How may the above knowledge be used in the design and construction of a useful bionic visual processing device? The understanding of the outer plexiform layer has already been utilized by Carver Mead and his co-workers [15] in the construction of a 'silicon retina' – more properly to be described as a 'silicon outer plexiform layer'. My own work on the retina was greatly stimulated by that development, and led to the model of [4]. It also made me realize that it was of value to model the transformation going on before consigning one's ideas too indelibly in silicon. Thus one can evaluate the advantages (or otherwise) of a particular connectivity of the outer plexiform layer. One might even have design specifications that would lead one to the use of several such layers in serial. Each layer will lead to a further enhancement of the spatial and temporal gradients; a theoretical study will lead to determination of the requisite number of such layers.

A similar advantage of obtaining a theoretical appreciation of the response of the inner plexiform layer is also evident. However, there is a difficult question that arises if one wishes to base a bionic eye on the living one. Which species should one take the information from? It has already been noted that there is a considerable difference between lower and higher vertebrates, in that in the former motion detection occurs in the retina, whilst in the latter it is performed first in the primary visual cortex. Which is the best choice? The question is difficult to answer partly because we do not yet know how to give a detailed description of the working of the visual cortex; there are even more unknowns in the subtleties of the neurones and synapses [5]. In spite of that, one may consider simplified models. However, if one consigns the motion processing to the cortex then one has also to face up to the problem that we do not yet know how to obtain fusion of the activity of the cortical neurones. In other words we are faced with the problem of how the complex information is handled at a later stage in higher animals; the later cortical areas, beyond the primary areas, must be of importance here. Thus it seems as if one may have to solve almost the whole problem of the brain before one can resolve this question. On the other hand, modelling more primitive vertebrates may allow one to avoid such very deep problems.

12.6 Conclusion

One should therefore try first to exploit the more primitive vertebrate retina, by modelling it in more detail at a theoretical level. In particular what is needed is a far better understanding of the process of motion detection. Is there a plastic period in such animals? There are NMDA-sensitive receptors in the inner plexiform layer [16]. Such receptors are regarded as being involved with memory in the cortex and the hippocampus. May they play a similar role in the retina?

It is possible to test if the above is a feasible proposal by simulation. If so, then it will be possible to build a bionic eye which would respond to suitably chosen moving objects. Such a device clearly has applications to a host of situations, from simple vehicle monitoring (with detailed recording even of the nature of the moving object) to burglar alarms to factory process monitoring. Further devices, of a much higher level of sophistication, will be available when the problems outlined above are solved.

References

1. Hsing, T.R. and Tzon, K.H. Visual communications and image processing. *Opt. Eng.*, **28**, 7, 691-692 (1989). Schreiber, W.F. Visual communications and image processing: an overview. *Opt. Eng.*, **28**, 7, 693-699 (1989).

2. Shamma, S.A. Speech processing in the auditory system II: lateral inhibition and the central processing of speech evoked activity in the auditory nerve. *J. Acoust. Soc. Amer.*, **78**, 5, 1622-1632 (1985).

3. Arbib. M.A. The Metaphorical Brain, 2nd edn., John Wiley, New York (1989).

4. Taylor, J.G. A silicon model of vertebrate retinal processing. *Neural Networks*, **3**, 171-178 (1990).

5. Major, G., Larkman, A.V. and Jack, J. Constraining non-uniqueness in passive electrical models of cortical pyramidal neurons. *Proc. Physiol. Soc.*, Oxford Meeting, 27-28 July, 23P (1990).

6. Taylor, J.G. Living neural nets. In Taylor, J.G. and Mannion, C.L.T. (eds.). *New Developments in Neural Computing*, Adam Hilger, Bristol 31-52 (1989)

7. Gorse, D. and Taylor, J.G. Towards a hardware realisable model of the neuron. In Cotterill, R. (ed.). *Models of Brain Function*, 465-482, Cambridge University Press, Cambridge (1989)

8. Aho, A *et al*. Low retinal noise in animals with low body temperature allows high visual sensitivity. *Nature*, **334**, 348-350 (1988).

9. Koch, C. Poggio, T and Vorre, V. Computations in the vertebrate retina: gain enhancements, differentiation and motion discrlmination. *Trends in Neurosci.*, **7**, 204-211 (1986).

10. Richter, J. and Ullman, S. Model for the temporal organization of X- and Y-type receptive fields in the primate retina. *Biol. Cyb.*, **43**, 127-145 (1982).

11. Terasawa, M.T., Sukuda, M.T. and Hauske, G. *Biol. Cyb.*, **60**, 239-246 (1989).

12. Enroth-Cugell, C. and Robson, J. The contrast sensitivity of retinal ganglion cells of the cat. *J. Physiol.*, **187**, 517-552 (1966).

13. Daugman, J. Non-orthogonal wavelet representations in relaxation networks: image encoding and analysis with biological visual primitives. In Taylor, J.G. and Mannion, C.L.T. (eds.). *New Developments in Neural Computing*, Adam Hilger, Bristol, 233-250 (1989).

14. Pollen, D.A., Gaska, J.P. and Jacobson, L.D. Physiological constraints on models of visual cortical function. In Cotterill, R. (ed.). *Models of brain function*, Cambridge University Press, Cambridge, 115-136 (1989).

15. Mead, C.A. and Mahowald, M.A. A silicon model of early visual processing. *Neural Networks*, **1**, **1**, 91-97 (1988).

16. Miller, R.F. and Slaughter, M.M. Encilatory amino acid receptors of the retina: diversity of subtypes and conductance mechanisms. *Trends in Neurosci.*, **7**, 211-218 (1986).

13
Conclusion

P. J. G. Lisboa,
University of Liverpool, England

13.1 Trends

The dozen or so examples of detailed applications reviewed in this book offer only a small sample of the current activity in the field of neural networks. More has necessarily been missed than included. Nevertheless, certain trends which are apparent in this small sample are typical of a wider scope of practical developments.

Thus, the multi-layered perceptron has established itself firmly as one of the most powerful and versatile general purpose classifiers in use today. Applications range from automated inspection running live on the factory floor [1], through real-time explosives detection in luggage at high-risk airports (reported here in Chapter 2 and in reference [2]), to span virtually the whole spectrum of digital signal processing, encompassing speech and image recognition, with particular success in hand-written character recognition. It is also used as a 'last ditch' classifier, whenever there is a signal, of any type, which has been manipulated into as much of a suitable representation as is possible, but still remains undecipherable without the help of an automatic classifier. Typical of this general purpose approach are applications to credit scoring and medical diagnosis. The neural classifiers also scored well against human experts, which underlines what is perhaps one of the more significant findings of this work: namely, the widespread potential for application of pattern recognition techniques to problems which might appear, at first sight, to be completely unrelated.

Direct comparisons of conventional and neural techniques are, clearly, a priority, but one which is often overlooked. In cases where they have been carried out, neural classifiers generally match, and often improve upon, the performance of traditional classifiers. Some examples were given in earlier chapters on character recognition – other instances and reviews can be found in references [3–6].

There are also overstated claims, and the capability theorems quoted in the literature do not, in general, prove the existence of any training algorithms capable of fully realizing the potential of the network [7–9]. Counter-examples to the performance claims about neural networks (namely conventional numerical techniques) have also been given, although these are, again, often unsystematic. Coming full circle from the deadlock of the 1960s, a case in point is the implementation of iterative solutions of the very parity problem highlighted by Minsky and Papert [10], as evidence of the requirement for multi-layered networks. The problem consists of automatically deciding, whether by counting or using other methods, whether the number of 'on' bits in a binary input state is odd, in which case the answer is 1, or even, answer 0. The simplest example of the parity problem is the 'exclusive-OR' task described in the Introduction. This is the two-dimensional version of the problem, because the input states have just two components, x and y.

Higher-dimensional parity problems have $2N$ states, which quickly grow very large in comparison with the size of the networks. Quite apart from being riddled with local minima, the lengthy calculations for order eight and higher which are incurred during training by back error propagation, make it far easier to handcraft a solution using, say, a counting method for the hidden layer, than to compute a genuinely distributed network. This is despite the obvious capacity of the network to support a solution to the problem, as it can be produced by hand. This is not surprising, however, since the generalized parity problem is just the type of problem which distributed training by back error propagation is not suited to. Every bit of information in the data is conflicting, and there is absolutely no redundancy. Solutions to it are reached, not by generalizing from sample data, but rather by reasoning about the problem as a whole at a much higher level.

To conclude about pattern classification, artificial neural networks are intended for low-level tasks, where reasonably successful generalization can be expected by choosing representative examples from each different class. In these problems, which include many real-life applications, distributed associative memories of the type produced with neural network techniques have an important role to play. A simple example outside of this class, albeit anecdotal, is J. S. Denker's trick problem of classifying the next digit when the set

(1,3,5,7) belongs to class 'A' and (0,2,4,6,8) to class 'B'. The answer, of course, depends on whether the number 9 is considered an odd integer, or a prime number. Despite this, there is a clear, and seemingly well-justified trend towards firmly establishing neural techniques near the top of the list of general purpose classifiers [3–6].

Other emerging trends have also been highlighted throughout this book. Modelling of dynamic processes, used in Chapter 3 for resource allocation, could be extended to many time varying processes, such as process control applications. Custom network architectures are now being developed for useful problems, for instance in robotics control (Chapter 6 and reference [11]). Applications in robotics extend to several other areas, including the analysis of complex vision processes, for instance concerning natural scene interpretation via image labelling (Chapter 8), but also related to obstacle avoidance [12] and joint visuo-motor coordination [13–15].

Data fusion [16] is another category of problems with room to expore the ability of neural networks for combining redundant information from multiple knowledge sources [17] in order to come to a decision. This opens the possibility of integrating neural techniques with knowledge-based systems [18], as well as building hierarchical neural network structures [19] with subnets forming appropriate redundant representations directly from sample data.

Moving on to optimization problems, judicious applications of several different network algorithms have demonstrated considerable power and flexibility of use in the solution of *NP*-complete problems [20–22], and also in various applications in image processing [23–25].

Neural approaches to feature coding, whether using self-organizing processes [26–28] or by analysing the representations formed in feedforward networks [29–31], are rooted in conventional signal processing applications but have reached out into novel areas of information technology, where their simplicity makes them attractive to use. These are reviewed in more detail in a later section. Significantly, one obvious trend is a concerted move of neural techniques away from the laboratory, to solve real problems in commerce and industry. First, a critique of the new approach.

13.2 Meek, myth or mirth?

This title categorizes three typical objections raised against artificial neural networks. They are approached here in an attempt to defy both extremes, proponents as well as objectors. Meekness refers to algorithms confined to toy problems; myth considers them simply a hyped-up re-discovery of algorithms that already existed; and mirth because of the requirement for carefully engineered pre-processors to achieve good performance with neural classifiers, which may be said to solve the problem before it ever reaches the network.

On the first point, some of the applications contained in this book already bridge the gap betwen test benches and the world of real-time and profit margins (e.g. Chapters 2 and 3). These examples offer a practical answer to the initial question about whether neural technology will ever be able to improve upon solutions offered by alternative specialist methods, and point towards replacing it with a more pertinent line of enquiry, about finding niches where the novel approach is to advantage, and working out how to extract maximum performance. Much work still remains to be done here, and the field is wide open to new solutions.

Regarding novelty, the new techniques owe much and borrow from established methods of pattern recognition (e.g. reference [32]). Examples of perceptron models, higher-order classifiers, and recursive least-square estimators date back many years [33–34], the back-propagation algorithm has been traced back to an old statistical approximation technique [35], stochastic optimization methods do use the very old Metropolis algorithm [36], pattern completion with Hebbian learning was demonstrated over two decades ago [37], holographic devices were related to information storage in the brain even earlier than that [38], hashing techniques have also been used to produce 'intelligent' learning behaviour [39] and are not unrelated to some of today's associative memories [40], and so on (viz. the bibliography in Chapter 1). These techniques have enjoyed considerable success in their own right, and remain powerful now. Some of the most important principles and neural network algorithms have also long been known, while others emerged unnoticed over the years. But there are some genuinely new developments which overcome the limitations of the early models, notably by introducing non-linear processing into usable algorithms, opening up solutions to a wide range of problems of practical interest, among them references [26], [41–46].

Finally, neural networks may be regarded as tools. They do not work by themselves, but only perform as well as they are applied. Knowledge about the domain of application is therefore as important as familiarity with the networks themselves. One way of including this knowledge is, of course, by means of data conditioning. In cases where prior knowledge is scarce, neural networks provide new techniques for analysing the raw data in a way which is robust against noise, adaptive to non-linearities, and potentially fast. This is still very useful both for constructing data representations and in classification, with a wide range of applications, some of which are listed below.

13.3 Application areas

This section gives an overview of neural network solutions to practical problems, grouped into broad subject bands, with brief comments about the state-of-the-art of the solutions, the names of the companies involved and references where available. It is just one snapshot of a continually developing and fast expanding field, and therefore cannot be complete. An attempt was made to include mostly applications already undergoing field tests, or directly related to practical use.

13.3.1 *Business and finance*

- Scheduling and inventory control applications, including the airline seat allocations which are described in Chapter 3.
- Bond rating and asset price forecasting in the stock market have good reports compared with econometric techniques, from Concept Logiciels, a subsidiary of Thomson-CSF Finance, France, TSB Bank, UK, IBM, USA, and Fujitsu Laboratories Ltd., Japan [47–49].
- Exchange rate forecasting, with comparable performance to human traders, carried out at Citibank, USA.
- Marketing and customer characterization, providing useful information for mail and retail operations, at Thorn EMI, UK.
- Credit scoring, one of the first applications in finance, works best for binary decisions, such as loan eligibility assessment.
- Mortgage underwriting, using several different algorithms, including modular architectures with multiple specialized subnets. Performs well where underwriters agree, and degrades only slowly for higher attempt rates [50].
- Hybrid connectionist-symbolic architectures, including an example for medical insurance underwriting described in Chapter 4, are

making progress in attempts to produce 'active experts', which implement distributed associative memories while providing symbolic explanation facilities. Another hybrid inference mechanism, from Chase Manhattan Bank, USA is reviewed in reference [51].

13.3.2 *Automated inspection and monitoring*

- Explosive detection in aircraft luggage, an example described in Chapter 2, is commercially competitive and in operation in Heathrow, Kennedy, Dallas, and other major airports.
- Industrial quality control, through visual inspection, is reported to give reliable judgements in several applications in the USA Spectral quality control is also successful e.g. for water analysis at Lyonnaise des Eaux, France, and also for detecting noisy car blower motors, at Siemens, Germany [1]. Further examples from the USA are described in references [52–54].
- Demand forecasting, important to the utility industries, is also an area where neural techniques can be employed, according to Lyonnaise des Eaux, France.
- Sonar signal identification, applied to submarine detection among surface and other noise, has been achieved successfully in the USA [29], [55–56] and at Thomson-CSF [57], France.
- Fault diagnosis is currently under investigation for combat aircraft [58] and, more generally, for sensor failure in industrial plant [59].

13.3.3 *Computer vision*

- Optical recognition of hand-printed digits has been one of the most successful applications of neural networks. The particular examples in this book (Chapter 10) show how neural networks can be used to form useful pre-processors, previously derived heuristically from domain knowledge, for high performance in a task where appropriate feature extraction is paramount (Chapter 7), and also one method of performing invariant classification for different fonts (Chapter 11). Several major establishments are active in this field, among them Siemens in Germany, IBM in

France and the USA, AT & T Bell Labs in the USA, and NEC in Japan [60–62]. Hand-printed character recognition is of particular interest in Japan, and prototypes for different Japanese scripts have been developed at ATR and Toshiba.

- Accurate facial feature recognition and location, at British Telecom, UK [63].
- Satellite image compression, using the back-propagation algorithm to discriminate between signals and noise, Royal Signals and Radar Establishment, UK [28].
- A difficult problem in image processing is the recognition of image invariants. An example of this, regarding the detection of faces in natural scenes, is described in Chapter 9.

13.3.4 *Speech processing*

- Single-letter speaker-independent recognition over a telephone line, incorporated into a demonstrator alphabetic Directory Enquiry system, and a single utterance Yes/No system with high recognition accuracy has also been successfully developed at British Telecom, UK [64].
- Medium-size vocabulary speaker-independent isolated word recognition, using partially connected networks, is among several demonstrations that neural techniques are able to match conventional recognition by dynamic time warping [65], and also scale considerably better when subject to noise from telephone lines on test vocabularies with up to 50 words, according to Standard Electrik Lorenz, in Germany.
- Reliable C/V set discrimination using networks with time delays was carried out with ATR Labs, Japan [66] and elsewhere [5,31], and modular networks were successfully applied to syllable recognition at NTT [67].
- Text-to-speech conversion has also been carried out using neural techniques, with good, although inferior, performance for English text, compared with conventional approaches, but achieved with much reduced man-power commitment [68].

13.3.5 *Robotics and control*

- Image labelling of natural scenes, as described in Chapter 8 resulted in useful additional knowledge about image representations, which can be included in expert systems for automatic vehicle navigation (British Aerospace, UK).
- Current research into neural network applications in robotics covers artificial vision for autonomous navigation [30], path planning with obstacle avoidance [12], and parallel computation of inverse dynamics (Chapter 6 and references [11,13,14]). Reference [15] reviews the subject as a whole. A practical application which demonstrates the shortcomings, as well as the capabilities of neural techniques in practice is described in reference [69].
- Operation guidance in blast furnace control by Kobe Steel in Japan, using two neural network architectures to perform pattern recognition and feature detection, resulted in a successful method of data acquisition for a regulatory expert system [70].
- Modelling non-linearities in pH level control, described in Chapter 5, demonstrates the relevance of neural techniques to chemical batch process control.
- An active area of research concerning general neural network techniques for non-linear control, aimed both at robotics and process plant [71–74], has produced promising results.

13.3.6 *Optimization problems*

- Load dispatching for electrical utilities, using the Hopfield algorithm with good results (Tokyo Electric Power Company, Japan [75].
- Solution of large combinatorial problems using self-organized neural networks, at Thomson-CSF, France [22].
- Research into neural optimization techniques covers a wide range of application areas, and is likely to profit largely from hardware implementations of the algorithms used [20–25,75–77].

13.3.7 *Medical applications*

- In applications to a standard test of automatic diagnostic systems, abdominal and low back pain, neural networks matched and sometimes improved upon the performance of alternative statistical classifiers, and consultants, in work related to the Research Initiative in Pattern Recognition, carried out at the Royal Signals and Radar Establishment, UK [6]. Similar studies were conducted elsewhere for the diagnosis of dyspepsia [78], with similarly promising results. The interaction between neural systems and diagnostic expert systems is also under investigation in France [79] and at NTT, Japan [80]. For a review of the role of neural techniques in medical diagnosis, see reference [81].
- Noise filters for cardiac signals suggest that non-linear neural networks perform better than traditional linear filters [82]. These techniques are able to usefully compress ECG signals for recording in Holter monitors, as well as being capable of discriminating signals from cardiac abnormalities [83], with potential for clinical use in patient monitoring.
- General neural network methods can also be applied to electronic signals in medicine, e.g. image processing applied to ultrasonograms [84].
- Finally, there is a wealth of research on artificial simulations of neuromorphological systems, with resulting benefits for both the technological and medical fields, the former through an ability to implement novel useful functions either in software, or even in silicon (e.g. Chapter 12 and references [85–87]), and the latter by providing a detailed understanding of aspects of human function.

The application possibilities are, of course, wider than this list, and extend to a broad range of engineering, scientific, financial and information technology applications. One of the earlier examples where neural networks perform 'better than anything else', for instance, was in deducing the secondary structure of a protein from its amino-acid sequence [88]. Another expanding practical area of research is the solution of inverse problems, where the end results for given sets of operational conditions are known, and the problem is to work out the correct operational settings to achieve desired end results. Examples of this class of problems abound, not only in computer vision and robotics, but also in manufacturing processes, for instance in plasma etching for chip manufacture, and to some extent also in robotics and process control.

A review of US patents in neural networks and related areas during the period 1963–89 is given in reference [89].

13.4 Perspectives

Artificial neural networks is an expanding subject area, in terms of financial investment, research and development. Substantial initiatives in this area have been launched nationally in the USA, Japan and across the European Community, involving government funding with additional support from numerous industrial concerns of all sizes. In Japan, the 'Fifth Generation Computer Systems Programme', due for completion in 1992, will be immediately followed by a new programme called 'New Information Processing' running over 10 years with a budget of over $300 million. Particular applications of artificial neural networks that are expected to yield useful results within that period are in the area of financial decision aids, image and pattern analysis and robotics. Tool-kits comprising the basic algorithms are available commercially, with comprehensive simulation environments aimed at different types of user, ranging from exploratory level to large-scale utilities, together with customizing facilities for integration with existing software, including the provision of source code [90].

The main selling points of this technology are its ability to adapt to the characteristics of example data, and classify it correctly among noise, distortions and non-linearities; the provision of simple tools for automatic feature selection which form useful data representations, and may be used as a front-end to expert systems; ease of integration with existing domain knowledge; and flexibility of use, with the ability to handle data from multiple sources and decision systems. In addition, artificial neural networks offer the potential for very fast optimization, especially when implemented directly in hardware, and similar prospects to speed-up on-line applications.

The prospect of an artificial neural chess master, operating by holographic memory, may remain distant, but the results achieved in applications to date amply justify continuing effort along that path. More important still, practical applications using these techniques have already reached the market-place – and all indications are that they will remain firmly rooted as useful new signal processing tools.

References

1. O'Reilly, B. Computers that think like people. *Fortune*, **119**, 5, 58-61 (1989).

2. Shea, P.M. and Lin, V. Detection of explosives in checked airline baggage using an artificial neural system. *Int. Joint Conf. on Neural Networks*, II, 31-34 (1989).

3. Huang, W.M. and Lippmann, R.P. Neural net and traditional classifiers. In Anderson, D. (ed.). *Neural Information Processing Systems*, American Inst. of Physics, New York, 387-339 (1988).

4. Lippmann, R.P. Pattern classification using neural networks. *IEEE Comm. Mag.*, **27**, 11, 47-64 (1989).

5. Lang, K.J., Waibel, A.H. and Hinton, G.E. A time-delay neural network architecture for isolated word recognition. *Neural Networks*, **3**, 1, 23-44 (1990).

6. Bounds, D., Lloyd, P.J. and Xathew, B.G. A comparison of neural network and other pattern recognition approaches to the diagnosis of low back disorders. *Neural Networks*, **3**, 5, 583-591 (1990).

7. Hornik, K., Stinchcombe, M. and White, H. Universal approximation of an unknown mapping and its derivatives using multilayer feedforward networks. *Neural Networks*, **2**, 5, 551-560 (1990).

8. Funahashi, K.I. On the approximate realisation of continuous mappings by neural networks. *Neural Networks*, **2**, 2, 183-192 (1989).

9. Girosi, F. and Poggio, T. Representation properties of networks: Kolmogorov's theorem is irrelevant. *Neural Computation*, **1**, 45-49 (1989).

10. Minsky, M. and Papert, S. *Perceptrons: An Introduction to Computational Geometry*, MIT Press, Cambridge, MA (1969).

11. Kawato, M. Computational schemes and neural network models for formation and control of multijoint arm trajectory. In Miller, T., Sutton, R. and Werbos, P. (eds.). *Neural Networks for Robotics and Control*, MIT Press, Cambridge, MA (1990).

12. Khatib, 0. Real-time obstacle avoidance for manipulators and mobile robots. *Int. J. Robotics Res.*, **5**, 90-98 (1986).

13. Kuperstein, M. and Wang, J. Neural controller for adaptive movements with unforeseen payloads. *IEEE Trans. Neural Networks*, 1, 1, 137-142 (1990).

14. Martinetz, T.M., Ritter, H.J. and Schulten, K.J. Three-dimensional neural net for learning visuomotor coordination for a robot arm. *Ibid*, 131-136 (1990).

15. Kung, S.Y. and Hwang, J.N. Neural network architectures for robotic applications. *IEEE Trans. Robotics and Automation*, 5, 5, 641-657 (1989).

16. Kam, M., Naim, A., Labonski, P. and Guez, A. Adaptive sensor fusion with nets of binary threshold elements. *Int. Joint Conf. Neural Networks*, II, 57-64, IEEE Press, Piscataway, NJ (1989).

17. Pawlicki, T. A neural network architecture for evidence combination. *Proc. SPIE*, **931**, Sensor Fusion, 149-153 (1988).

18. Handleman, D.H., Lane, S.H. and Gelfand, J.J. Integrating neural networks and knowledge-based systems for intelligent robotic control. *IEEE Control Syst. Mag.*, 10, 3, 77-87 (1990).

19. An unusual and commercially successful application to robotic behaviour control can be found in Nagata, S., Segikuchi, M. and Asakawa, K. Mobile robot control by a structured hierarchical neural network. *Ibid*, 69-76 (1990).

20. Casotto, A., Romero, F. and Sangiovanni-Vicentelli, A. A parallel simulated annealing algorithm for the macro-cells. *IEEE Trans. Comp. Aided Des.*, **CAD-6**, 5, 838-847 (1987).

21. Takefuji, Y. and Lee, K.C. A parallel algorithm for tiling problems. *IEEE Trans. Neural Networks*, 1, 1, 143-145 (1990).

22. Angeniol, B., de La Croix Vaubois, G. and Le Texier, J.Y. Self-organising feature maps and the travelling salesman problem. *Neural Networks*, 1, 289-293 (1988).

23. Bilbro, G.L. and Snyder, W.E. Range image restoration using mean field annealing. In Touretzky, D.S. (ed.). *Advances in Neural Information Processing Systems I*, Morgan Kaufmann, San Mateo, CA, 594-601 (1989).

24. Roth, M.W. Neural networks for extraction of weak targets in high clutter environments. *IEEE Trans. Syst. Man and Cybern.*, **SMC-19**, 5, 1210-1217 (1989).

25. Bedini, L. and Tonazzini, A. Neural network use in maximum entropy image restoration. *Image and Vision Computing*, **8**, <u>2</u>, 108-114 (1990).

26. Kohonen, T. Self-organized formation of topologically correct feature maps. *Biol. Cybern.*, **43**, 59-69 (1982).

27. Nasrabadi, N.M. and Feng, Y. Vector quantization of images based upon the Kohonen self-organizing feature maps. *IEEE Int. Conf. Neural Networks*, I, 101-108 (1988).

28. Luttrell, S.P. Image compression using a neural network. *Proc. IGARSS – 88 Conf. on Remote Sensing*, Edinburgh, 1231-1238 (1988).

29. Gorman, R.P. and Sejnowski, T.J. Analysis of hidden units in a layered network trained to classify sonar targets. *Neural Networks*, **1**, <u>1</u>, 75-89 (1988).

30. Touretzy, D.S. and Pomerleau, D.A. What's hidden in the hidden layers? *Byte*, 227-223, Aug. (1989).

31. Waibel, A. and Hampshire, J. Building blocks for speech. *Ibid*, 235-242 (1989).

32. Widrow, B., Winter, R.G. and Baxter, R.A. Layered neural nets for pattern recognition. *IEEE Trans. Acoust. Speech and Signal Proc.*, **36**, <u>7</u>, 1109-1117 (1988).

33. Widrow, B. and Hoff, M.E., Jr. Adaptive switching circuits. *1960 IRE WESCON Convention Record*, **4**, 96-104 (1960).

34. Duda, R.O. and Hart, P.E. *Pattern Classification and Scene Analysis*, Wiley, New York (1973).

35. Robbins, H. and Monro, S. A stochastic approximation method. *Annals of Math. Stat.*, **22**, 400-407 (1951). For a review, see White, H. Learning in artificial neural networks: a statistical perspective. *Neural Computation*, **1**, 425-464, Winter (1989).

36. Metropolis, N., Rosenbluth, A.W., Rosenbluth, M.N., Teller, A.H. and Teller, E. Equations of state calculations by fast computing machines. *J. Chem. Phys.*, **21**, 1087-1093 (1953).

37. Harth, E.X. Brain models and thought processes. In Caianiello, E.R. (ed.). *Automata Theory*, Academic Press, New York, 201-217 (1966).

38. Van Heerden, P.J. Theory of optical information storage in solids. *J. Applied Optics*, **2**, 4, 393-400 (1963). For a review, see [39].

39. Andreae, J.H. *Thinking With the Teachable Machine*, Academic Press, New York (1977).

40. For example, the WISARD machine, which is reviewed in Aleksander, I. and Morton, H. *An Introduction to Neural Computing*, Chapman and Hall, London (1990).

41. Grossberg, S. *Studies of Mind and Brain: Neural Principles of Learning, Perception, Development, Cognition and Motor Control*, Reidel Press, Boston, MA (1982).

42. Hopfield, J.J. Neural networks and physical systems with emergent collective computational abllities. *Proc. Natl. Acad. Science USA*, **79**, 2554-2558 (1982).

43. Klopf, A.H. *The Hedonistic Neuron: A Theory of Memory, Learning and Intelligence*, Hemisphere, Washington, DC (1982).

44. Reilly, D.L., Cooper, L.N. and Elbaum, C. A neural model for category learning. *Biol. Cybern.*, **45**, 35-41 (1982).

45. Werbos, P. Applications of advances in nonlinear sensitivity analysis, in Drenick, R. and Kozin, F. (eds.). *Systems Modelling and Optimization: Proc. 10th IFIP Conf.*, New York (1981), Springer-Verlag, New York, 762-777 (1982).

46. For a review of early practical applications see Crick, F. The recent excitement about neural networks. *Nature*, **337**, 129-132 (1989).

47. Dutta, S. and Shekkar, S. Bond rating: a non-conservative application of neural networks. *IEEE Int. Conf. Neural Networks*, II, IEEE Press, Piscataway, NJ, 443-450 (1988).

48. White, H. Economic prediction using neural networks: the case of IBM daily stock returns. *Ibid*, 451-458 (1988).

49. A very brief critical analysis can be found in Halquist, C.H. and Schmoll, G.F., III. Neural networks: a trading perspective. *Tech. Anal. of Stocks and Commodities*, November, 48-54 (1989).

50. Collins, E., Ghosh, S. and Scotfield, C.L. An application of a multiple neural network learning system to emulation of mortgage underwriting judgements. *IEEE Int. Conf. Neural Networks*, II, 459-466 (1988).

51. Marose, R.A. A financial neural-network application. *AI Expert*, 50-53, May (1990).

52. Draper, J.S., Frankel, D.S., Hancock, H. and Mize, A.S. A microcomputer neural net benchmarked against standard classification techniques. *IEEE Int. Conf. Neural Networks*, IV, IEEE Press, Piscataway, NJ, 651-658 (1987).

53. Mathai, G. and Upadhyaya, B.R. Performance analysis and application of the bidirectiornal associative memory to industrial spectral signatures. *Int. Joint Conf. Neural Networks*, I, 33-37 (1989).

54. McAvoy, T.J., Wang, N.S., Naidu, S., Bhat, N., Gunter, J. and Simmons, N. Interpreting biosensor data via backpropagation. *Ibid*, 227-233 (1989).

55. Gorman, R.P. and Sejnowski, T.J. Learned classification of sonar targets using a massively parallel network. *IEEE Trans. Acoust. Speech and Signal Proc.*, **36**, 7, 1135-1140 (1988).

56. Maloney, P.S. and Specht, D.F. The use of probabilistic neural networks to improve times for hull-to-emitter correlation problems. *Int. Joint Conf. Neural Networks*, I, 289-294 (1989).

57. Ammirati, Y., Lemer, A. and Legitimus, D. Identification automatique de bruits en acoustique sous-marine par reseaux multicouche. *Proc. Int. Workshop Neuro-NIMES*, Nimes, France, 269-278 (1989).

58. McDuff, R.J., Simpson, P.K. and Gunning, D. An investigation of neural networks for F-16 fault diagnosis: I. System description. *AUTOTEST CON '89 Conf. Record – The System Readiness Technology Conf.*, IEEE Publ. Cat. No. 89, CH25684, 351-357 (1989).

59. Naidu, S.R., Zafiriou, E. and McAvoy, T.J. Use of neural networks for sensor failure detection in a control system. *IEEE Control Syst. Mag.*, **10**, 3, 49-55 (1990) .

60. Le Cun, Y., Jackel, L.D., Boser, B., Denker, J.S., Graf, H.P., Guyon, I., Henderson, D., Howard, R.E. and Hubbard, W. Handwritten digit recognition: applications of neural network chips and automatic learning. *IEEE Comm. Mag.*, **27**, 11, 41-46 (1989).

61. Yamada, K., Kami, H., Tsukumo, J. and Temma, T. Handwritten numeral recognition by multi-layered neural network with improved learning algorithm. *Int. Joint Conf. Neural Networks*, II, 259-266 (1989).

62. Krzyzak, A., Dai, W. and Yuen, C.Y. Unconstrained handwritten character classification using modified backpropagation model, in Suen, C.Y. *Frontiers in Handwriting Recognition*, Publ. CENPARMI, Montreal, Canada (1990).

63. Hutchison, R.A. and Welsh, W.J. Comparison of neural networks and conventional techniques for feature location in facial images. *1st IEE Conf. Neural Networks*, Conf. Publ. 313, IEE, London (1989).

64. Woodland, P. and Millar, W. Fixed dimension classifiers for speech recognition. In Wheddon, C. and Linggard, R. *Speech and Language Processing*, Chapman and Hall, London, 231-243 (1990).

65. Bottou, L., Fogelman Soulie, F., Blanchet, P. and Lienard, J.S. Speakerindependent isolated digit recognition: multilayer perceptrons vs. dynamic time warping. *Neural Networks*, 3, 4, 453-465 (1990).

66. Waibel, A., Hanazawam, T., Hinton, G., Shikano, K. and Lang, K. Phoneme recognition using time-delay networks. *IEEE Trans. Acoust. Speech and Signal Proc.*, 37, 3, 328-339 (1989).

67. Matsuoka, T., Hamada, H. and Nakatsu, R. Syllable recognition using integrated neural networks. *Int. Joint Conf. Neural Networks*, I, 251-258 (1989).

68. McCulloch, N., Ainsworth, W.A. and Linggard, R. Multi-layer perceptrons applied to speech technology. In Wheddon, C. and Linggard, R. *Speech and Language Processing*, Chapman and Hall, London 291-305 (1990).

69. Sanner, R.M. and Akin, D.L. Neuromorphic pitch attitude regulation of an underwater telerobot. *IEEE Control Syst. Mag.*, 10, 3, 62-68 (1990).

70. Konishi, M., Otsuka, Y., Matsuda, K., Tamura, N., Fuki, A. and Kadoguchi, K. Application of a neural network to operation guidance in a blast furnace. *3rd European Seminar on Neural Computing: The Marketplace*, London, (1990).

71. Psaltis, D., Sideris, A. and Yamamura, A.A. A multilayered neural network controller. *IEEE Control Syst. Mag.*, **8**, 2, 17-21 (1988).

72. Narendra, K.S. and Parthasarathy, K. Identification and control of dynamical systems using neural networks. *IEEE Trans. Neural Networks*, **1**, 1, 4-27 (1990).

73. Nguyen, D.H. and Widrow, B. Neural networks for self-learning control systems. *IEEE Control Syst. Mag.*, **10**, 3, 18-23 (1990).

74. Kraft, L.G. and Campagna, D.P. A comparison between CMAC neural network control and two traditional adaptive control systems. *Ibid*, 36-43 (1990).

75. Matsuda, S. and Akimoto, Y. The representation of large numbers in neural networks and its appliction to economical load dispatching of electric power. *Int. Joint Conf. Neural Networks*, I, 587-592 (1989).

76. Hiramatsu, A. ATM communications network control by neural networks. *IEEE Trans. Neural Networks*, **1**, 1, 122-130 (1990).

77. Kelly, M.F., Parker, P.A. and Scott, R.N. Myoelectric signal analysis using neural networks. *IEEE Eng. in Medicine and Biology Mag.*, **9**, 1, 61-64 (1990).

78. Scalia, F., Marconi, L., Ridella, S., Arrigo, P., Mansi, C. and Mela, G.S. An example of back propagation: diagnosis of dyspepsia. *1st IEE Conf. Neural Networks*, IEE Conf. Publ. 313, 332-336 (1989).

79. Pham, K.M. and Degoulet, P. MOSAIC: a macro-connectionist organization system for artificial intelligence computation. *IEEE Int. Conf. Neural Networks*, II, IEEE Press, Piscataway, NJ, 533-540 (1988).

80. Saito, K. and Nakano, R. Medical diagnostic expert systems based on the PDP model. *IEEE Int. Conf. Neural Networks*, I, 255-262 (1988).

81. Reggia, J.A. and Sutton, G.G., III Self-processing networks and their biomedical implications. *Proc. IEEE*, **76**, 6, 680-692 (1988).

82. Widrow, B. and Winter, R. Neural nets for adaptive filtering and adaptive pattern recognition. *IEEE Computer Mag.*, **21**, 3, 25-39 (1988).

83. Iwata, A., Nagasaka, Y. and Suzumura, N. Data compression of the ECG using neural network for digital holter monitor. *IEEE Eng. in Medicine and Biology*, **9**, 3, 53-57 (1990).

84. Silverman, R.H. and Noetzel, A.S. – Image Processing and Pattern Recognition in Ultrasonograms by Backpropagation. *Neural Networks*, **3**, 593-603 (1990).

85. Lyon, R.F. and Mead, C. An analogue electronic cochlea. *IEEE Trans. Acoust. Speech and Signal Proc.*, **36**, 7, 1119-1134 (1988).

86. Eisenberg, J., Freeman, W.J. and Burke, B. Hardware architecture of a neural network model simulating pattern recognition by the olfactory bulb. *Neural Networks*, **2**, 4, 315-325 (1989).

87. Taylor, J.G. A silicon model of vertebrate retinal processing. *Neural Networks*, **3**, 2, 171-178 (1990).

88. Qian, N. and Sejnowski, T.J. Predicting the secondary structure of globular proteins using neural network models. *J. Molecular Biology*, **202**, 865-884 (1988).

89. Wenskay, D.L. Intellectual property protection for neural networks. *Neural Networks*, **3**, 2, 229-236 (1990).

90. Treleaven, P.C., Recce, M. and Wang, C. Neural network programming environments: a review. *European Seminar on Neurocomputing '91: Putting Networks to Work*, IBC, London (1991).

Appendix A: Glossary

Artificial neural network (ANN). Collection of simple interconnecting computing elements usually forming a regular network. The name derives from the nature of the component processing elements, called artificial neurones, which are based on simple models of the behaviour of neuronal cells in the brain.

Artificial neurone. Simple mathematical model of the activity of neurones in biological nervous systems. This usually takes the form of a threshold logic unit with a graded response between two saturation levels.

Associative memory. Information storage devices which when queried with new data respond in a way that is similar to the response to similar data already stored in the network. These devices can be regarded as performing some form of interpolation between the elements in the training data set.

Back-propagation. Algorithm for supervised training of multi-layered artificial neural networks. The name derives from the procedure for updating the weights in the network. It is based upon gradient descent techniques, which result in propagation of the errors generated at the output layer back through the network to each link weight.

Central Processing Unit (CPU). Highly complex computational devices capable of performing logical and arithmetic operations on data with great speed and accuracy.

Content addressable memory. Information storage devices arranged in such a way that presenting them with partial or corrupted data is likely to elicit the corresponding completed or corrected stored data.

Credit assignment problem. The problem of assigning values to the hidden nodes during the training process. A major strength of the back-propagation algorithm for artificial neural networks was to solve this problem, thus overcoming the limited capabilities of single-layer networks.

Distributed processing. Form of information processing where a particular concept is not determined by the state of a single processing element, but rather is a property of the state of the system as a whole.

Expert systems. Computational decision systems which encode expert knowledge from a particular domain within a framework of explicit logical rules. They comprise a database containing predicates and conditional statements together with an inference engine which uses the elements in the database to form decisions. Expert systems have the property that the route taken in coming to a decision can usually be identified.

Feedforward network. Networks where information is processed in only one direction, from the input layer through the network to the output layer.

Fuzzy logic. Formalism to perform logical operations on classes of objects where the transition from one logical state to another is gradual rather than abrupt.

Generalization. Key property of artificial neural networks which involves the correct response of the network to test data based on information contained in a restricted set of training data.

Graceful degradation. Reduction in the performance of an information processing system due to inaccurate operation of its components.

Gradient descent. Mathematical technique which seeks to minimize a performance-related quantity, e.g. classification error, by progressively moving the state of the system, at each point in time, along the direction of maximum gradient. This process is similar to rolling a ball down to the bottom of a hill.

Hebbian learning. Training mechanism based on the assumption that the simultaneous excitation of two neurones strengthens the link between them.

Hidden layer. Array of processing elements whose activity is not determined directly by external information either at the input or at the output of the network. See also under credit assignment problem.

Holographic memory. Storage mechanism with similar properties to a holograph, where images are stored without a one-to-one correspondence between a section of film and a part of the image. Reducing the area of film used to reproduce the image simply degrades the quality of reproduction across the whole image.

Input layer. Processing elements which collect the information supplied as input to the network and distribute it without alteration to the elements in following layers. For this reason, elements in the input layer are sometimes termed sensor elements.

Knowledge-based systems. See Expert systems.

Lateral inhibition. Mutually inhibitory link between two processing elements in the same layer. This type of link plays an important role in biological sensors.

Learning. See training algorithm and training data.

Multi-layered networks. Networks comprising one or several hidden layers, in addition to an input layer and an output layer. Usually only the active layers are counted, namely the hidden layers and the output layer.

Network architecture. Configuration of the connectivity between processing elements in an artificial neural network.

Neurone. Key elements in biological nervous systems. They act as information processors because they respond to signals transmitted to them via dendrites by generating electrical impulses which are transmitted outwards usually along a single axon.

Non-linearity. Nature of the relationship between variables in a system, which cannot be represented simply in terms of linear combinations. Non-linearities may result in the occurrence of saturation.

Output layer. Layer of processing elements which encode the response of the network to the input data. Because of their role, elements in the output layer of early perceptron networks were also referred to as associator elements.

Perceptron. Originally the name of one of the earliest machine learning algorithms using threshold logic units. It now refers to any layered neural network, with that type of unit, which is capable of supervised learning.

Processing element. Basic component in any information processing system, where information received from other elements is transformed before being relayed to the remainder of the system. This may be a CPU or an artificial neurone, respectively, in conventional computers and artificial neural networks.

Recall. Eliciting a response from the network to a trial input. This may involve a single forward pass through the network, perhaps resulting in a classification of the input data into a particular class, or it may involve repeated iterations in recursive networks.

Recursive network. Processing system with return links which bring information from the output layer back to the input to the network. This causes information to circulate around the system until a stability is reached, where data presented at the input layer simple replicates itself at the output. This iterative process may correspond to the dynamics of a system sliding down an energy surface, in which case the final stable states represent optimal configurations, and the purpose of the network is to elicit the optimal configurations most appropriate to the input data.

Robustness. Property of an information processing system of being able to achieve approximately correct response in the presence of unpredictable errors in its components.

Saturation. Property of some non-linear functions which limit their values between finite maximum and minimum values. This is important in the study of artificial neural networks because it allows a very high degree of interconnection between artificial neurones.

Self-organization. Generation of a stable pattern of response directly from data without the intervention of a tutor or any external correcting influence. Self-organized networks usually operate as clustering mechanisms, exploiting correlations in the data to find significant features.

Sigmoid. S-shaped curve used to define the behaviour of a class of threshold logic units. It has the property that its differential is simply expressed in terms of the original function, which speeds up computer simulations.

Supervised learning. Process of training a neural network by repeatedly comparing the output from the network against a reference, or target output, and adjusting the weights in the network until the desired output is achieved.

Synapse. Connection between an axon carrying the excitation from one neurone and a dendrite which will transmit the effect of this excitation to another neurone, in a biological system. The strength and sign of the synapses is believed to contain the key information stored in nervous systems. Synapses are represented in networks of artificial neurones by weights.

Test data. Data used to validate the information stored in an artificial neural network. By recalling a set of test data through the network at regular intervals it is possible to monitor the training process to achieve maximum generalization capability.

Threshold logic unit. Simple device which weighs up incoming data and derives a response by comparing the sum with a reference threshold value. This response may be analogue with saturation, or binary. These units are extensively used in fuzzy logic.

Training algorithm. Mathematical procedure by which information is stored in a neural network. The main function of the network is often interpreted as retrieving the stored data most closely associated with the input signal. The process of supervised learning is sometimes referred to as teaching the network, which thus acts as a machine learning device conditioned to provide the desired response to the stimulus provided by the training data.

Training data. Data used to load-up, or train, the network. The choice of this data can be critical to the performance of the network in generalization.

Unsupervised training. See self-organization.

Weights. Numbers representing the strength of the link between two processing elements. They can be positive, indicating an excitatory link, or negative, resulting in an inhibitory link. Both of these types of links are found in biological systems, and they are essential for the operation of most types of neural network.

INDEX

Activation 3, 17, 71, 73-77, 81, 85, 112
  function 95, 165, 166, 169, 209
Adaptive network 50-54, 59, 61, 63, 156
Adaptive system 40, 53, 79
Ahmad, Z. 111, 112
Ahuja, S.B. 67, 88, 89
Airline revenue 51, 52, 55
Annealing
  simulated 54, 170-172
Artificial intelligence 2, 35, 49, 70, 71, 81, 123, 144, 156
Artificial neural network 1, 4, 7, 10, 35, 123, 131, 143, 164, 252, 253, 260
Artificial neural systems 40-47, 129
Artificial neurone 11, 37, 58, 269
Associative memory 10, 17, 73, 83, 198-200, 202, 207, 215, 225, 252, 269
Associative recall 197-200
Automated inspection 251,256
Axon 4, 234, 235

Back propagation 40, 42, 44, 46, 91-93, 95, 100, 101, 103, 106-108, 138, 139, 164, 192, 193, 202, 210, 254, 257, 269
  learning by 58, 93
  network 97-99, 101, 185, 188

Back error propagation 15, 23, 26, 95, 112, 114, 137, 141, 151, 156, 252 (see also Perceptron, multi-layered)
Bell, T.M. 49, 66
Bhat, N.V. 91, 109, 265
Bichsel, M. 30, 163, 183
Bionic 233, 244, 246, 247, 239
Biosensor 91, 93, 105, 271
Boltzmann machines 40
Boser, B. 186, 194, 265

Center-surround cell types 237
Central processing unit (CPU) 42, 269
Chemical process control 99
Computer
  conventional 7
Computer vision 123, 126, 128, 129, 143, 144, 149, 150, 160, 164, 259
Connectionism 156
Connectionist expert system 80, 85
Content addressable memory 10, 13, 15, 17, 269
Cortex 8, 20, 124, 125, 233, 234, 243, 247
Cortical neural network
  receptive field 245
Credit assignment problem 16, 269
Cun, Y. Le 29, 186, 194, 195, 265

Dendrite 4, 234, 235, 238
Denker, J.S. 186, 194, 195, 265
Distributed associative memories 10
Distributed processing 7, 270
Dynamic modelling 40, 52, 92, 99-101, 117, 253
Dynamical associative memories 198
Dynamics 104, 111, 117, 118, 120, 227, 258

Expert systems 72, 81, 83, 86, 87, 270

Faces
    detection of 123, 143, 176, 178
Fault tolerance 43
Feature extraction 189, 198, 218, 219, 222, 227
Feature selection 260
Feedforward 39, 40, 124, 151, 163-166, 200
    network 7, 39, 43, 45, 46, 112, 118, 182, 213, 214, 218, 219, 222, 227, 253, 270
Fuzzy logic 270 (*see also* 207-210)

Gaussian classifier 96, 116, 124, 245, 246
Generalization 186, 199, 227, 252, 270
Graceful degradation 81
Gradient descent 15, 94, 131, 151, 200, 270
Grossberg, S. 264
Guez, A. 111, 122, 262

Hand-written digits 185, 186, 192, 193
Hebbian
    learning 168, 169, 254, 270
    rule 198, 200, 203
Henderson, D. 186, 194, 265
Hidden layer 16, 93, 189, 190, 223, 252, 270
Higher-order networks 17, 197, 198, 212, 215, 219, 226, 228
Holographic (hologologic)
    representation of information 254
    memory 260, 271
Hopfield model 11, 12, 14, 15, 17, 40, 164, 197-200, 202-205, 207, 227, 233, 258
    application to travelling salesman problem 49
    minimal energy concept 12
    optimization and 15
Howard, R.E. 186, 194, 195, 205
Hsiung, A. 67
Hubbard, W. 186, 194, 265
Hutchison, W.R. 49, 53, 64, 65, 66
Hyperplane 44, 130, 137, 178

Information 2, 47, 130, 168, 185, 246
    holograph representation of 254
    retrieval of 199, 205, 227
    flow 4, 20
Information-processing models of memory
Input layer 271, 188
Insurance
    medical 68

Intelligence
artificial (*see* Artificial Intelligence)
Invariance 130, 174, 189, 197, 198, 200, 208, 212-218
Inverse KinematicRobotics 111, 117, 258

Jackel, L.D. 186, 194, 195

Knowledge-based systems 73, 81-83, 271 (*see also* Expert Systems)
Kohonen 78, 130
networks 20-24, 130-132, 134, 136, 138, 140, 233
Labelling
image 149, 156, 157, 253, 258
Learning 15, 54, 67, 72, 81, 92, 118-121, 131, 150, 159, 163, 165, 168, 186, 193, 271
by back propagation 97, 99, 151, 181, 192, 193
by back-propagation paradigm 15
network 185
paradigms 81, 85
rule 172, 173, 181
Linear decision boundaries, or problems 57
Lisboa, P.J.G. 1, 29, 123, 144, 146, 231, 251

McAvoy, T. 91, 100, 109, 265
McCulloch-Pitts neurons 2, 165
Medical 251
insurance 68
risk 67, 68-70, 86
Memory 199

Minderman, P.A. Jr. 91
Moments 198, 218, 222
Monitoring 247
Multi-layered networks 16, 17, 20, 188, 271
Multi-layered perceptron (*see* Perceptron, multilayered)
Multi-layered structures 15

Nearest neighbor method 21, 40, 42, 75, 79, 149, 156, 159, 207
Neorecognition 190
Network architecture 3, 10, 15, 17, 18, 23, 27, 51, 52, 72, 73, 77, 111, 117, 131, 181, 185, 190, 193, 213, 214, 219, 226, 253, 258, 271
Neural networks 1-10, 13, 15, 23, 26, 35, 71, 73, 75, 81, 85, 111, 113, 114, 117, 123, 124, 149-151, 160, 163-165, 168, 169, 173, 175, 178, 181, 182, 197-199, 207, 208, 215, 218, 219, 227, 233-235, 251-256, 258
Neurone 2-11, 15, 23, 25, 26, 36, 37, 71, 92, 93, 95, 102, 130, 131, 163-166, 168, 169, 171-174, 177-179, 181, 182, 188, 189, 212, 234, 247, 271
Node, active 74-76, 132, 135
Non-linearity 6, 7, 10, 26, 36, 37, 40, 44, 49, 58, 91-93, 103, 106, 244, 254, 255, 260, 271

Optimization 13, 15, 26, 50, 52, 59, 60, 62, 98, 170-172, 174, 253, 254, 258, 260
Output layer 93, 271

Parallel distributed processing models 7
Parallel processing 77
Perantonis, S.J. 27, 29, 146, 197, 229, 230
Perceptron 19, 114, 136, 138, 142, 198, 200, 202, 203, 254, 272
  Rosenblatt 3, 16
  comparison with Bayes procedures 161
  decision regions formed by XOR problem 16-19, 43, 252
  multi-layered 15, 16, 113, 130, 137, 138, 140, 149-151, 153, 197, 207, 251
  parallel nature of computation process 91, 117
  single-layer 137-139, 141, 142, 205, 210, 213
Processing
  element 37, 79, 245, 270-272
  units 9, 151
  image 125, 129, 163, 165, 173, 176, 177, 253, 257, 259
  non-linear 151, 245

Reading 7
Recall 10, 11, 20, 272
Recursive network 272

Reinforcement
  models 25
  learning 23, 54, 55
Relaxation property, of network 149, 150
Resource allocation 51, 52, 54, 55, 61
Retina 4, 124, 233, 235-247
Robot 111, 112
Robotics 1, 44, 111, 112, 253, 258, 259, 260
Robustness 7, 8, 123, 133, 150, 164, 175, 176, 255, 272

Saturation 272
Scheduling task 60-62
Seitz, P. 30, 163, 183, 184
Self-organization 130, 132, 141, 253, 258, 272
Selinsky, J. 111, 122
Sigmoid 38, 273
  nonlinearity 92, 114
  function 169, 178
Simulated annealing (*see* Annealing, simulated)
Speech processing 257
Statistical classifiers 81
Stephens, K.R. 49, 57, 64, 65, 66
Supervised learning 23, 25, 131, 164, 273
Synapse 4, 165, 234, 239, 244, 247, 273

Taylor, J.G. 233, 248, 268
Test data 225, 273
Threshold logic unit 2, 273
Training 9, 13, 17, 25, 91, 114
  algorithm 3, 9, 13, 252, 273
  data 94, 101, 225, 273

Unsupervised learning 67, 71, 190

Vibration control. 45
Visual cortex 20, 123-125, 233-235, 237, 245-247

Wang, N.S. 91, 265
Weights 17, 21, 74, 79, 94, 95, 103, 113, 114, 118, 124, 131, 132, 135, 136, 138,

151, 154, 157, 159, 160, 165, 169, 170, 174, 189-191, 193, 198, 199, 210, 214-216, 222, 226, 274
Works, G.A. 35
Wright, W.A. 149, 162

Zernike moments 218, 219, 222, 223
Zipcode 185-187, 193